RACISM IN METROPOLITAN AREAS

Culture and Politics / Politics and Culture

General Editors:
Laura Nader, *University of California, Berkeley*
Rik Pinxten, *Ghent University, Belgium*
Ellen Preckler, *Ghent University, Belgium*

Cultural Identity, whether real or imagined, has become an important marker of societal differentiation. This series focuses on the interplay of politics and culture and offers a forum for analysis and discussion of such key issues as multiculturalism, racism and human rights.

Volume 1
Europe's New Racism: Causes, Manifestations and Solutions
Edited by **The Evens Foundation**

Volume 2
Culture and Politics: Identity and Conflict in a Multicultural World
Edited by **Rik Pinxten**, **Ghislain Verstraete** and **Chia Longman**

Volume 3
Racism in Metropolitan Areas
Edited by **Rik Pinxten** and **Ellen Preckler**

RACISM IN METROPOLITAN AREAS

Edited by
Rik Pinxten and Ellen Preckler

Berghahn Books
New York • Oxford

First published in 2006 by

Berghahn Books
www.BerghahnBooks.com

© 2006 Rik Pinxten and Ellen Preckler

Library of Congress Cataloging-in-Publication Data
Racism in metropolitan areas / edited by Rik Pinxten and Ellen Preckler.
p. cm. -- (Culture and politics/politics and culture ; v. 3)
Includes bibliographical references and index.
ISBN 1-84545-088-4 (alk. paper) --- ISBN 1-84545-089-2 (pbk.)
1. Group identity. 2. Intergroup relations. 3. Racism. 4. Visual perception.
I. Pinxten, Rik. II. Preckler, Ellen. III. Series

HM753.R33 2005
305.8'009173'2--dc22

2005043629

British Library Cataloguing in Publication Data
A catalogue record for this book is available from the British Library.

Printed in the United States on acid-free paper.

CONTENTS

Part Two: Empowering to Combat Racism

INTRODUCTION:
RACISM IN METROPOLITAN AREAS

Rik Pinxten and Ellen Preckler

After the terrible annihilation of peoples because of their so-called racial features in the Second World War, the United Nations Organization was founded to work on the basis of the Universal Declaration of Human Rights. The basic creed of this attempt at worldwide negotiation and interaction in a common forum was not so much 'no more war', but rather 'human rights and human dignity for all'. One could indeed say that the UN's purpose is to prevent and eventually to remedy violations of basic rights of anyone by combating structural humiliation, exclusion and enslavement. The establishment of such an organisation and the implementation of the Declaration of Human Rights in actual policies throughout the world have never been attempted on such a large scale in the history of humankind. Over the past five decades, we have witnessed an increase not only in knowledge, but also in behavioural patterns accordant with Human Rights: an unprecedented historical milestone. But not all is well. A political discourse that incites exclusion and hatred for those who are seen as different is unfortunately gaining in appeal, most notably in affluent and developed countries, where certain groups are excluded from the benefits and privileges of mainstream society because of their ethnic, racial or religious identity. Two decades ago it would have been utterly impossible to publicly defend the atrocities of the Holocaust or any other racist policies. Today, however, certain political parties actively support such opinions by drawing upon racist discourses (often disguised as cultural fundamentalist proposals) which are finding massive appeal in the older Western democratic societies (see Ford, this volume). Racism is back, and antiracism is no longer accepted as an argument that suffices in itself.

Our first international conference held on these issues highlighted the topic of new manifestations of racism in Europe (Evens, 2002). The second international conference, held at Ghent University focused on the worldwide context of large cities and racism. One obvious reason for this is that nowadays about half of the entire human population resides in cities and urban areas, thus accelerating the growth of the metropolis. This reality led us to investigate whether this form of settlement would show universal features of (new) exclusion of groups that differ from the nationalistic or territorial ethnic basis for racism of the past. In what sense does the larger city induce forms of collaboration or of structural exclusion that would be typical in some sense for the anonymous, necessarily multicultural and intrinsically dynamic context of the large city? This was the focus of the second conference from which the present volume emanates.

The format of the conference differed from what is commonly followed in academia. As racism is a social, cultural and political problem, and not a merely scientific topic, we have attempted to involve a series of relevant agents in dialogue with each other. Scientists, politicians, cultural brokers, captains of industry and media people were engaged in a constant forum of discussion during the conference.

The book expresses a similar mix of voices and competencies. Unfortunately, not all of the speakers were able to submit a written contribution. Racism is on the agenda of all these agents in contemporary society and our aim was to present an ongoing dialogue in this book. Moreover, we remain mindful that a printed dialogue is not really comparable with the dynamism of the real event.

Taking into consideration the focus of this publication, we begin the book with a short contribution by the chairman of a social democratic party with government responsibility in Belgium (Janssens, this volume). We end this part with the perspective on policies against racism at the European level by a member of the European Parliament who has a distinguished reputation on these issues (Ford, this volume).

The present introduction and the synthetic conclusions and propositions by Laura Nader in the final chapter thus encapsulate a set of contributions that is deliberately varied as a result of the particular professional interests of the authors. We would like to express our gratitude to the participating scholars, but even more so to the people 'from the field' for their willingness to participate in this endeavour.

The general structure of the book divides the contributions into two categories: those that discuss ways of empowerment and those that detail processes of disempowerment. Duster gives a detailed analysis of how employment policies in larger American cities can offer opportunities or keep racially identified youth away from the job market. Seward examines recent attempts to deal with surging racism in British cities. His involvement in this field in insightful in delineating a series of potentially effective measures. Hervik on the other hand, stems from a double background: that of academia and of policy-making institutes. He focuses on the situation in Denmark and proposes to negotiate with the people about limits of tolerance. Three authors then offer different perspectives on the questions of racism in India's caste society.

In the second part we present a set of authors highlighting cases of empowerment. Again we drew specialists from academia (e.g., Marx, Gingrich) and from the field. In the latter group journalists (Peirs) as well policy makers (Leman) offer their expertise.

Finally, we want to thank sponsors who enabled the symposium or the preparation of the book: the Evens Foundation, the Triodos Bank and the Foundation for Scientific Research of Flanders.

Reference

Evens Foundation. 2002. *Europe's New Racism?* Oxford: Berghahn Books.

PART ONE

Disempowering through Racism

How a Dream was Shattered

Patrick Janssens

At a symposium on racism in metropolitan areas at one of our distinguished universities, a group of eminent international speakers were giving lectures. I wanted to address them as common inhabitants of the city. Politicologists, anthropologists and sociologists have undoubtedly offered important contributions to the analysis of a phenomenon that is spreading like a cancer throughout our cities. Strangely enough, their analyses often do not coincide with the daily practice of the urban citizens who experience racism, or – and this is probably more important – who generate racism. I've always stated that it is easy to be an antiracist in the green suburbs. The highly literate children of the baby-boom generation – the progressive legacy of the 1960s – have settled there. From their suburban dwellings, they write with indignation about the growing intolerance in the city. It is from there – behind their desks with a view of the green lawn outside their doors – that they brood on terms such as 'inequality', 'bad neighbourhoods' or 'multicultural life' and wag their fingers at the 'scared white man'.

I wanted to do something slightly different. I declined the role of the sociologist addressing his fellow sociologists. The introduction I wanted to give would deal with the daily experience of people in the city. It was the experience, moreover, of my parents. They were two hard-working citizens, who at the end of the 1950s had had a dream. They wanted to open a butcher's shop; much like my father's father had done before him: in a nice neighbourhood, a popular area, where people loved to eat a good piece of meat. My parents opened their butcher shop in 1958 in *het Zuidkwartier*, the South Quarter of Antwerp. This area is part of the nineteenth-century extension of what is now the region of Belgium with the most important economic expansion rates. Antwerp is one of the most successful European harbours, situated on the shores of the river Schelde. Being once one of the largest towns in Europe, it is now a mere modest city of approximately half a million people. The South Quarter, where my parents ran their shop, is situated near the outskirts of the town. At that time, it had an outdoor swimming pool that drew massive crowds from the city. On one of the inbounds to the city there was a decent shopping street, right around the corner from my parents' business. The future looked bright. It would be hard work, but this was a neighbourhood with potential. The shop was a success. My parents knew that a good butcher's shop would prosper and bring home a good bit of money. They were confident that they, in time, would sell their shop at a profit. That money would be a nice supplement to their pension. The shop was in that regard their personal savings for retirement. People would always eat meat, so all's well that ends well. They lived through the 'golden sixties' and its optimism. The belief in progress was never as high as then, the economy was booming. In fact, there was so much work available that people were invited to Belgium to fill all the vacant jobs. First came the Italians and Spaniards, they worked in the coalmines in the province of Limburg. Then Turkish and Moroccan people came over. There was plenty of work on the docks of the Antwerp harbour, and the large infrastructural works, like the subway in Antwerp, needed unskilled labourers. These people had to set up residency somewhere. The South Quarter was an appropriate area for them. Old bourgeois houses from the 1900s went out of fashion in the 1960s – they were too big for the smaller average families of that time, and the houses were too costly to heat after the oil crises of the 1970s. Local people, who could afford to, left the neighbourhood. Only the smaller 'blue-collar worker' houses in the quarter were still inhabited by locals. The outdoor swimming pool degenerated and was replaced by high-rise apartment buildings, looking out on the network of highways at the border of the city. The buzz of bizz (business) in the shopping street around the corner vanished or was replaced by shops with foreign signatures.

Immigrants moved into the neighbourhood. The large bourgeois houses were appropriate for the larger immigrant families. Moreover, they were very cheap, and, with minor costs for renovation, they were habitable. A satellite dish connected these nineteenth-century houses with the country of origin of the new occupants. My parents began to worry. All these new inhabitants turned to the Turkish or Moroccan butcher's to buy their meat. They occasionally came into my parents' shop, but only to buy a small jar of mayonnaise. The neighbourhood started to lose its appeal. Some houses were left empty. Others became ruins. My parents' dream was shattered, loudly and abruptly. Their retirement trust was jeopardised. When they finally sold their shop in 1998, they were pleased to have been able to sell the house at all. The profit they had hoped for was out of the question.

My parents' story is the story of those who 'stayed behind'. It is one that has seldom been told – unfortunately, because it is precisely this group of people that was prone to the first signs of racist urges. This group is susceptible to the extreme right discourse. Radical right groups who seized their chance to construct an image as 'protectors of common people' fuelled their fears and frustrations. Meanwhile, the leftist intellectuals in green suburbia pushed those 'who remained behind' deeper into their misery by portraying them as intolerant scum.

A similar dynamic can be found in the high-rise, blue-collar worker apartment buildings in Kiel, another nineteenth-century neighbourhood on the outskirts of Antwerp. The situation there was even worse. Kiel was more distinctively a 'blue collar' neighbourhood than the South Quarter. The city council invested large sums in housing projects here during the 1950s. In keeping with the times, the majority of housing problems in Kiel were solved vertically, the housing towers followed the recipe of modernist architects. Antwerp actually did a brilliant job. Le Corbusier had created a master plan for the neighbourhood on the left bank of the river. A pupil of his, Renaat Braem, did the same for the settlements of Kiel.

Braem was a visionary architect, who wanted to achieve social equality and social justice with bricks and concrete. A socialist by conviction, he was determined to make the blue-collar workers happy by means of a new vision of urban development. Without a doubt, the towers he constructed in Kiel were an example of modernist high-rise buildings. The families who settled in were more than satisfied. They had modern and comfortable flats, with a magnificent view of the town. The apartments were well situated and had easy access to public transport. For most of the inhabitants, these flats in Kiel were appreciated as a token of upward social mobility. They experienced progress.

Almost half a century later, however, things have changed for the worse. The buildings are ageing, and with them the once young occupants grow old. Children have left home, and because the residents have less family to take care of, their rent has increased; but not the quality of the building. At the same time new residents have moved in – immigrants. And the policy of the city council has changed; no more political favouritism determining who gets what type of flat. Those who acquired a flat through this practice were asked to move out, in favour of the immigrants. And so the locals said: 'We have to go, and they ... ' Since then the us–them contrast is undermining social relationships in the high-rise buildings, just as time has started to gnaw away at the concrete. What was then a token of upward social mobility, is now turning into social degradation for those who remain behind.

As for me, this context is determinant for the problem of racism. A danger is that the care and attention for the locals who stay behind could be interpreted as a rejection of the problem of foreign newcomers. Concern for the local people can also – with or without bad intentions – be confused with the monocultural view of the extreme right. I refuse to become entangled in these sorts of arguments. As a politician, and as a socialist, it is my wish to defend a society of equal opportunities for everyone, newcomers as well as locals who stayed behind. Our story must be grounded in reality, not simply in a theoretical framework, and in a willingness to listen to all those concerned, while respecting their particular problems. Only then shall we be able to work towards the recognition of the European metropolitan area as a radically new environment, with new challenges and in need of yet unseen solutions. It is in this 'new city' that I wish to live.

EXPLAINING INCREASED RACIAL CONFLICT IN POST-INDUSTRIAL SOCIETIES: THE CREATION OF SYSTEMIC 'COMPETITIVE' YOUTH UNEMPLOYMENT

Troy Duster

When in a Eurobarometer survey of attitudes in 1988, respondents were asked, 'When you think about people of another race, whom do you think of?', respondents in all the fifteen except France and Britain cited black people in first place, indicating a perception of the greatest difference. The French cited 'Arabs' first and the British 'Indians'. When asked a similar question about people of another nationality, the French indicated a preoccupation with North Africans, the Germans with the Turks, and the British with Asians. A survey nine years later (Eurobarometer 1997) noted a lack of embarrassment on the part of 33 percent of respondents who said they were 'very racist' or 'quite racist'. It concluded that self-reported racism was growing in direct proportion to dissatisfaction with life circumstances, fear of unemployment, etc.

Of fifteen countries, the eight with the highest percentages of respondents classifying themselves as *very racist* or *quite racist* were: Belgium, 55 percent; France (48); Denmark (43); Austria (42); Germany (34); U.K. (32); Netherlands (31); and Italy (30) (Banton 1999: 6).

Rob Witte (1995) tried to explain it this way:

> What seems to be true for all groups victimized by racist violence is that in furious and highly publicized debates on asylum and migration policies, they are or were portrayed as the main representatives of people under discussion. Such public and political debates occurred, for instance, in Britain during the late 1960s and the 1970s, in France during the early 1970s, the early 1980s and in the early 1990s, in the Netherlands during the early 1980s and especially in the early 1990s, and in Germany during the early 1990s. (Witte 1995: 8)

Three massive social-economic developments have converged over the last three decades to provide the context for the emergence of increased racial and ethnic tensions and conflict that are now being experienced in postindustrial societies, most especially in Western Europe. It is the convergence and integration of these forces that are the necessary backdrop to understanding before we can move to a meaningful discussion of the sources of inter-group conflict. In order, these three forces are: (1) deindustrialisation, the movement of capital investment across national boundaries to newly industrialising sites, and the concomitant shift to tertiary economies; (2) the movement of labour across national boundaries from less-developed nations to postindustrial societies, and the concomitant 'hour-glassing' of the social stratification system of tertiary economies; and finally (3) the creation of an endemic and systemic pool of high youth unemployment.

As national borders are made porous by the movement of cheap labour, we are witnessing a shifting tension between the local resident workforces in postindustrial societies, and the migrants and sojourners who come to take the lower-paying jobs. Many of these migrants and sojourners are from nations in which there are not only linguistic, cultural and religious differences (from the host country), but also phenotypically marked racial and ethnic differences. The combination of ethnic and racial differentiation, of the new workers, alongside high rates of unemployment and a sense of 'displacement' by local resident workers, produces a volatile situation.

While the United States has witnessed this problem for a full century, with rural to urban and Southern to Northern migration (of poorer blacks and Latinos), and the consequent racial and ethnic tensions and violence, this has been a relatively recent phenomenon in Western Europe. When it happens, it often catches the locals by surprise. For example, in several towns in the southeastern area of Spain in early 2000, there were three days of rioting in areas overwhelmed by mobs of residents chasing Moroccan and other African immigrants through the streets, shouting racist slogans, and vandalising the shops and cars of foreign labourers. In response, the Foreign Minister, Abel Matutes, said on state radio: 'We must think about how we need to change in a pluralist society, where every day we will need more immigrants to take our country forward.' Spain is hardly a pluralist society by most measures. Instead, the country has mainly exported its people for centuries, first to the new American colonies, and later to Northern Europe. But this trend was reversed during the last two decades, when Spain joined the European Union and the economy began to prosper. The flatlands around Almeria, just east of Malaga, have grown rich from intensive and successful agriculture, now able to supply Europe with fruits and vegetables during the winter. Even today, only 2 percent of Spain's population is foreign-born. However, a floating population estimated as high as 100,000 migrant labourers, mostly Moroccan, harvest olives and oranges around Andalusia, or pick strawberries and tomatoes. They cross the Mediterranean in shabby boats to earn the equivalent of $25 per day. And while this is low for Europe, it is more than four times what farm labourers earn in Morocco. In the villages of Almeria, where the core of the racist violence was focused, 25 percent of the people living there are poor foreign migrant workers. This is the highest concentration of such workers anywhere in Spain, and the majority live in hovels without light or running water.

Germany has had a much longer history of migrant labour, or guest workers. When Turkish workers began arriving in Germany in the 1960s, it was widely believed that they would be sojourners. Scores of thousands remained as 'guest workers' and a second generation has now settled into several major metropolitan areas. However, a combination of factors, including the uniting of East and West Germany, the movement of labour into Germany from many other parts of Europe, and the unprecedented construction boom in Berlin during the last decade has fuelled a new level of interethnic and interracial tensions.

> In Germany, since September, 1991, in Hoyersweda (ex-East Germany) there has been a sharp increase in attacks against immigrants from Central Europe, as well as against Turkish and Moroccan immigrant workers: according to *Verfassungsschutz* (State security police) there were 270 racist actions in 1990 and 1483 racist actions in 1991. That number sharply increased to 2286 in 1992, and of this total 696 were acts of violent destruction of property, 598 attacks on people, 701 criminal fires and bomb attacks, and 17 murders. (Wieviorka, 1996: 340)

A Larger Context for Youth Unemployment

In both academic and policy circles, there is a notable, even remarkable consensus about the nature of the great economic and social transformation of Western industrialised societies over the last quarter century. In particular, there is general agreement that the important and decisive shift from predominantly industrial to mainly service economies has been accompanied by select and patterned 'dislocations' that are true for all nations which have a declining manufacturing sector. Perhaps most significantly, without regard to ethnic or cultural variation, what is common to declining secondary-sector economies is the attendant sharp increase in youth unemployment.[1]

In Australia, for example, while there has been a growth in employment overall and for adults in the last few decades, for youth (aged 19–24) there has actually been a substantial loss of jobs. Indeed, over one-third of the jobs available to teenagers in the 1960s in Australia disappeared by the middle of the 1980s (Polk and Tait 1990).

Economists, sociologists, public policy analysts and social demographers are in general agreement on these basic facts, but there are fierce disagreements about the implications of these developments for policy and the lessons that rising youth unemployment provide about the changes in national economies. All postindustrialising societies share this relatively new development but, as Tolstoy told us, 'each family [substitute 'nation'] is unhappy in its own way'. Local outbreaks of racial and ethnic violence represent decidedly particularistic narratives of what is an increasingly common phenomenon.

Those analysts who are inclined to see cycles express a strong faith that 'the crisis' of youth unemployment will work itself out. They advise that economies should continue along the same general path as had been their course in the heyday of industrial-sector domination. Others see more structural change, and thus advise strong readjustments in state policy to limit the haemorrhaging of capital and/or the underwriting of new methods to generate employment. Still others have suggested explicit planning to better articulate schooling with work. In any event, comparative studies across nations and regions hold out the promise of increasing our insights about the larger picture that youth face in the new service economies. There are two quite distinct approaches to this matter of comparative youth unemployment. First, there is the strategy of comparing whole societies – for example, France with Germany, the U.S.A. with Japan, or Australia with England – regarding the fate of youth. These comparisons are made with regard to rates of youth unemployment, or with regard to public policy on employment and employment training. As Osterman (1995) points out, this allows us to see how youth in general are doing in different settings, and how large societal issues and policies (or a lack thereof) relate to the transition from school to work. The other strategy involves comparing the fate of particular segments of the youth population within the same society, e.g., youth from the dominant society with youth from immigrant groups, from ethnic, or racial and cultural minorities.

There is a major methodological problem in studying youth unemployment by cross-national comparisons of the status of racial and ethnic populations. The Nuremburg injunctions against identifying citizens by race mean that many nations just do not keep statistics by race and ethnicity, or they have rejected a basis for collecting such data. Several researchers have come up against this barrier when trying to do comparative work in Europe. Gordon (1992) notes how Italy has very poor record keeping by race and ethnicity, Witte (1995) notes the same problem in France; and it is certainly true in several other European nations. Moreover, there is no agreed-upon poverty line in most countries; and even where there is, the differences between rural and urban poverty are considerable. It is difficult, in short, to address the issue of the comparative centrality of race or ethnicity in different countries without some minimal agreement on a baseline and an empirical database for making measurable comparisons. We can nevertheless salvage some important insights from specific kinds of comparative data. For example, most of the immigrant labourers have 'fallen' into secondary labour market employment in the last decade. There is a general tendency for the largest migrant groups in each country to experience the highest rates of unemployment. However, it is equally important to assess the ways in which the native population characterises and perceives the sense of 'their own displacement'. The massive economic and structural changes that occurred with German unification have been well chronicled. One of the 'local stories' was the sharp increase in ethnic and racial tensions and violence noted above, at the beginning of the 1990s.

On the surface, immigrant minorities and indigenous minorities would seem to experience much the same fate, i.e., the greatest vulnerability to high rates of youth unemployment. Nevertheless, it is a mistake to lump together immigrant youth with indigenous minorities in cross-national comparisons. In the United States, it is the indigenous minorities that have the highest rates of unemployment; immigrant Asian minorities on the two coasts, and immigrant Cubans in Florida fare much better (Portes and Rumbaut 1990; Portes and Zhou 1992).

By staying within a single country, we can compare youth unemployment between immigrant minorities recently arrived, and long-term indigenous minorities (where such records are kept). The U.S.A. has a history of recordkeeping regarding this difference, and mainly in the 1980s, there was important empirical and theoretical work in this arena. Ogbu (1978, 1983, 1990), Portes and Rumbaut (1990), Light and Bonacich (1988), Bourgois (1995), Bailey and Waldinger (1991), Waldinger (1986) and Wilson and Martin (1982) each made a contribution to our increased understanding of the relationship between ethnicity and economic destiny in postindustrial nations. Portes shows how immigrant solidarity in ethnic enclaves can be a buttress, even sometimes an economic advantage (trust, working with kin, extended and fictive, etc.). But this must be contrasted with Ogbu's work on indigenous cultural minorities where enclaves do not serve this advantage.

Because of the putative link between socialisation, credentialing and the workplace, comparative research on educational achievement of cultural minorities has been especially instructive. Gordon shows that West Indians fare relatively poorly in the United Kingdom's school system, John Ogbu (1990) points out that West Indians, however, do relatively well in the educational system of the United States. Since American-born blacks do relatively poorly in the U.S.A., Ogbu has theorised that the often dramatically different educational achievement successes of immigrant minorities versus indigenous minorities can be explained by the 'active resistance' of the latter, and is in sharp contrast to the 'active assimilation' strategy of the former. Today's immigrants soon become tomorrow's second and third generation, who either assimilate into occupational structures or act (and/or are treated) increasingly like indigenous minorities, who are visibly isolated to low-wage marginalised employment. Theoretically, comparison strategies (cross-national global comparisons versus internal differentiation, then comparative) can be related. As a matter of either practical empirical investigation or of social theorising, analysts tend to make a choice and favour one over the other. With respect to national policy planning related to the transition from school to job, at one end of the continuum is the German model. Germany integrates schooling with apprenticeships and, among nations, has the best articulation with industry and other sectors of the economy with actual post-training placement into first adult jobs.

At the other end of the continuum, the United States has one of the looser connections between schooling and employment, with a period of flux, adjustment and uncertainty. Current critiques at the most general level argue that U.S. education does not articulate well with either the changing white-collar technical segment or with the changing vocational economic organisation of the service sector. In the United States, about one-third of those who only complete high school fail to find stable employment by the time they are 30 (Osterman 1995: 11) In Germany, only about 10 percent of the population has not found stable employment by age 30.

When youth populations are disaggregated by immigrant, native-born, and ethnic or racial minority status, both internal and cross-national comparisons are dramatic and illuminating. At the beginning of the 1990s (Osterman 1995: 17) unemployment among all American high school dropouts, ages 16–24, was very high. However, for Blacks in America, it is over 70 percent. Germany, Luxembourg, and the Netherlands have virtually no families in persistent poverty (when that is defined as less than 50 percent of the median income for a period of over three years). Yet, using this same definition, Canada and the U.S.A. have a substantial portion in persistent poverty (Duncan, et al. 1995:7). For Quebec, Canada, the figure was one in eight. In the United States, for whites it was one in seven, but for Blacks, two in five.

There is a pyramid shape to income distributions of both agricultural and industrial economies, but an hour-glass shape (perhaps even 'coke bottle') of income distribution as the economy shifts from secondary-to service-sector domination (Plunkert 1990; Tienda, et al. 1987). Sassen's (1988) work on New York City economy shows that the immigrant population is engaged in the 'informalisation' of the New York City economy. Expanding high-income populations demand customised service, and this could produce the bulge above the middle squeeze of the hour-glass. Meanwhile, expanding low-income populations increase the demand for low-cost goods and services, thereby producing the bulge below the middle squeeze of the hour-glass. It is this lower bulge that is served by the proliferation of new small vendors or services and goods among the immigrant populations. Burgeoning private services can sometimes be handled by highly competitive small entrepreneurs developing out of the secondary labour market, and this is a direct link with what Sassen-Koob (1984) described in New York. In a related way, the work of Bonacich and Light (1988) on Koreans in Los Angeles, and Portes and Rumbaut (1990) and Bailey and Waldinger (1991) on ethnic enclaves in Miami (Cubans) and New York (Dominicans and Chinese) make similar points about vertical integration and entrepreneurial success.

The salience of this discussion is that there are two very different social policy implications here. If we think that it is the situation of youth in general that is worsening, we will consider general policy initiatives. On the other hand, if we think that the general situation is working, we need only tinker with the parts or direct policies at specific target groups and develop fine-tuned remedial strategies for those groups.

Blacks in America may simply be the first to have experienced massive structural youth unemployment in the service sector. They are soon to be followed by parallel developments in a number of other nations experiencing a sharp increase in the service sector of their respective economies. We should not be surprised when skyrocketing rates of youth unemployment happen to the most vulnerable youth populations, for example: the Turks in Germany; North African and Caribbean immigrants in France; Pakistanis and Jamaicans in the

United Kingdom; Vietnamese, Greeks, and Italians in Australia; and African immigrants (North and sub-Saharan) in Italy.

As noted above, Australian youth unemployment has run at about 15–20 percent for the last decade (Polk and Tait 1990). Australia obviously has no black youth unemployment problem, and the Aborigines are mainly in rural areas. But the fact that Australia has what seems to be an intractable youth unemployment problem forces us to reflect on whether this problem is a consequence either of 'neutral systemic forces' or policies and practices that impact one part of the population more than others. Phrasing the matter this way, it is clear why it is a severe analytic error to analyse spiralling youth unemployment in tertiary economies as either systemic or a feature of vulnerable populations. Both are true.

Deindustrialisation in the History of the Shoe: *The Nike Story* as both Metaphor and Literal

Nike, based in Beaverton, Oregon, began as a wonderfully simple American business story. For its first three years of operation, from 1969 to 1972, Nike was a fledgling company with little to distinguish it among shoemakers. Then, in 1972, a running coach at the University of Oregon, William Bowerman, placed a piece of malleable rubber on a waffle iron and demonstrated to Nike owner Phillip Knight an idea that would 'take off, running'. By attaching such a cushioning piece of rubber to the soles of shoes, they would become both lighter in weight and more durable. In twelve years, sales rose from $ 2 million in 1972 to $919 million by 1984 (*The Economist*, 2 December 1989: 84).

Nike discovered the profits that could be turned by closing its U.S.-based factories and replacing them with much cheaper labour in Asia. In 1988, Nike was paying an average of $6.94 per hour to American workers. However, in Korea, workers were earning less than one-third that amount. And so in 1989, Nike closed its last American factory in Saco, Maine. They had turned at first to South Korea in the early 1980s, and contracted with the Sung Hwa Corporation (Ballinger 1992: 46). Things were going well enough there until the South Koreans earned the right to unionise and to strike by the last third of that decade. In 1988, Nike bought 68 percent of its shoes from South Korea – but when the labour trouble hit, Nike struck quickly, and with Sung Hwa as intermediary, opened factories in Tangerang, Indonesia, a squalid industrial boomtown on the outskirts of Jakarta. There, a worker in the shoe factory is paid 14 cents per hour, or approximately $1.08 per day. Contrast this with the $55 per day average wage of the U.S. footwear factory worker, and we get a glimpse of how Nike's sales exceeded $3 billion in 1991, profits surged to $287 million that year (the highest ever), and why less than one percent of its more than 88 million pairs of shoes sold annually are made outside of Asia. To repeat, not a single pair of Nikes is now manufactured in the United States. And while South Korea was making nearly 70 percent of Nike shoes in 1988, cheaper and unorganised labour in China (Clifford: 1992), Indonesia and Thailand produced a precipitous drop to only 42 percent of production coming from Korea.[2]

As Ballinger (1992) points out, the Indonesian worker in that Tangerang factory, working six days a week, for ten and a half hours per day, takes home a paycheck at the end of a month equivalent to $38. A single pair of Nikes routinely sells for double that price.

However, job loss through the export of labour to other parts of the world is only one part of the story. In late 1995, American Telephone and Telegraph announced the elimination of 44,000 jobs. This was less a function of export, more a feature of downsizing to accommodate the new technologies that are replacing American workers, not with a labour force outside the country, but with sophisticated computer circuitry. The same thing goes for the recent trend to merge banks. While the lead paragraphs in these stories emphasize the increased size, volume and wealth that will result from creating the mega-banks, buried in some later paragraphs there is always the account of the loss of 6,000 to 14,000 jobs.

If the 1950s and early 1960s were economic boom periods for whites in the U.S. labour force, then the 1980s and 1990s were contrasting decades of economic downsizing/busts, with a corresponding decline of purchasing power – and of course, a declining sense of job security. In this context, politicians have a very important choice. They can elect to take the issue of job loss head on, and confront the political and economic policies that are generating that job loss. Or, they can purposefully try to deflect from the real issue of a shrinking labour force to focus attention on 'racial preferences' and 'racial quotas'.

The deflection is purposeful and inflammatory, since pollsters know that if the question of affirmative action is posed as a matter of social justice, of reducing discrimination against disenfranchised and excluded groups, even American white males are inclined to support it. But by naming the same practices[3] as 'race preferences' – the bull is guaranteed not only to charge, but to charge at the wrong target.

New Competing Labour Segments in the Service Economy

Employers in the industrial sector are more likely to be concerned with a worker's productivity than with how that worker relates to the outside world. That is the nature of employment in the manufacturing sector. Conversely, employers in the service sector are more likely to be concerned with a worker's way of relating to the customers, clients and the general public. This helps explain the findings by Culp and Dunson (1986) and Struyk et al. (1991) cited above regarding the different fates of matched pairs of white and black youth seeking employment in these two different occupational spheres.

For analytic parsimony, economic and social analysts of employment patterns usually emphasise one or the other side of the relationship between employer/employee and the job market. However, in an increasingly competitive economy with a low rate of growth, employment in the service sector involves a more complex set of conditions, which notably constrain economic opportunities, entry-level employment, and career trajectories for all workers. The problems here are exacerbated for young workers, and even more particularly for young workers with styles of presentation and demeanour employers see as threatening or less attractive. These employers are particularly sensitive to behaviours, attitudes and social and physical attributes that make up a certain 'presentation of self' because they assume that prospective customers will find these behaviours and attributes undesirable, and take their business elsewhere.

In this setting, more mature female workers replace younger male workers; immigrant workers replace native-born workers from racial and ethnic minorities (Segura 1984, 1989); and suburban workers replace workers from the more ethnic urban cores. The new demographic reality of two-worker households has meant that more women are engaged in the part-time or full-time workforce (Tienda et al. 1987, Bianchi and Spain 1986). This combines with the flight of retail trade, supermarket grocery and discount stores to the suburban periphery. It is now part of the taken-for-granted assumptions and of common observations and understandings how jobs migrate away from 'certain parts of town'.

For example, nearly all new export and regional-serving jobs moved north of Atlanta during the 1980s; the vast majority of low-income, black neighbourhoods are on the south side of town. In Dallas, nearly all new jobs have been created in the north and northwest quadrants of the metropolitan area; the black and Hispanic populations are concentrated to the east and south. In the Philadelphia metropolitan area, from 1970 to 1990 the number of export and regional-serving jobs that located in the high-income Main Line to the northwest of the city, as well as in the white middle-income areas of lower Bucks County to the northeast and New Jersey to the east, increased by more than 50 percent. The number of these types of jobs in the increasingly black and Hispanic city dropped by 15 percent over the same time period (Leinberger 1992).

A good summary of the empirical literature on this topic appears in Moss and Tilly (1991). There is also recent comparative work on geographical location and employment opportunities for young black males in New York and Los Angeles (Jargowsky and Bane 1991). The misfit between the location of urban young minority workers and suburban service jobs complements the employer preference for female and white workers to serve the predominantly white and female suburban retail trade and services clientele.

Wilson (1987) has argued that the exodus of the black middle class from the inner city to housing in more affluent neighbourhoods has effectively destabilised the situation for the poor blacks in the urban core. Wilson posits that the combination of the absence of role models and the lack of networks, connections or links by way of job referrals are at the core of the problem. Yet there is a sharp contradiction here that needs to be addressed both theoretically and empirically. In the early part of the century, it was common for immigrant minorities to settle in working-class and very poor areas of our cities. In succeeding generations, some sizeable proportion of this early group would accumulate enough wealth to move up and out of the area. This is the well-documented social history of the lower east side of Manhattan, where working-class Jews (garment district) and Italians (Little Italy) lived for a time, then the more economically successful moved up and out to Scarsdale and New Rochelle and Long Island. The Bowery served in a similar manner as the first home to the Irish. As some of these Irish became more affluent, they moved out. These three groups did not leave behind them an underclass of Jews and Italians and Irish, trapped in persistent unemployment, persistent and seemingly intractable poverty, and saddled with high rates of teenage pregnancies and high rates of incarceration. Rather, they left behind working-class Jews and working-class Italians and working-class Irish.

These groups left behind a working class for the elegantly elementary and simple reason that there was still a strong industrial sector at that period in American history. It had little to do with the absence of role models or the 'connection to jobs' that is provided by ethnic linkages and kin ties. Indeed, ethnic networks were and are important, and referrals to jobs in the police departments, the garment industry and the restaurant business were very much intact and in operation irrespective of the proximity or physical or geographical location or the making of the network (Glazer and Moynihan 1970). Thus, it is important to restate and emphasise that job referrals were done by kin, fictive kin and ethnic associates and connections, even from the distance of Scarsdale and New Rochelle. No underclass developed for the Jews and Irish and Italians, not because the middle class stuck around to provide role models (they didn't), not because the middle class stuck around (they didn't) to provide referrals (they did, but not from contiguous geographical locations), but because there was a strong manufacturing sector, a vital factory system which sustained a working class. The working class never needed the middle class to provide them with role models in order to work. In fact, where this topic has been the subject of empirical investigation, the working class often rejects the middle class as model and instead configures and creates its own image of appropriate class-related behaviour (Bernstein 1975; Bourdieu 1984; Cohen 1955; Miller 1958; Willis 1981).

If we reexamine the question of why the 'underclass' (or persistent poor) phenomenon has peculiarly visited itself upon African Americans (Jencks 1992), and if we reexamine why we did not have a Jewish 'underclass', despite the exodus of Jews to Scarsdale (Glazer and Moynihan 1970), we will stumble upon the answer because we can't get very far without tripping over it. Why? The data Wilson (1987) presented in the first chapters of *The Truly Disadvantaged* tell an important story about the economic transformation of this society. Wilson's argument about black middle-class exodus is special and interestingly idiosyncratic when we place it up against his earlier formulation about the decreasing significance of race in explaining persistent poverty. If this situation (of leaving behind an 'underclass') was experienced only or mainly by blacks, then are we not left with the glaring probability that there is something peculiar and unique about the circumstance of blacks in America? Race, perhaps?

Yet, if we leave it only at that, we have only part of the answer. Wilson was actually onto something important in the first part of his analysis of structural changes and its effects upon a new kind of development broadly affecting African Americans. However, rather than shifting the level of analysis to a general jobs policy and submerging the saliency of race, it makes more sense to acknowledge the saliency of greatest vulnerability. Social policy needs to take into account the specific and particular needs of the most vulnerable youth populations, and to fine-tune those policies in ways that address those particular vulnerabilities. This is not a zero-sum problem, where, to accept and promote a fine-tuning strategy requires that one must then abandon a quest for general strategies that will improve the conditions of labour market access for youth in general. It is important to pursue both strategies simultaneously.

Conclusion and Policy Implications

The United States, like almost every other nation that was an industrialised power in the first part of the twentieth century, has experienced a fundamental change in its social and economic organisation. The shift to service-sector domination has brought along with it substantial and sometimes massive youth unemployment. In the U.S.A., youth unemployment has had a particularly disproportionate effect upon blacks.

In an earlier time, there was a need for unskilled and semi-skilled labour. Today, we have an economy, which has few avenues of access for the young, inexperienced and unskilled. In the factory system, and in ancillary employment around the factories, there was usually employment for young males. However, in the service economy, new competition entering the labour force – from women and immigrant minorities – produces a considerable 'displacement' of these youth.

In other countries, a parallel development is occurring, and will affect the most vulnerable youth populations. We are bound to see alternative and underground economies springing up with greater frequency and with deeper penetration throughout post-industrialising societies across the globe. In these societies, youth from the most vulnerable immigrant, ethnic and indigenous minority populations will be most recruited to these alternative economies. Africans in Rome and Turks in Berlin will both experience these developments before Italian youth or German youth. Thus, rather than seeing African American youth as possessing particular attributes that make them unique, we may find some useful insights into the future if we reconceive the situation of high black youth unemployment as systemically derived and thus a harbinger of things to come for other vulnerable youth populations.

What are the social policies available to us to gain some control over these problems? Two basic approaches are available. The first is a control strategy, which is limited strictly to an attempt to contain and/or control the specific problems of crime that come hand-in-glove with alternative and underground economies. The second I will call a developmental strategy, designed to provide positive alternatives to the basic core of economic problems, within which urban education will play a central role. While control strategies might be appealing in some quarters, they leave the underlying problems intact.

We can expect too much from schools. The basic source of the contemporary crisis among young blacks resides in the shifting structure of the economy and the nature of work. Any attempt to work with schools must be accompanied by policies designed to address labour market conditions as well. Put another way, while there may be too many inadequate schools in the United States, the current crisis is not the result of bad schooling.

If we wish to take seriously the question of how to organise new futures for large numbers of young people currently trapped in a cruel structural reality and dominated by despair, we must be willing to consider the possibility of broad and wide-ranging new economic and educational policies. If we are to hold out for young people new hope in terms of work, then whole new job structures will need to be created. The term 'job structures' is used deliberately here, since more is at issue than simply creating jobs. Many young people today are trapped because they are excluded by a job world that requires high levels of skill, experience, credentials and qualifications. New forms of career ladders are required which make it possible for young persons who lack skills, experience or qualifications to make the climb upward into viable careers.

European Experience and Selective Importation

With all the caveats in place, we still need to ask what we might learn from selective European experiences. One of the interesting models is in Germany, where there has been a long and strong history of schooling that is directly tied in to employment at the end of the training and school. If a nation's leadership decided to rebuild or refurbish its mass system, it could have such a policy of articulating our schools with employment in the subway system. If a nation's leadership decided to build a super-magnetic levitation train system it could have a policy that could be articulating its schools with employment in super-magnetic levitation train systems. More than one step will be necessary to move school dropouts into the growing arenas of work such as computers (and related technologies), health, law, the environment, education, and new commercial enterprises.

Several steps will have to be created, and these steps involve two essential ingredients. First, new jobs have to be created which make it possible for a person to move upward (in ways not currently possible) in a step-by-step fashion in a career structure. For an example, at the present time, one becomes a teacher by finishing a university-level degree and obtaining a teaching certificate. However, it should be possible to have as an additional route a path where one works first as a tutor, then as a teacher's assistant, then as a teacher's aide, then perhaps as a teaching intern. Such routes would provide an alternative portal of entry into the role of teacher. The 'career ladder' assumes the creation of a linked set of new jobs, and is, therefore, above all else a job-creation strategy.

The second ingredient is some combination of education and training. This component is essential to ensure that through the upward movement in the career ladder there is the progressive learning of professional skills and experience, combined with credentialing. Such new forms of schooling would provide settings for the teaching and learning of specific skills, as well as the framework for ensuring that such learning is appropriately recognised through official recognition in the form of progressively developed qualifications. Explicitly organised to ensure movement upward in work careers, these would have a clear articulation with existing labour markets. The very notion of career ladders would then hold out for young workers the possibility of long-term employment with potential career mobility, a welcomed change from the current dominant scene in postindustrial societies.

I began by referring to a French and English exceptionalism in describing who the major image of 'the racial other' is in their population's dominant view. I want to conclude by providing what I think is a plausible explanation for this 'exceptionalism'. The fact that the British perceive the Indian population as 'the other' in a parallel manner that the French see the Arabs as 'the other' has to do with the convergent nature of these three forces. In order, these are (1) de-industrialization, the movement of capital investment across national boundaries to newly industrializing sites, and the concomitant shift to tertiary economies; (2), the movement of labour across national boundaries from 'less-developed' nations to post-industrial societies, and the concomitant 'hour-glassing' of the social stratification system of tertiary economies; and finally (3) the creation of an endemic and systemic pool of high youth unemployment. In Great Britain, Pakistani and Indian minority populations have become the most visible pool of high youth unemployment, and it follows that the British xenophobia towards this group is the highest of any European nation. In France, north Africans have become the most visible pool of high youth unemployment, and the French xenophobia towards this group is the highest of any European nation. It is more than just 'suggestive' therefore, to conclude that racial and ethnic conflict will be unevenly spread across Europe and Great Britain, but that there will be patterns to that conflict. We can expect the Dutch to have similar responses to the Surinamese, and the Spanish towards the Moroccans. To even suggest that there is random violence towards 'people of color' is not the way to approach a better understanding of the Eurobarometer findings. In order to reduce these new levels of inter-ethnic conflict, no amount of exhortation to be tolerant or civil will be as effective as developing long-term strategies of addressing systemic and endemic youth unemployment, across the continent, and across the divide between native and immigrant youth.

Notes

1. To a greater degree than any other nation, Germany, especially the former West Germany, has been able to buck the trend, with a relatively higher employment rate in the industrial sector, by remaining competitive in the manufacture of automobiles, chemicals and machine tools.
2. Spring in Their Step', *Far Eastern Economic Review*, 5 November, 1992: 56–57.
3. Set-asides for government contracts to small minority-owned businesses where there has been demonstrated racial exclusion

References

Bailey, T. and Waldinger, R. 1991. 'Primary, Secondary, and Enclave Labor Markets: A Training Systems Approach'. *American Sociological Review.* 56, 4: 432–45.

Ballinger, J. 1992. 'The New Free-Trade Hell'. *Harper's.* August, 285: 46–47.

Banton, M. 1999. 'National Integration and Ethnic Violence in Western Europe'. *Journal of Ethnic and Migration Studies.* 25, 1: 5–20.

Bernstein, B. 1975. *Class, Codes and Control, Volume 3, Towards a Theory of Educational Transmissions.* London: Routledge & Kegan Paul.

Bianchi, S.M. and Spain, D. 1986. *American Women in Transition.* New York: Russell Sage Foundation.

Bluestone, B. and Harrison, B. 1982.*The Deindustrialization of America.* New York: Basic Books.

Body-Gendrot, S. 1995. 'Urban Violence: A Quest for Meaning'. *New Community.* 21, 4: 525–36.

Bound, J. and Freeman, R.B. 1992. 'What Went Wrong? The Erosion of Relative Earnings and Employment among Young Black Men in the 1990s'. *Quarterly Journal of Economics.* 285: 201–32.

Bourdieu, P. 1984. *Distinctions: A Social Critique of the Judgement of Taste.* Cambridge, MA: Harvard University Press.

Bourgois, P. 1995. *In Search of Respect: Selling Crack in El Barrio.* Cambridge: Cambridge University Press.

Cohen, Albert K. 1955. *Delinquent Boys: The Subculture of the Gang.* Glencoe, IL: The Free Press.

Cole, R.E. and Deskins, D.R. Jr. 1988. 'Racial Factors in Site Location and Employment Patterns of Japanese Auto Firms in America'. *California Management Review.* 31, 1 (Fall): 9–22.

Cross, H., with Kenney, G., Mell, J. and Zimmerman, W. 1992. *Employer Hiring Practices: Differential Treatment of Hispanic and Anglo Job Seekers.* Washington, DC: The Urban Institute.

Culp, J. and Dunson, B.H. 1986. 'Brothers of a Different Color: A Preliminary Look at Employer Treatment of White and Black Youth'. *The Black Youth Unemployment Crisis,* R.B. Freeman and H.J. Holzer eds. Chicago: University of Chicago Press: 233–60.

Duncan, G., Gustafsson B., Hauser, R., Schmaus, G., Jenkins, S., Messinger, H., Muffels, P., Nolan, B., Ray, J.-C. and Voges, W. 1995. 'Poverty and Social Assistance Dynamics in the United States, Canada, and Europe'. *Poverty, Inequality, and the Future of Social Policy,* K. McFate, R. Lawson and W.J. Wilson eds. New York: Russell Sage Foundation.

Eurobarometer Opinion Poll No. 47.1, 1997. *Public Opinion in the European Union.* European Commission. Report 47, Directorate-General X, Brussels: 1–83.

Farley, R. 1984. *Blacks and Whites: Narrowing the Gap.* Cambridge, MA: Harvard University Press.

Farley, R. and Allen, W.R. 1987. *The Color Line and the Quality of Life in America.* New York: Russell Sage Foundation.

Flanagan, T.J. and Maguire, K. eds. 1990. *Sourcebook of Criminal Justice Statistics 1989.* U.S. Department of Justice Statistics, Washington, DC: USGPO.

Freeman, R.B. 1991. 'Crime and the Employment of Disadvantaged Youth', National Bureau of Economic Research, NEBR Working Paper No. 3875.

Glazer, N. and Moynihan, D.P. 1970. *Beyond the Melting Pot: The Negroes, Puerto Ricans, Jews, Italians, and Irish of New York City.* Cambridge, MA: MIT Press.

Gordon, I. 1992. *The Impact of Economic Change on Minorities and Migrants in Western Europe*. Washington, DC: Joint Center for Political and Economic Studies.

Hacker, A. 1992. *Two Nations: Black and White, Separate, Hostile, Unequal*. New York: Scribner's.

Jargowsky, P.A. and Bane, M.J. 1991. 'Ghetto Poverty in the United States 1970–1980'. *The Urban Underclass*, C. Jencks and P.E. Petersen. Washington, DC: The Brookings Institute.

Jencks, C. 1992. *Rethinking Social Policy: Race, Poverty and the Underclass*. Cambridge, MA: Harvard University Press.

Leinberger, C.B. 1992. 'Business Flees to the Urban Fringe'. *The Nation*. 255, 1: 10–14.

Light, I. and Bonacich, E. 1988. *Immigrant Entrepreneurs: Koreans in Los Angeles, 1965–1982*, Berkeley: University of California Press.

Lorence, J. 1991. 'Growth in Service Sector Employment and the MSA Gender Earnings Inequality: 1970–1980'. *Social Forces* 69, 3: 763–83.

Miller, W. 1958. 'Lower-Class Culture as a Generating Milieu of Gang Delinquency'. *Journal of Social Issues* 14, 3: 5–19.

Moss, P. and Tilly, C. 1991. *Why Black Men are Doing Worse in the Labor Market: A Review of Supply-Side and Demand-Side Explanations*. Social Science Research Council, New York.

Ogbu, J.U. 1978. *Minority Education and Caste: The American System in Cross-Cultural Perspective*. New York: Academic Press.

————— 1983. 'Minority Status and Schooling in Plural Societies'. *Comparative Education Review* 27, 2: 168–90.

————— 1990. 'Minority Status and Literacy in Comparative Perspective'. In *Daedulus*, 119, 2: 141–68.

Osterman, 1995. 'Is there a Problem with the Youth Labor Market, and if so, How Should We Fix It? Lessons for the United States from U.S. and European Experience.' *Poverty, Inequality, and the Future of Social Policy*, K. McFate, R. Lawson and W.J. Wilson, eds. New York: Russell Sage Foundation: 387–413.

Plunkert, L.M. 1990. 'The 1980's: A Decade of Job Growth and Industry Shifts'. *Monthly Labor Review* September: 3–16.

Polk, K. and Tait, D. 1990. 'Changing Youth Labour Markets and Lifestyles'. *Youth Studies* 9: 17–24.

Portes, A. and Rumbaut, R. 1990. *Immigrant America, A Portrait*. Berkeley: University of California Press.

Portes, A. and Zhou, M. 1992. 'Gaining the Upper Hand: Old and New Perspectives in the Study of Foreign-Born Minorities'. *Poverty, Inequality and the Crisis of Public Policy*. Joint Center for Political and Economic Studies.

Sassen, S. 1988. *The Mobility of Labor and Capital*. New York: Cambridge University Press.

Sassen-Koob, S. 1984. 'The New Labor Demand in Global Cities'. *Cities in Transition*, M.P. Smith ed. Beverly Hills, CA: Sage: 139–71.

Segura, D. 1984. 'Labor Market Stratification: The Chicana Experience'. *Berkeley Journal of Sociology* 29: 57–91.

————— 1989. 'Chicana and Mexican Immigrant Women at Work: The Impact of Class, Race and Gender on Occupational Mobility'. *Gender and Society* 3: 37–52.

Struyk, R.J., Turner, M.A. and Fix, M. 1991. *Opportunities Denied, Opportunities Diminished: Discrimination in Hiring*. The Urban Institute, Research Paper Sales Office, P.O Box 7273, Dept. C., Washington, DC, 20044.

Tienda, M., Smith, S.A. and Ortiz, V. 1987. 'Industrial Restructuring, Gender Segregation, and Sex Differences in Earnings'. *American Sociological Review* 52: 195–210.

Waldinger, R. 1986. *Through the Eye of the Needle: Immigrants and Enterprise in New York's Garment Trades*. New York: New York University Press.

Wieviorka, M. 1996. 'Violence, Culture and Democracy: A European Perspective'. *Public Culture* 8: 329–54.

Willis, P. 1981. *Learning to Labour: How Working-Class Kids Get Working Class Jobs*. New York: Columbia University Press.

Wilson, K. and Martin, A., 1982. 'Ethnic Enclaves: A Comparison of the Cuban and Black Economies in Miami'. *American Journal of Sociology* 88: 135–60.

Wilson, W.J. 1987. *The Truly Disadvantaged: The Inner City, the Underclass, and Public Policy*. Chicago: University of Chicago Press.

Witte, R. 1995. 'Racist Violence in Western Europe'. *New Community* 21, 4: 489–500.

Racial Conflicts in British Cities

Eric Seward*

The summer of 2001 saw some of the most serious disturbances in England's northern towns and cities for twenty years. It also, in two towns, involved Asian youths for the first time. It was certainly not a summer of love.

The events have caused people to question what is happening. How is it that after thirty-three years of comprehensive race equality legislation and a new, strengthened Race Relations Act, which was passed by the British Parliament in 2000, have we arrived at this situation? In 2000, a number of reports were produced on what has happened. They included specific reports on the disturbances in Burnley (Clarke Report) and Oldham (Ritchie Report), a report known as the Cantle Report which visited a range of towns and cities in the U.K. to learn about positive experiences in multiracial areas as well as negative ones, and a Government report (Denham Report) pulling together things from these various reports and other enquiries.

I want to set out here the thinking of the Commission for Racial Equality and, in particular, our perspective from the North of England on what has happened and what is the way forward. I do this having worked in race relations for nearly thirty years and having spent most of that time working in various capacities in the North of England. I have to say, at the outset, that whilst I have always believed that good race relations require continuous work and nourishment, if I had been asked when I started work in the North of England in 1977 that we would be witnessing what has happened in 2001 I would have been disappointed. It is certainly not what the Commission, along with many others, has been working to achieve.

The main disturbances, all of which had racial connotations, were in Burnley, located in the hills of Northeast Lancashire, Oldham on the east side of Greater Manchester and Bradford in West Yorkshire. The common feature of all of these towns/cities is that they were former centres of the textile and cotton industry

* Director for the Commission for Racial Equality in the North of England.

and for the last twenty years have suffered economic decline as the textile industry has collapsed and new industries and economic opportunities have moved elsewhere, particularly to the growing financial centres in Manchester and Leeds. As an illustration, in Oldham in 1971 over 18,000 people were employed in textile manufacture. Thirty years later, this figure had fallen to just over 3,000. Between the mid-1960s in Bradford and 2001, the number of people employed in the city's textile industry declined from 70,000 to 7,000.

All of these towns have significant Pakistani communities. Many came from the Miripuri area of Pakistan from the late 1950s/early 1960s onwards. The men arrived first and for many their initial intention was to earn sufficient money to support their families in Pakistan and then return. As time went on, this was no longer an economically viable option. Also, tightening immigration control meant that it was advantageous for families to join their men folk. When men arrived in these towns they joined relatives and friends already there. They used the private housing market, often renting properties first, and then purchasing low-priced houses in the same area later. They also used this kinship network to find jobs, mainly in the textile industry. They often worked on night shifts and had little contact with the indigenous white workforce who worked during the day. Even as late as 1984, 44 percent of Pakistani males in Britain were still working on night shifts across industries. With the collapse of the textile industry in the mid-1970s, many Pakistani men were thrown out of work and have struggled ever since to find alternative employment. Research in the early 1980s in a town adjoining Oldham in Greater Manchester, Rochdale, found that over 60 percent of Pakistani men aged over 50 were unemployed. Where they have found employment, it has been within jobs arising out of their own community – in the garment trade, the fast food and restaurant market and taxis. It has not always provided secure or high-earning employment. They have often been followed by their children (particularly their sons) into this work. Many of their children came to the U.K. halfway through their school lives. They did not always benefit from completing a full education in the U.K. They struggled in the new jobs market – financial services and communications – which frequently required good levels of education and communication skills.

I have briefly looked at the history of migration of the Pakistani community to northern towns and cities because it provides an important background to the current position of this community. Also, in Burnley and Oldham there is a smaller Bangladeshi community whose path to the U.K. and economic and life experience is similar to the Pakistani community I have just described. In Bradford, there is also an Indian population and a black or Afro-Caribbean population. The last reported census in the U.K. was in 1991 and we are expecting figures on the 2001 census to provide much needed and helpful information on what has happened to the various communities. However, we already know from the 1991 census and from further studies and our own observations, certain patterns that have taken place. In 1991, in Oldham, the census found that 8.7 percent of the population were of black and ethnic minority origin (mainly Asian). They live in four electoral wards clustered around the west and south of the town centre and most of them still live in these areas. In Burnley, the 1991 census showed the black and minority ethnic population at just over 5 percent. At that time, nearly 90 percent were living in just two electoral wards and this remains the case. In Bradford 11.5 percent of the population was of black and ethnic minority origin in the 1991 census. It has grown significantly since this time but some different patterns have emerged over where people live. Within the Pakistani community, the majority in 1991, and now, live in some five wards clustered around the town centre. Originally, many members of the Indian and black communities lived in the same areas. However, many of these Indian and black communities have become much more mobile over where they live. The Indian community, in particular, is moving to suburbs in the city. Essentially, when looking at population figures on the Indian community, you find that a significant minority of the community, often because of lack of economic success, have remained in their traditional areas of settlement around town centres. Others, however, who have been more economically successful, have moved out of traditional areas of settlement. Even by 1991, this was already marked in Huddersfield, a town adjoining Bradford and with a very mixed ethnic minority population. Just over 50 percent of the Indian community were living in two electoral wards in the former textile manufacturing area of the town. However, another 40 percent of the Indian community were already spread across ten other electoral wards.

I now turn to outlining the events around the disturbances. I deal with Bradford first. It has first to be said that there were previous disturbances in the city in the early and mid-1990s to which urgent action was promised and review groups were established. The first disturbance was on Sunday 15 April in an area to the west of the city centre, where a group of white males descended on a public house known to be used by Sikhs and Hindus and where people were also attending a Hindu wedding party. It was an area with no history of racial violence. The white males racially abused the Asian customers in the public house and arguments broke out. Word quickly spread by mobile telephone that a racial fight was going on and a large number of Asian (Pakistani) youths hurried to the scene. Three public houses and a chemist's shop were badly damaged, eight vehicles were destroyed and a number of windows broken. In the ensuing melée white passers-by, East Europeans leaving a local community centre, and a Hindu chemist's shop were attacked by the Pakistani youths. Most of the white males who had originally caused the trouble had left the area when the Pakistani youths arrived. There were complaints about the slowness of the police response, but it was the Easter weekend. The next disturbance in Bradford was on Saturday 7 July. An Anti-Nazi League rally against far right political organisations was held in the centre of the town. At the time, there was a banning order on all marches and processions, but meetings could take place. The Anti-Nazi Rally proceeded peacefully. However, as the rally was breaking up, rumours spread that a number of white males in the nearby shopping centre who had come out from a public house had attacked an Asian youth. This was true. There is also good reason to believe that these white males were associated with, or had sympathy with, far right political groups. Significant groups of Pakistani youths began gathering. The police moved them out of the shopping centre of the town towards an area known as Manningham to the north of the city centre, which has a large Pakistani community. There a long stand-off took place in which missiles, including petrol bombs, were thrown at the police. At its peak, 400–500 Asian youths were involved and over 200 police officers were injured. It should be stressed that there were other members within the Pakistani and Asian communities who were aghast at what was happening. There are well-documented stories of Asians protecting their own and white businesses as well as a young Asian man helping elderly white residents to a safer place when disturbances spread to the streets where they lived. The following Monday night more limited disturbances occurred on some white council housing estates in other areas of Bradford as white youths, stirred up by the far right, sought to exploit the situation. There were also some minor disturbances again in early November involving firework celebrations. The opportunity for disturbances therefore still exists. It is also worth saying that the courts are taking a tough line on the perpetrators of the violence. In some of the first cases to reach the courts, two Asian youths were sentenced to over six years, and four years imprisonment respectively for their involvement in the disturbances.

In Oldham, racial tension gradually increased since the end of 2000. There had been some well publicised reports in the local media, first of a young white male being violently attacked by a group of Asian youths in January and then in March a 76-year-old white war veteran. Figures were made public by the local police that showed that more white people were complaining of racial attacks than Asians. Far right political groups, in particular the British National Party, sought to exploit the situation and accused the police of not protecting the white community. These events started to attract national media attention and on the BBC radio news an interview was carried out with anonymous young Pakistanis who stated that areas of the town were 'no-go areas' for whites. This kind of comment fuelled racial tension. The government placed a banning order on marches in Oldham in order to preserve public order. However, it did not prevent British National Party (BNP) members gathering for informal meetings in public houses in the centre of the town. They also announced their intention to contest the two parliamentary constituencies in the coming General Election for the U.K. Parliament in June. On Saturday 26 May, in the early evening, following a minor argument between two Pakistani youths and a white youth in an area south of the city centre, a gang of white males, called by mobile telephone, attacked Asian homes and businesses. This led to an angry response from Pakistani youths who believed that the police were not protecting their community. (Many members of the Asian communities in Oldham were already not visiting the shopping centre in the town at weekends because of the presence of the British National Party). This led, as the evening progressed, to Asian youths seeking to leave the Glodwick area of Oldham where they lived to march to the police station in the centre of Oldham to protest and to the police stopping them. The youths also attacked a number of public houses where rumours were spreading that the far right political members had retreated to. Four or five hours of disturbances followed. Thankfully, only a small number of injuries were sustained. On the following Sunday and Monday nights, further incidents arose but on a much smaller scale. However, there were attempts by far right political groups to stir up white residents in adjoining white council housing areas to march on Asian areas that in turn drew a response from Asian youngsters. In the ensuing General Election, the British National Party received over 16 percent of the vote in one Oldham parliamentary constituency and 11.5 percent in the other. These were their best votes in any constituency in the General Election.

In Burnley, the violence began with minor incidents early in the morning of Saturday 23 June, involving initially a neighbours' dispute over a noisy party and then some stones being thrown at a Pakistani taxi driver as he was driving home. This led to increased tension and it peaked on the evening of Sunday 24 June. The most serious disorders started in the early evening when the police had to move in to prevent clashes between white and Asian youths in an area just outside the main shopping centre. Petrol bombs were thrown at the height of the disorder, a sex shop was burnt out and two public houses were badly damaged. Eighty-three police and twenty-eight members of the general public were injured. It is also know that disputes over territory for supplying drugs partly influenced what took place. The far right political party, the British National Party, has always had a small organisation in Burnley and in the General Election received just over 11 percent of the vote, which, after Oldham, was the best vote they received in the U.K. There were some local authority or council by-elections in Burnley at the end of 2001. In all these elections, the BNP fielded candidates. They received around 20 percent of the vote in each electoral ward where they stood, but this was a long way from being successful.

I have spent a little time detailing what happened as it helps our understanding. The disturbances that took place could easily have occurred in other northern towns with a similar population make-up and economic experience. The fact that they did not was due to luck, to effective community leaders discouraging Asian youngsters from responding to rumours about their communities being attacked, and to the far right not finding incidents that they could exploit. It also has to be said that these disturbances did not involve the black or Indian communities and that many Pakistani community leaders, businesspersons and people generally were appalled by what their male youngsters had done. It certainly was against their economic interests as it discouraged people from all communities from visiting many Asian restaurants located in these towns. The other important thing to remember is that all these disturbances arose initially out of small incidents that were provoked by white males who were at the very least hostile to the Pakistani community and had some sympathy with the political far right.

The question is, where now? The problem is clearly taxing the government and many other people.

I deal first with the political far right. They thrive on the media reporting on – and in particular showing pictures of – Asian youngsters throwing petrol bombs and bricks at the police and destroying property. Their tactic is to create fear in the Pakistani and Bangladeshi communities and then hope they violently react. Increasingly, their propaganda is not directed at the removal of all black and ethnic minority people from the U.K. but says that Muslims are not part of modern Britain and, if they can't be repatriated, should live in their own areas and have businesses located in their own areas along the lines that separate the Catholic and Protestant communities in parts of Belfast. They are not a large political party organisation in England and have no local authority councillors, let alone members of Parliament. The British electoral system, under which the candidate with the highest number of votes placed directly for them wins the seat, makes it more difficult. However, their determination to contest council elections indicates the need for them to be defeated remains. Also, questions need to be asked about whether orders banning marches and processions are sufficient to prevent far right political groups from creating unnecessary fear and damaging race community relations in our towns. We will have to look again at our legislation on this as well as whether our laws making incitement to racial violence a criminal offence are adequate. Currently, there are only some four successful prosecutions a year for this offence.

A characteristic of all the areas where these disturbances took place was poverty. They have all been subject over the years to a variety of government regeneration schemes but that has not removed high levels of unemployment, poor educational qualifications, poor housing and low incomes. Poverty and deprivation will always make communities inward-looking, territorial and anxious to protect the few things that they have, and which make them feel secure. It is no different for the Asian communities in these towns than it is for the white communities. All of these towns have white communities that are poor and deprived. In Oldham, government figures show that in 2000 nearly one third of the population (white and Asian) were living in income-deprived families. In Burnley, over 9 percent of the housing stock is empty, much of which is in the private sector and can be purchased, if ever any buyers can be found, for a few thousand pounds. A similar story exists in parts of Bradford. What has to be emphasised is that however bad deprivation is amongst some white communities, it is as bad, if not worse, amongst some of the Pakistani and Bangladeshi communities. In the main electoral ward where the Pakistani population lives in Burnley, government figures show that it ranks in the top 1 percent of deprived wards nationally. In a central electoral ward in Bradford, government figures show that it is the third most deprived area in terms of housing in England. Government regeneration money has been directed at these areas. However, it still causes resentment. As one Pakistani youth leader in Oldham said to me shortly after the disturbances, 'Why is Oldham having all these riots in areas where regeneration schemes are taking place?' It also produces resentment from deprived white communities who believe that Asian communities are getting all the money and they are not. What is needed is for regeneration schemes to be more closely identified with need, actually do something about high unemployment levels and be directed not at specific communities defined by racial group but at all poor communities.

Whilst talking about regeneration schemes, it is worth mentioning that another common feature in all the areas where disturbances took place was the absence of adequate facilities for young people for leisure and social purposes. The youth service run by local councils in the U.K. is not a statutory service and is frequently the target of expenditure cutbacks. It is also a service which, to survive, funds many time-limited and short-term projects. A more permanent funding basis is needed. In addition, the needs of young people, even within Asian communities, need to be taken account of. Research conducted by the Commission for Racial Equality in East Lancashire, which included Burnley, found strident complaints from young Pakistani and Bangladeshi women about the lack of leisure facilities for them, and which was even worse than it was for their male counterparts. In Oldham, a brand-new community centre built with regeneration money has met a real need in the Asian community for a proper venue for large meetings including Asian weddings. However, its opening led to the closure of a nearby youth facility used by many young Pakistani males. They are extremely bitter about this and see the needs of the elders in their community being met, but not their own. They also complain that when they go to meetings with the police all that is talked about are problems facing Pakistani taxi drivers in Oldham and not the topics they want to discuss.

A common feature in all the towns and cities where the disturbances took place was how the communities, in particular the Pakistani and Bangladeshi communities, had become separated in their work and lives from other communities in the town. It was best summed up in a report produced by former Commission for Racial Equality Chairman, Lord Ouseley, entitled 'Community Pride Not Prejudice – Making Diversity Work in Bradford', which was written before, but published shortly after, the troubles in that city. He stated:

> The key concern in the district (Bradford) is that the relationships between different cultural communities should be improving but instead they are deteriorating. There are signs that communities are fragmenting along racial, cultural and faith lines. Segregation in schools is one indicator of this trend. Rather than seeing the emergence of a confident, multicultural district where people are respectful and have understanding and tolerance for difference, people's attitudes appear to be hardening and intolerance towards differences is growing.

I referred earlier to population figures showing how communities are often living in different areas along ethnic lines. Where this happens, it can be reflected in the ethnic composition of pupils in schools. This is most likely to happen at primary schools that cater for children between the ages of 5 and 11. They normally attend the most local school. In Bradford, there are twenty-six primary schools where 70 percent+ of pupils are of Asian origin and in some primary schools, it is 100 percent. There are also forty-nine primary schools where the pupils are almost wholly white. A similar situation exists in Burnley and Oldham. In Oldham, there are seventeen primary schools where the majority of pupils are of Asian origin. There are also sixty-six primary schools that are almost wholly white. In secondary schools, which pupils attend from the age of 11 until 16 or 18, the ethnic composition of pupils can be more mixed as these schools attract pupils from a wider area. However, there can still be concentrations of pupils of particular ethnic groups. In Bradford, there are six secondary schools where Asian pupils form over 70 percent of the population. There are also three secondary schools that are almost wholly white. In Oldham, at secondary school level, there is one secondary school that is almost wholly composed of Bangladeshi pupils and another secondary school that is comprised almost wholly of Pakistani pupils. Over the last decade, white parents have gradually declined to send their children to these schools, even if they are the nearest school. Some Asian parents have also declined to send their children to a school where most pupils are of Asian origin. In Bradford, Burnley and Oldham there are also successful multiracial schools. An added factor with regard to ethnic composition of schools depends on whether the schools are maintained by the State or if they have Church (Roman Catholic or Church of England) affiliation. These schools exist in all three towns and cities where the disturbances took place. Some of these schools take pupils who are not of their religious faith. They are often multiracial. However, other schools only admit pupils of their faith. As a result, you have both a Roman Catholic and a Church of England secondary school in Oldham, which are wholly white, even though they are located close to areas where the Asian community lives.

We have therefore, in multiracial towns, a situation where some school pupils are being largely educated amongst children of their own racial group and in Oldham it can mean that if you are a Pakistani you only see Pakistani kids at school and if you are Bangladeshi only Bangladeshi kids. Because of the size of the indigenous white community, there will always be monocultural white schools in the U.K. The issue is what is taught in these schools to pupils about respect for pupils of other cultures, faiths and ethnic origins. In addition, monocultural schools should not exist in towns where there is a diverse ethnic population, particularly at the secondary level. The other important factor is that schools, regardless of the ethnic composition of their pupils, need to have high attainment levels. One of the factors that has discouraged white and a minority of Asian parents from sending their children to secondary schools where there are significant numbers of Asian pupils is poor attainment standards. For a number of years, Pakistani and Bangladeshi pupils have been achieving exam results at age 16 that are only half as good as white pupils. It is also worth noting that pupils of Indian origin are often some of the highest performers in these exams.

Having described the situation which exists in these three towns/cities and which, as I have previously stated, also exists in some of our other northern towns and cities, I now turn to potential solutions. I list them as follows:

1. The need to *build on the goodwill and tolerance of the key stakeholders* and the majority of people in all three towns/cities where the disturbances took place. In the General Election in June 2001 in Oldham, 86 percent of people did not vote for the far right British National Party. In more recent local

elections in Burnley, 80 percent of the people did not vote for the far right political party.

2. *In education, high educational attainment in all schools is a key factor.* If schools are successful in academic terms parents, regardless of ethnic group, will want to send their children there. Schools also need to have a clear and public ethos about welcoming diversity and not tolerating to racial discrimination and harassment. There is also a need to learn from and build on success stories in multiracial schools that are working.

   The United States' experience may be able to help. Court-enforced legal directions to desegregate schools have not always been successful. More recent evidence from the United States suggests that encouraging multiracial schools through a voluntary approach may produce better results. The 'Magnet School Model' seeks to promote the racial desegregation of schools through equity for all pupils and excellence of education. The quality of the education programmes in these schools is upgraded by, for example, having smaller classes and making improvements to school premises and facilities. Funding from the private sector is involved in these schools and there is strong networking between different Magnet Schools.

3. *Unacceptability of incitement of racial violence and racial attacks.* A climate needs to be created where racial attacks by any group are unacceptable and are reported as such in the local media. The police have a key role in encouraging the reporting of such attacks and successfully investigating these cases so that the perpetrators can be caught. In Oldham, for example, there are persistent complaints from the Asian community that the police will do nothing about their complaints of racial attacks and therefore they do not bother to report them. The government also needs to look again at whether our laws dealing with incitement to racial hatred and allowing meetings of political organisations to take place which stir up such hatred can any longer be tolerated and whether the law needs to be tightened.

4. *Government regeneration schemes.* As previously said, there has not been a shortage of money under regeneration schemes going into Bradford, Oldham and Burnley. The issue is around whether real needs are being met and whether one deprived group feels it is not getting something that another group is getting along ethnic lines. A more area-based approach is needed. For example, a health education programme in Oldham could be directed at all deprived communities, but it might be more concerned with heart disease and diabetes amongst Asian women and more concerned with combating smoking amongst white working-class women.

5. *Wealth creation.* All of the towns where the disturbances took place face economic decline. There are other northern towns in a similar situation. There is a real need to stimulate local employment, including use of the

entrepreneurial skills of the Asian communities, as well as encouraging other employers to invest in these areas. Government and European funding will be necessary. These places need to be reinvigorated in the same way that new towns and industries alongside them were created in different parts of the United Kingdom in the 1950s and 1960s.

6. *Bringing communities together.* Funding programmes for community activity need to give greater priority to schemes that bring different ethnic communities together. Funding will always be needed for community groups servicing particular community needs and this may be on ethnic lines. However, much more needs to be done to fund schemes that bring people together. For all the difficulties, that the United Kingdom faces in Northern Ireland, the community funding programmes there are much better directed at bringing the divergent Catholic and Protestant communities together. There may be lessons for the rest of the United Kingdom here.

7. *Planning future location of communities.* Where people work, live, socialise and are educated is a matter of choice. However, if this is to take place in an environment where diversity is encouraged and separateness is not, then where we locate houses, schools, shops and facilities in future must take diversity into account. In the United States there are some examples where using strong local leadership, public subsidies, tax breaks and imaginative planning, diverse communities have remained diverse and some inroads have been made into communities segregated along racial lines. The future location of shops, places of worship, schools, leisure facilities and work needs to bring people of different ethnic groups together, even if they might live in streets that are segregated along ethnic lines. There is no reason why the halal butcher should not be on the same street as the non-halal or traditional English butcher. Shops selling South Asian cloth and clothes could easily be located on the same street as our main chain stores such as Marks & Spencer, Next and British Home Stores. Schools need to be positioned in a place where they can attract pupils in their catchment's area from different ethnic groups. Places of work, particularly where employees meet members of the public, need to be located in areas that attract different ethnic groups. Underpinning all of this must be a strong ethos that removes racial harassment and the fear of violence from all communities so that where people live, choose to work and send their children to school is not governed by these factors. Changes in the United Kingdom's planning criteria, financial incentives and the encouragement of housing across a wider price range will all help to bring this about.

When race discrimination legislation was first passed in the U.K., the government Minister then responsible (Home Secretary) talked about creating a society that was culturally pluralistic but based on racial equality: not integration but based on a respect for difference of culture, faith and ethnic groups. That respect applied both to how the black and minority ethnic communities approached the white community and how the white community approached and saw the black and minority ethnic communities in the United Kingdom. It is not all a depressing story. We now have in leading positions in the United Kingdom persons from black and minority ethnic communities in public institutions and private business. There are many areas of employment previously denied to black and minority ethnic communities that are now available to them. Some of the highest educational achievers in the United Kingdom are pupils of Indian and African origin. Much, however, remains to be done and the disturbances discussed in this chapter, with their racial connotations, are a ready reminder of this. The government has a key leadership and influencing role. Desegregation cannot be left to economic market forces alone. The Government is looking for a national debate about what multicultural Britain means in the new twenty-first century. It might not be a comfortable debate and it will not always be easy to keep to the key issues. For example, some are already saying that racial segregation is happening because the Pakistani and Bangladeshi communities do not speak English. They conveniently forget that the Asian youths attacking the police can all speak and write English. Most were born here. A debate, however, must take place and it must have a successful outcome.

LIMITS OF TOLERANCE AND LIMITED TOLERANCE: HOW TOLERANT ARE THE DANES?

Peter Hervik

A recent survey by the European Monitoring Centre on Racism and Xenophobia (EUMC) has shown that Denmark is one of the most polarised countries in the European Union. Denmark had some of the highest tolerant *and* racist answers (EUMC 2001). These data suggest that the notion of tolerance relates to racism either in opposition or in a more delicate relationship. The EUMC opted for the first and concluded, 'Denmark is a quite polarized country' (EUMC 2001: 12).[1]

During classes in Copenhagen and Oslo, I played a little game that may further illustrate the complexity of this relationship. To introduce discussions about the nature of racism, I asked the students if they felt they were 'racists'. A unanimous and prompt 'no' followed. Then I asked, 'is "racism" widespread in Denmark or Norway?' Again, the answer came out strongly and instantly 'yes'. I asked these questions at the beginning of the class to illustrate the complexity that lies in the exercise and to trigger the urge to seek an explanation.

The affirmative answer 'racism is widespread in Denmark', is consistent with the EUMC findings. Racism *is* widespread and would therefore produce many racist answers. The other answer tells us that the students do not identify themselves as 'racists' instead they see themselves as tolerant. According to the EUMC typology, Danes scored high on 'not being disturbed by people from different minority groups', which in the survey terminology is called 'actively tolerant'. In other words, the students in the class could also produce both racist and tolerant answers. How can one at the same time produce tolerant and racist answers?

One of the tools that opened up the classroom discussion is indeed the Eurobarometer Opinion Poll of 1997. Or rather, one of the questions posed in the survey. Instead of asking, 'do you consider yourself racist?' approximately

16.000 people in the European Union were asked to rate their opinion on a scale between the two extremes, 'not at all racist' to 'very racist'. Applying this question in the classroom students would no longer deny their own racism, but admitted 'some degree' of racism. Besides perhaps demonstrating the fragile nature of quantitative research, this little experiment also suggests that tolerance and racism appear in a delicate, intimate, and perhaps unequal relationship.

At no point did I present a definition of racism and neither did the researchers conducting the Opinion Poll. This was for different reasons. I continued the discussion in a way, which would bring up and out connotations of racism including its relationship to tolerance and antiracism. The opinion poll assumed that all knew and understood the definition of racism, and alluded simply to the 'commonly used' way of describing 'a process of prejudice which leads to groups being stigmatized, discriminated against and considered as inferior because of particular characteristics of their group' (Eurobarometer Opinion Poll 1997). This is an analytic definition that does not necessarily reflect the range and complexity of popular associations. Research, including my own, has shown that several clusters of related meanings dominate the Danes' discussion of racism. First of all, the term is associated with German Nazism, white supremacist movements such as the American Ku Klux Klan and South African apartheid. Secondly, racism also simply refers to 'not liking' people of a different colour or cultural background. Thirdly, racism may be acknowledged, but is associated with various problems ethnic minorities represent for the host society (Hervik and Jørgensen 2002, Hervik 2003). Taking these popular connotations of racism into consideration, we can no longer be sure what the Eurobarometer Opinion Poll exactly showed.

I use this information to illustrate my general argument: that the discourse of tolerance is intimately connected to racism.[6] In the last decade, tolerance has been challenged in Denmark by the emergence of new nationalism and new racism seeking an end to what is called 'blue-eyed' tolerance. In the general definition of UNESCO:

> Tolerance is respect, acceptance and appreciation of the rich diversity of the world's cultures, our forms of expression and ways of being human. It is fostered by knowledge, openness, communication and freedom of thought, conscience and belief. Tolerance is harmony of difference. It is not only moral duty; it is also a political and legal requirement. (UNESCO 2001: 9)

Definitions like this go hand in hand with multiculturalism (Hastrup 2001: 2) and are being challenged by critics who claim that there should be no tolerance of people who do not rightfully belong in Denmark. Such contestation has led to two observations that I wish to look closer at in this paper.[3] On the one hand, when tolerance is challenged and limits are crossed, we could expect that the notion of tolerance should be defended by sanction if necessary, and appeals to moral education or otherwise restored. Only in an idealistic setting would there be no intolerance. Nevertheless, there is a limit to tolerance; otherwise, it would not have made sense as a shared value or ideology. The limit of tolerance is not an absolute, but dynamic and debatable. Obviously, tolerance is not applicable to all actions. There seems to be a general agreement that tolerance should not accept acts of murder, violence, physical harm or denials of exercising the right to fully express diverse beliefs and practices (Kurtz 1996: 1). Social claims of where the limit of tolerance runs in Denmark are one of the key issues in this paper. One can easily imagine people arguing that the limit of tolerance has been overstepped and followed by claims of cultural difference that are seen as incompatible and not to be tolerated. If the headscarf (head covering of Muslim women) is contested, does that express a limit of tolerance that has been crossed or does it express something entirely different, such as racism? Ideally, two responses may occur. Either the discourse of tolerance is evoked and defended or it is abandoned. However, regardless of what occurs, when the limit of tolerance is challenged by racism, the position of power held by tolerators is exposed and separated from people who are the objects of tolerance. Tolerance is at the mercy of those who practise tolerance. I will show how this is demonstrated through political discourse and popular understanding.

On the other hand, Denmark has witnessed the unfolding of limited tolerance, which appears as racism that takes tolerance as a cover for attempts to contest and dominate ethnic minorities associated with non-Western origins. Tolerance is evoked in discourse (we are tolerant), but the appearance of cultural others is not tolerated (we should not accept the headscarf) – then we can speak of 'limited tolerance'. Those who are culturally distinct are inferior for holders of power, who use inferiorising as a basis for denying access to public resources, material as well as symbolic. This we can refer to as 'limited tolerance' for racism. In my opinion racism must include the culturalist division typically between an 'in-group' of a positive, unspecified, majority of 'we' and an 'out-group' of unbridgeable others, but only insofar as the distinction is used by the 'in-group' as a rationale to manage, control and dominate the 'out-group' (see Hervik 1999, 2001).

Tolerance is best seen as an attitude, and toleration, the active form of tolerance. Toleration is therefore never a matter of non-discrimination, but of engaging the value of difference (Hastrup 2001). By introducing this distinction, Hastrup (inspired by Michael Walzer) rhetorically seeks to shift the significance of tolerance from a passive attitude of acceptance to an active outreach and commitment to engage positively in the difference. Michael Walzer introduces a useful idea of shades of tolerance that allows for different practical engagements in toleration. The first is simply 'a resigned acceptance of difference for the sake of peace' associated with religious toleration of the sixteenth and seventeenth centuries. The second refers to a 'passive, relaxed, benignly indifferent to difference' attitude that sees that it is necessary to have 'all kinds to make a world'. Thirdly, there is the attitude that '"others" have rights even if they exercise those rights in unattractive ways'. The fourth concerns openness, curiosity, and even respect to learn from the difference of others. The fifth is the 'enthusiastic endorsement of difference. Since difference is either seen as God's creation or liberalism's condition for flourishing' (Walzer 1997: 10–11). The first three types of engagement – 'resigned acceptance', 'benignly indifferent' and accepting the right to practise 'unattractive ways' – tolerate the existence of what is perceived as fundamentally different. The fourth and fifth type of engagement in difference seem to be the most actively and positively gained since the imperative is 'learning' and 'endorsement of diversity'.

Walzer (and Hastrup) does point to the inherent positions of power and tacit assumptions about who is tolerant of whom. However, while he expands the concept to allow for different degrees of tolerance, he does not address the relationship between tolerance and racism – issues, which I argue, are intimately connected. At this point, he may be prisoner of his own liberal perception of the individual. If tolerance 'presupposes the value of the individual, his or her autonomy, and freedom of choice' (Kurtz 1996: 1), then there is an inherent risk in the tolerant society to de-emphasise the dialectic, and usually asymmetric, relationship between tolerator and tolerated (Vanges 2001). What happens, for instance, if tolerators declare that there are certain cultural practices of other people that they do not want to tolerate, and insist on ending tolerance towards certain groups and their beliefs? This seems to be the case in Denmark.

If tolerance refers to the attitude that some ideas, beliefs and practices of other groups of people are permitted, then how does that relate more specifically to the growing culturalist perspective that sees differences as incompatible and antagonistic? This is the question for my first section, where I will analyse the political discourse on tolerance and racism that has gradually emerged since 1989. In the second part of this text, I turn to the popular discourse that regards the Danes as tolerant. In the third section, I deal with basic assumptions of tolerance and racism behind quantitative research examining Danish attitudes towards immigrants and refugees. Then, in sections four and five, I will present and discuss hidden beliefs and assumptions of tolerance, including the separation of tolerators and tolerated and the so-called threshold of tolerance.

Discourse of Tolerance and Discourse of Unbridgeable Cultural Differences

Following the radical events of 1989 (i.e., the fall of the Berlin Wall), Europe witnessed in 1990–91 a drastic increase in racially motivated violence and polarized attitudes towards immigrants (and refugees). These incidents were followed by new demands for tougher policies restricting the number of non-Westerners coming into Western Europe and calling for tougher requirements of those already within the European Union. At that time the discussion revolved around comprehensive changes in the former Soviet Union, the Balkans and the idea of 'Fortress Europe' with its vanishing internal borders and fortified external borders.

This relationship between international turbulence and global processes, accompanied by leading politicians' warnings about hungry Russians and Africans threatening the 'safety' of the West European middle class, can perhaps best be illustrated by a referendum on the expansion of the European Union.

Denmark voted in 1992 on the so-called Maastricht treaty, which questioned whether the country could agree on further European integration. The referendum – ending in a surprising rejection of the treaty – revealed a large gap between politicians and the voters, who in fear of abolishing borders reacted against the politicians and the idea of a United States of Europe. This gap was further consolidated during the second referendum less than a year later, where the treaty, although with some reservations, was passed.[4]

In 1997 a newly formed right-wing party, the Danish People's Party (*Dansk Folkeparti*) and a tabloid paper, *Ekstra Bladet*, teamed up and succeeded in capitalising on the discrepancy between the politicians and the voters by launching a campaign. It was known as 'The Foreigners' against the presence of immigrants and refugees. Danish culture is presented by the journalists of the paper and the commentators from Danish People's Party, who frequently appear in *Ekstra Bladet's* campaign, as being threatened not only by immigrants and refugees, but also by the political and cultural elite who allow 'foreigners' to enter the country and exploit the Danish welfare system.

This nationalist upsurge reached a new peak when immigrant and refugee presence became *the* dominant issue in both local and national elections. In these discussions, nationalist demands for a strengthening of Danish values emerged in tandem with growing racism targeted at the 'foreigners in Denmark'.

The emergence of a new racism in Denmark unfolded and became strong in a dialectic relationship between the international events and global process of the post-1989 world and distinct Danish circumstances. Through the efforts of political entrepreneurs and opportunistic leaders of newspapers, a distinction between a 'we-group' of seemingly unproblematic, open-minded, democratic people was produced as different from the 'out-group' of unbridgeable different cultural others. The elements mobilised to construct the positive 'we-group' and the negative 'out-group' are syncretistic, since they are formed by any available argument, regardless whether they are internally inconsistent. This culturalist distinction does not constitute a new racism in itself, but becomes a new racism, when the dichotomy denies the out-groups' rights to access to political office, the labour market or welfare and public recognition. In Denmark, the discriminated 'out-group' consists of people associated with what Ghassan playfully has labelled 'Third World-looking people' (Hage 1998: 57ff).

With this development, one would perhaps expect that there are vast numbers of immigrants, refugees and asylum seekers in Denmark. This is not the case and the relative number of immigrants and their descendants is not much different from other European countries. Foreign citizens in Denmark constitute 4.8 percent of the population (statistics from 1 July 2002). The number of immigrants and their descendants, regardless of citizenship, amounts to 7.8 percent or almost 421,715 of the 5,374,255 Danes (Nyt fra Danmarks Statistik 2002). Of these, approximately 170,000 are Muslims, including all degrees of religious conviction.

In the late 1990s leading Social Democrats (the big brother of the government's coalition) felt they needed to contain growing anti-immigrant sentiment. To do so they appointed a new hard-line Minister of the Interior,

Thorkild Simonsen. He was given the task of passing a new Integration Act that supposedly would increase the quality of integration and curb the growing racism. In the situation of growing racism, the new minister tried to locate tolerance at the national level. He summarised his concern for tolerance:

> Some Danes speak about a threat against the national values. And *they* have stirred up worries about Danish 'hygge', culture, language, and economy. But there is a national value, which is very important in the future of *our* society – a value that is really threatened. Still, many fall short of defending it. That value is tolerance. Tolerance does not mean that *we* should blindly accept everything foreign. But tolerance means that *we* shall be open to each other without too many biases. Tolerance means that *we* should not stigmatize people who look different from *us* and not belittle other people's way of living and *their* religion. (T. Simonsen in *Ekstra Bladet*, 15 December 1999, emphasis mine)

The Minister of the Interior identified tolerance as a Danish national value that needs to be cared for. The culturalist division is clearly present. 'We' is not specified but refers to Danes, while 'they' are 'foreign', some of whom 'look different from us' and have a different 'way of living' and religion. Tolerating is something 'we' the unmarked Danes should do, rather than 'blindly accept everything foreign' without too many biases, 'stigmatize' or 'belittle' those, who are to be tolerated. Simonsen's reflections suggest than Danes should be tolerant (which they are not) towards those who are foreign, appear physically different or practise different religions. Thus, he addresses racism by promoting tolerance, but ends up establishing and reproducing the same culturalist and nationalist distinction that new racism builds upon.

Another politician, John Vinter, has also addressed the theme of racism and tolerance. But this member of the Conservatives disavows racism and attempts to promote tolerance by referring to Denmark's international reputation:

> Racism is really not a genuine problem in this country. On the contrary, Denmark is known for its tolerance, and by those, who really have felt racism on their body, they recognize Denmark as a people whom without hesitation helps other people, for instance the Jews during the war. (John Vinter in *Politiken*, 23 May 1997)

During his celebration of tolerance and denial of racism, Vinter uses Denmark's historical reputation to argue that contemporary Denmark is not racist. In other words, tolerance is evoked to trivialise racism.

Pia Kjærsgaard, leader of the Danish People's Party, is an example of the evolving new racism as well as an entrepreneur appropriating intercultural differences for political purposes. Kjærsgaard exploits and capitalises on the contradiction between political rhetoric of equality and people's social experience of cultural difference as a problem which is important in the organisation of collective action and which the party utilises to near perfection. Thus, Kjærsgaard explained in an emotional appeal:

> I don't care about what the political establishment says and thinks. What is important to me is that local storekeepers agree with me. (*Berlingske Tidende*, 4 October 1997)

Denmark is not a country of 'racist' people. We are an open minded and tolerant
people, and meet foreigners in a natural manner of friendship. But, we refuse to let
ourselves be abused. That is what it is all about. In the Danish People's Party we do
not hide the fact we are against having Denmark turn into a multi-ethnic society.
(Speech at the party's annual meeting 1997, *Dansk Folkeblad*, 1997)

In meetings around the country, I experience daily the insecurity that prevails among
Danish citizens. And the many letters that I receive daily say the same: Everyone is
disconcerted, insecure, and feels that it is no longer safe to walk around freely.
(*Ekstra Bladet*, 19 September 1997)

The fundamentalist perception of Islam still lives in the Middle Ages, and is
incompatible with the Danish society. We can not simply give free scope to people
who in our opinion are more than 100 years behind in terms of norms and ways of
living. (*Weekend Nu*, 21 September 2001)

Kjærsgaard's statement that we are 'tolerant' but 'refuse to let ourselves be abused'
is obviously pure rhetoric. Placing people according to socioevolutionary stages
of development and systematic calls for restrictions on people of diverse cultures
from outside the Western world constitute limited tolerance.

Claims of tolerance emerge with a culturalist/nationalist division between a
'we-group' of Danes and an 'out-group' of foreigners. The politicians appeal to
the notion of tolerance, but the appeals are rhetoric. The Minister of the
Interior reminds people to remember to be nice. John Vinter denies the obvious
and ongoing contestation of ethnic minorities in order to care for Denmark's
historical reputation, which is at stake. And Pia Kjærsgaard's 'limited tolerance'
turns the presence of ethnic groups in Denmark into a security issue and a
cultural threat.

The discourse of tolerance and antiracism prevails in Danish society, but it
either competes with or is subdued by the stronger and more motivating
discourse of culturalism that sees cultural differences as unbridgeable and even
hostile. When the discourse of culturalism embeds a more or less articulated
sentiment directed at individuals and groups who are identified as 'culturally
diverse', with the purpose of making them inferior, marginal, and excluded, we
call it a discourse of neoracism. This is the case when the 'out-group' is placed
on a different rung of the socio-evolutionary ladder a hundred years behind in
terms of 'norms and ways of living'. In this way, neoracism is one radical version
of the discourse of culturalism.

I will now turn from politicians' representations to popular talk (as
represented through our interviews).

'Danes Have Become More Tolerant'

In this section, I will discuss if popular talk concerning the cultural expressions
of Denmark's ethnic minorities relates to the notion of tolerance or to racist
discourse implicit in discussions about tolerance.

'Danes have become more tolerant' was the sales slogan of the Danish daily newspaper *Politiken* on 13 March 1997. The text appeared on a placard that also displayed an eye-catching photo of a dark-haired female wrapped in a Danish flag. She used the flag as a veil, thereby displaying two immensely powerful symbols: the Danish flag and the veil generally used as a metonym for Islam. This captivating image appeared as an artefact of *Politiken's* discourse in the upbeat Danish debate about which rights and obligations immigrants and refugees should meet.

Many Danes had their curiosity aroused and perhaps satisfied at the news-stand when they glanced at the large front-page colour photograph that added a headline to the sales slogan: 'We have become accustomed to foreigners.' The text itself revealed that in the last years, we (the Danes), have become more tolerant as a result of declining media coverage.

Months later, we – in the research project – acquired a copy of the placard and used it to facilitate conversations with Danes about their concerns and anxiety relating to the emerging multiculturalism in Denmark. Here are some reactions from our interviewees:

> It is a ridiculous message; I do not know what could be behind it. (Pia, 24, student)

> It seems to me that she is being covered up in the Danish flag, like covering up foreignness. (Thomas, 24, student)

> I too see an ambivalence between the text that says we are becoming more tolerant and then we go on to shield ourselves in the flag. (Morten, 29, student)

> What does: Danes have become more tolerant mean? It might just be a slogan for selling the paper. (Morten)

> Besides that her veil is the foremost symbol of xenophobia. I also think there is a curious ambiguity in that the Danes have become more tolerant and then we are shown a picture of what we like the least and use it as a symbol. (Erik, 31, teacher)

> I just feel like in the text it is the foreigners who say this, right? And that makes me a little upset. They should not think so. (Anna, 19, unskilled worker)

> We have been tolerant, but I don't think we are anymore, and I don't think we should be. (Anna)[5]

Talk about the placard photo and text left all interviewees perplexed. Their perplexity arose from the ambivalence between text and photograph and the startling news that contradicted interviewees' experience of what was going on in Denmark at the time. Either they reasoned that the symbols, the headscarf and the flag, contradicted each other. Or, they looked for a subtext that could explain the surprise as to why someone would come up with a statement that so obviously contradicted the popular common sense notion that Danes were becoming increasingly intolerant. All in all, the interviews dispute the assertion that Danes have become more tolerant.

In terms of accepting (tolerating) different cultural markers, most interviewees would agree with Agnete and Lola, who explained:

That women wear scarves is provocative for many Danes. (Agnete, 34, economist)

Head scarves are provocative, either because they did not themselves choose to wear head scarves, or because they do not want to do anything else. (Lola, 32, editor-in-chief)

They are simply foreign by their appearance. (Grethe, 61, secretary)

I do get offended when I see groups of girls on their way to school. Their headscarves, I wonder, are always nicely ironed with beautiful laces, and look very clean in the mornings, but I must say it annoys me. (Grethe)

One informant, Helle, had a hard time tolerating immigrants who commit criminal acts and wished to send them back to their country of origin. She argues:

Regardless of how tolerant one wishes to be in relation to different groups of people I cannot help being offended. (Helle, 25, teacher)

These interviewees were annoyed with cultural difference, but they did connect their feelings with the idea of tolerance. The idea of tolerance was not an available option. If Danes were tolerant in the past, they are now no longer. A social worker's commentary epitomises the change:

Headscarves mark a difference, but it is a difference that I can live with. I think it is nice and I think it is exciting to experience, how these women dress differently ... [pause] ... They should do as they please, I cannot see why wearing a headscarf would annoy anyone, but then of course it marks a difference. I mean, I think they should be allowed to, but it might be that it would be smart of them not to wear it, since some people may be offended by it. (Marianne, 53, social worker)

At first, Marianne talks about tolerance in the sense of tolerating different cultural markers. However, it becomes clear that the same markers are difficult for her to accept and that they represent something provocative.

In both the politicians' discussions and the interviews, we have seen a culturalist distinction between a 'we-group' of Danes and an 'out-group' of foreigners. Any such construction of others also serves the constitution of groups (Wodak 1995). In the case of Marianne, we saw an example of the denial of personal responsibility and a displacement of responsibility onto the group as a whole. Rather than demanding that immigrant women cease to wear the headscarf, Marianne displaces her stand from herself to the anonymous 'we-group', when she says 'it might be that it would be smart of them not to wear it, since some people may be offended.' To avoid harassment and discriminatory remarks these women – in their own interests – should not wear the headscarf. Like the previous informants, Marianne does not evoke the discourse of tolerance.

The aim of such discourse of self-justification, says Ruth Wodak, is a way of allowing the speaker to present herself or himself as free of prejudice or even as a victim of so-called reverse discrimination (ibid.). Even when respondents were asked for their views concerning named individuals known to the wider public, they would automatically leap into the general 'we' and 'they' categories, as if everyone understood who 'we' and 'they' were (Hervik 2003).

Annoyance or even irritation has now reached an extent to which even intimate items such as food and clothes (in particular the headscarf) cannot be accepted. Vibeke associated ethnic clothing with the worst category of 'foreigners' in Denmark, whom she saw as exploiting the welfare system:

> Clothing is – in my opinion – most provocative regardless if foreigners keep one or the other form of dress. (45, official)

Abelone cannot accept the sight of religious activity:

> I believe that when they kneel five times a day during work, that I can't tolerate. They should follow Danish customs. (Abelone, 83, retired)

Anders explains the notion of integration (in the sense of assimilation):

> Integration means not to wear the head scarf and carry out Muslim practices. (Anders, 37, public administration)

Cultural differences are experienced and constructed as incompatible and unacceptable. Therefore, my argument is that the cultural practice that cannot be tolerated does not refer to an idea of tolerance. The interviewees relate to intimate issues such as clothes and food, items that most people would normally agree belong to the realm of what is tolerable. Danes may not like the headscarf, the turban, the colour, or the unfamiliar name, but if the idea of tolerance is to make any sense, then it would as a minimum entail the coexistence of different lifestyles and expressions of cultural and religious beliefs, or what Walzer (in his shades of toleration) called 'benignly indifferent to difference'. Likewise, it seems fair to argue that if a person cannot exercise the right to wear a headscarf, and then the denial of this right cannot be done in the name of tolerance. However, if these comments do not express the limits of tolerance, then is it limited tolerance as it pretends to shield against racist attitudes?

Solomos and Wrench have argued that a novel characteristic of contemporary forms of racism is intensified struggles around 'the expression of racism that often claims not to be a racism' (Solomos and Wrench, cited in Hervik 2003). The shift from culturalism to racism and from the acceptance of intercultural tension to racialised prejudice is present in the case of Anna (19, unskilled worker).

Anna explained that immigrants do not care about Danes. They only come here to receive the benefits of the state. They think they can do whatever they want. As she went on, it became clear that racism is associated with things one does not like about the other. But, then she explicitly dismissed racism, by arguing that disliking each other is a two-way thing:

So, we do not like the way they dress or smell or talk and they probably also think we are strange. (Anna)

At this point, Anna talked about intercultural differences and tensions, which are not in themselves racist. But the culturalisation of differences would soon enough be used in racist reasoning. A few minutes later in the interview, she spoke about crime (including murder and theft):

Well, now, there is another robbery, where some person is attacked by a black person. It is always a black person. It might be because we don't hear about the Danes, but I don't believe so. I really believe blacks commit the majority of crimes. (Anna)

There is no statistical evidence showing that blacks commit more crimes than 'white Danes' of similar social background. By ascribing negative characteristics to a category of people to whom she obviously does not belong, Anna supports a positive image of her own white group.

Line, another interviewee, noted that women who wear the headscarf are associated with being Muslim. And being a devoted Muslim stereotypically associates with foreignness and fanaticism, whereas Danes are not similarly provoked by someone who enters 'the bus with a stick in his nose or green hair' (Line, 42, teacher).

In other words, only some cultural differences are seen as incompatible and therefore intolerable. Cultural markers, like the headscarf, objectify something unwanted and are therefore more than a simple and practical problem.

This argument then raises the question of who is tolerating whom and when? I shall return to that in a moment. First, however, I wish to look more closely at the research behind the headline 'Danes have become more tolerant', which our interviewees responded to.

'Have Danes Become More Tolerant?'

'Danes have become more tolerant' referred to the publication of a survey by political scientist Lise Togeby (1997) that relates to earlier work (Gaasholt and Togeby 1995). The material used for research consists of telephone interviews where respondents give quick answers to questions about immigrants and refugees according to a scale ranging from 'in complete agreement' to 'total disagreement'. Accordingly, Gaasholt and Togeby use methods similar to the EUMC survey. Therefore, a scrutiny of the assumptions behind their use of tolerance can be used to further reveal how tolerance and racism connects in the Danish public sphere.

A series of assumptions define what the authors named 'ethnic tolerance'. Ethnic tolerance is not the tolerance of ethnic minorities, but a label given to the respondents' perception of non-Danish immigrants assumed to be of non-Western origin. Answers to these questions make up the 'ethnic tolerance' and are measured as tolerant or non-tolerant answers. By comparing the original count of tolerant answers from 1993 with a new, follow-up study in 1996, numbers can be compared. The results showed that there were more tolerant answers in the later survey than the first.

Measuring 'ethnic tolerance' in terms of a percentage can hardly be compared to popular perception of tolerance inferred from in-depth interviews. Therefore, it is hardly surprising that the reactions we found in the interviews contradicted the news report about the quantitatively based study that Danes were becoming more tolerant.[6]

Togeby's method and argument begs an answer to the question: what are the features of tolerance? Based on a theoretical discussion, she and Gaasholt argued that tolerance consists of fighting off the internal reluctance one may be nourishing and despite this feeling treat the immigrants and refugees in a decent manner (Gaasholt and Togeby 1995: 20). Accordingly, Gaasholt and Togeby take the libertarian humanist position that the inner thoughts and conscience are parts of the inviolable private sphere (Kurtz 1996).

'All things considered, it is reasonable to assume that resistance towards immigration and immigrants is a natural reaction – a very normal and perhaps also necessary adjustment in a society – which is exposed to immigration from foreign cultures' (Gaasholt and Togeby 1995: 13). Liking or disliking each other is not the important thing when it comes to tolerance; of greater importance is, treating each other in a decent manner. Tolerance consists of fighting the internal aversion and despite it treating others decently. In fact, tolerance is what keeps racism away.

However, Gaasholt and Togeby's assertion is fragile in its actor-oriented liberal focus. If tolerance consists of fighting off the inner natural intolerance, then toleration has shifted its focus from the object to be tolerated to the individual tolerant subject. Consequently, toleration cannot embrace an active effort of listening and learning (Walzer's fourth possibility). Moreover, when the public space is opened up for expressions of intolerance and racist views, then doesn't it undermine tolerance, threatening to turn it into flabby humanism? In both cases, we see clear limitations of tolerance subdued to the grace of antihumanist and racist discourse and practices.

Gaasholt and Togeby explained that xenophobic reactions were only to be expected when Denmark comes under pressure from increased immigration. However, this assumption of xenophobia rests on a false basis. Xenophobia is not natural but naturalised. Naturalising xenophobia is precisely what cultural fundamentalism is about. Cultural fundamentalism is Verena Stolcke's term for denoting the shift of rhetoric of the political right (Stolcke 1995). 'Rather than asserting an endowment of different human races, contemporary cultural fundamentalism emphasizes differences of cultural heritage and their incommensurability' (ibid. 4).

Cultural fundamentalism recognises the equal status and rights of the other, but stresses the incommensurability of cultures in such a way that the alien is opposed to the natural. People naturally belong to certain territories. When they are deterritorialised, the incommensurable cultures will evoke antagonistic reactions unless their bearers assimilate. Karin Norman has pointed out that if xenophobia is in play, then one should avoid 'the foreign' at all costs. But in the case of refugees and immigrants from Third World countries, hostility and aversion still makes room for contact, and then at some historical moment there is an attack. This then is not xenophobia. 'Xenohostility' would be a more appropriate concept than the medicalising xenophobia (Norman 2002). Also, if xenophobia is a medical condition, all foreigners would cause outbursts of 'xenophobia'. But this xenophobia is selective and follows a hierarchy of rejected groups.

In the previous sections, I have dealt with tolerance and the construction of 'we-groups' and 'out-groups' that fell roughly along the lines of nation (we) and the foreign (the other). Now, I will turn to the relationship of inequality between tolerators and tolerated. In Walzer's words: 'To tolerate someone else is an act of power; to be tolerated is an acceptance of weakness' (Walzer 1997: 52).

Tolerance and Tolerant Individuals

The EUMC report noted that Danes had more racist and tolerant answers than most other European countries. This contradiction of simultaneously presenting racist and tolerant answers must be seen in relationship to an inherent asymmetry of power between tolerant individuals and those who should be tolerated, which belies the equality it professes (Hastrup 2001).

In Jan Blommaert and Jef Verschueren's terminology, the 'tolerant majority' is the producer of the nationalist discursive construction of 'we' and 'the other'. It is nationalist since the 'we' (according to the nation-state ideology) is seen as consisting of those people who share an imagined cultural sameness and belong 'naturally' to the territory that makes up the state. The conditions are set then within a nationalist framework where the tolerant majority captures 'the layer of society, which also professes the virtues of openness and tolerance' (Blommaert and Verschueren 1998: 11–12).

According to the two Belgian scholars, this tolerant majority shares with the extreme right the view of cultural diversity as a problem to be managed. Management is always in the hands of the powerful, and the management of diversity is not an exception. The 'managed' have little say in all this. Therefore, the debate is really about the 'other', viewed from the perspective of the majority (ibid. 15). In the light of the interviews above, tolerance disappeared rapidly and was substituted by the management view. In other words, the solution to the problem of diversity lies in the hands of the managers or even the tolerators.[7]

The tolerating group of antiracist activists may construct a 'we'-group, that is hardly visible by the tolerators themselves. American anthropologist Ruth Frankenberg showed that American middle-class women engaged in various antiracist activities, constructing themselves as a group 'without culture', since they did not seem different to each other. In this process, ethnic minorities of colour were visible and carriers of culture. Whiteness was unmarked, invisible and without a specified content, but still normative and determining (Frankenberg 1994).

When people enact privileged positions based on their group position as white, we can follow David Wellman and call it 'white privilege'. Wellman maintains that the rationale used by white people to justify their relative location to blacks in society is due to the preservation of privilege (1993).

During the growth of new nationalism in Denmark in the 1990s, Danes discovered that 'they were white'. The privileged position is white and Danish, while immigrants of colour are the 'out-group'. The political right wing seeks to manage these visible immigrants by denying their right to difference as a means for the allocation of public symbolic or material resources. This strategy seems to rest on the idea that if difference is ignored then 'the immigrant problem' will vanish. At the opposite end of the political spectrum, we find an acknowledgement of difference. However, since the left wing also see the cultural distinctness of ethnic minorities as a problem, it turns to programmes and acts of integration that can remove the disturbing differences (see also Blommaert and Verschueren 1998).

I do not want to exaggerate the racial dynamics of the construction of 'whiteness' in itself. One can easily gain the impression (a false one, I would argue) that the presence of people of different shades of colour and culture is the prime reason for growing intolerance. Nationalism and the growth of the middle class are also producing marginal groups and enemies. I see the growth of nationalism and the middle class as responses not so much to Denmark's ethnic minorities but to the collective self-scrutiny or identity-formation in the post-1989 world of rapid international changes and global processes.

The majority's management of cultural diversity is an approach that depends on two premises. First, ethnic minorities must be recognised as Danes and part of Danish society like anyone else. This is also crucial for safeguarding the collective rights of ethnic minorities to be different. The cultural fundamentalists contest this right by arguing that these 'foreign' cultures do not belong in the Western world to begin with. Second, and merging from the first, when ethnic minorities are accepted as Danes, the tolerant majority and the state elite will fiercely deny that they are enacting privileged white positions and possibly committing ethnic discrimination, regardless of existing documentation. The national image of Denmark as an exemplary case of an egalitarian society will endlessly deny discrimination and racism, since such an acknowledgement would imply that egalitarianism is no longer present.

Threshold of Tolerance

Balibar has described the subtle ways in which the notion of cultural relativism has shifted from an emancipatory weapon against cultural imperialism and evolutionism to an argument in defence of cultural fundamentalism, i.e., the idea of incompatible and hostile cultures (Balibar in Blommaert and Verschueren 1998: 4). In a similar manner, nationalism embodies two aspects. The first is nationalism applied in struggles for independence and freedom from dominant external powers or directed towards other nations within the larger complex of nation-states. The second refers to the internal dominance and chauvinism within the nation-state that sees ethnic differences as threats for the 'imagined cultural community'. Likewise, tolerance requires a positive acceptance of difference. Nevertheless, the fact is, tolerance is at the mercy of tolerant individuals and can be severely limited, therefore, giving way to racism.

> In Western democratic countries, where tolerance is highly valued as a self-ascribed property, the radical elimination of diversity in the form of segregation, undisguised discrimination or the expulsion of foreigners is not available as a public option – though it is openly advocated by a growing number of people at the extreme right of the political spectrum. (Blommaert and Verschueren 1998: 4)

Tolerance in this way forms part of the positive self-image, but then coincides with the practice of ethnic discrimination and racism. The crucial point in this coexistence occurs when tolerance is challenged (regardless of whether it is imagined or real). Indeed, 'in nationalist ideology the nation is envisioned as a natural entity characterized by its culture', which again 'is understood in a somewhat atomistic fashion as a collection of traits integrated to form a unique object in the real world' (Handler 1984: 61). Tolerance is objectified when the limit of tolerance is reached. The objectification of this limit can be seen through the metaphor of a 'threshold' of endurance. Tolerance can be abused and threatened to the extent that the tolerators will no longer be able to manage or contain diversity and therefore give in to discrimination and racism.

In the Danish debate, we saw this idea of a threshold of tolerance in press reports about 'annoying' Somalis. In March of 1997, newspapers reported similar stories from four of the biggest cities in Denmark. Mayors in Odense, Esbjerg, Aarhus and Aalborg, all of them Social Democrats, came out with similar stories about how approximately 1,000 Somali refugees in each city had become too much of a problem. The 'breaking point has been reached', 'the city is flooded with refugees', and 'we cannot absorb anymore', were some of the descriptions to be found in the media. Somalis and Somali culture were described as annoying, impossible to integrate and incompatible with Danish culture. With the increasing number of these extremely different refugees, the threshold of acceptance had been reached.

The Somalis were described as extremely different, but tolerance was not evoked as the relevant strategy for relating to this cultural difference. Instead, the Somalis represented a burden that needed to be managed properly. The diversity-as-a-problem attitude became objectified in terms of 'a threshold', where problems became unbearable.

Blommaert and Verschueren (1998) have also observed the tension between the tolerant majority's self-image and the observable expressions of racism and xenophobia (1998: 77). Too many 'foreigners' or immigrants in one area is considered particularly problematic, whether residential areas, schools or some other administrative unit. They go on to theorize the threshold of tolerance, which they see as:

> An objectifying socio-mathematical concept that defines the conditions under which all-European tolerance and openness may have been cancelled without affecting the basic self-image. The European does not become intolerant until this threshold is crossed. Just let him or her step back over the same threshold, i.e. just reduce the number of foreigners again, and the good old tolerance will return. (1998: 78)

In other words, even in moments of intolerance, the European is still tolerant at heart, and the observed behaviour is completely due to the factual circumstances, which render it impossible to exercise this essential openness (ibid.).

Permissiveness, then, is defined as excessive tolerance for deviations from one's traditions. This is not tolerable, since it threatens one's own identity.

Concluding Remarks

Let us now look back to the EUMC survey referred to at the beginning, which showed Denmark on top with most tolerant *and* racist answers. We obviously still do not know exactly what was measured, nor for that matter do the political scientists, Gaasholt and Togeby, who sparked the headline 'Danes have become more tolerant'. To find out what was measured we would need to conduct research on the research. This could be fruitful for some purposes, but not for increasing our knowledge about the phenomenon of tolerance itself.

In the nationalist self-image tolerance is seen as good. Yet, the term is dealt with ambivalently by the Danes, since excessive tolerance is considered naive and counterproductive for sustaining Danish national identity. Consequently, tolerance may be severely limited and give in to a new form of racism. This racism is subtle, indirect, often unintentional, and uses terms such as 'culture' and 'difference' instead of 'race' and 'racism', although the terms frequently refer to the same trope of ultimate, irreducible difference between groups or adherents of specific belief systems (Gates 1985: 8).

In everyday usage, racism is not included in the self-image of Danes or Europeans. Therefore, charges such as the one above, on the basis of an analytic concept of new racism, are heavily disputed despite existing documentation. Racism can simply not be acknowledged, as I argued, within an egalitarian ideology, neither the Scandinavian nor any other. When racism and ethnic discrimination are acknowledged, it is then immediately explained away as a natural reaction due to the increasing problem of diversity. In this scheme, integration and restrictions on who can enter the country becomes a cultural, psychological, and even biological self-defensive measure.

The notion of tolerance operates within this framework that separates the managers of diversity and tolerance from those who are to be managed and tolerated. Tolerators inhibit the same privileged position as those who ethnicise, culturalise, and racialise immigrants from non-Western countries, naturalise xenophobia, and deny racism between Danes and the people of non-Western countries. These tolerators are also the ones to maintain the self-image of tolerance.

Rather than ensuring the 'right to be different' (which could be done as long as social, cultural, religious and other differences do not lead to physical harm of other people, to crime or violence), the response to difference that occurs in Denmark is to enforce strict limits of tolerance and self-defence. When the limits of tolerance are strictly defined to encompass clothes, lifestyle and religious practices, the notion of tolerance must be regarded as discontinued. The right to self-defence is celebrated and is referred to as something natural that happens when 'incompatible cultures' meet. These widely different cultures are presented as embedding an irreducible, undeniable essence which cannot be changed but has consequences for how we deal with it. Furthermore, by referring to this 'natural' difference, the national 'we-group' can displace any responsibility for the outcome of the meeting with cultural others, whether limited tolerance or outright hostility, from themselves to the 'out-group'.

Acknowledgement

For the preparation of this manuscript, I wish to acknowledge the outstanding efforts of Ulla Fadel and Rikke Egaa Jørgensen.

Notes

1. The survey does not reveal whether the same individuals give the polarised answers, or if answers are divided between different groups of people who are either racist or tolerant.
2. The material I draw upon stems from various research projects and activities I have been engaged in for the last six years. First, I make use of a pool of fifty-two interviews conducted in the Metropolitan area of Copenhagen. The interviews were conducted as part of a team research project dealing with Danish Responses to Emerging Multiculturalism. Secondly, I draw from a media analysis that formed part of the same project. Thirdly, I refer to an ongoing study of the Danish media coverage of religions in Denmark in 2001. Fourthly, I take information from ongoing engagements of various sources in media coverage of issues of racism, incorporation of ethnic minorities and ethnicity. Some of these were conducted while I was a lecturer in Oslo from 1999 to 2001.
3. The idea of tolerance appears within humanism, which again associates with the uprising against religion and authorities through an emphasis on rationality and science that began in the fourteenth and continued to the sixteenth century. Humanism also evolved as an ideology that emphasised human principles such as respect (individualism), rationality (against the belief in the Original Sin), and tolerance. According to this view, each person had the right to an independent moral development, implying tolerance towards people, who sought other answers than oneself.
4. Through the combined efforts of an unholy partnership, the Progressive Party (*Fremskridtspartiet*) and the Socialistic People's Party (*Socialistisk Folkeparti*), both opposed to the Maastricht treaty, the focus of attention shifted from the foreign outside Denmark, to foreigners in Denmark. The 'no'-campaign contributed further to this process through slogans such as 'Say yes to the treaty, and you will not have to vote anymore'. I am not saying that the opponents of the Maastricht treaty brought about the shift, but rather than they were able to capitalise on an emerging reaction set within wider changes.
5. Anna goes on to explain that she believes the sign 'Danes have become more tolerant' is a foreigner's observation. Since foreign immigrants do not want to become Danish, the message upsets her.

6. According to Togeby's thesis, fewer media stories about immigrant and refugee issues will increase the tolerance of the population. Reading Togeby, one could easily be led to believe that the alleged immigrant problem will disappear with less media coverage.

7. The asymmetric relationship between those who practise tolerance and those who do not is perhaps especially clear in religious tolerance. Religious tolerance, which is the father of the modern liberal forms of toleration, also reveals the strong power held by the tolerators. A Catholic handbook defines religious toleration:

> Understood [as] the magnanimous indulgence which one shows towards a religion other than his own, accompanied by the moral determination to leave it and its adherents unmolested in private and public, although internally one views it with complete disapproval as a 'false faith'. (Catholic Encyclopedia s.d.)

References

Blommaert, J. and Verschueren, J. 1998. *Debating Diversity. Analysing the Discourse of Tolerance*. Routledge: London and New York.

Catholic Encyclopedia, n.d., *New Advent* (online version) www.newwadvent.org

Dansk Folkeblad. 1997. Vol. 1, (6), October. (Newsletter for Danish People's Party).

Eurobarometer Opinion Poll No. 47.1. 1997. 'Racism and Xenophobia in Europe'. First results presented at the Closing Conference of the European Year Against Racism. Luxembourg, 18–19 December.

EUMC (European Monitoring Centre on Racism and Xenophobia). 2001. Attitudes Towards Minority Groups in the European Union. A special analysis of the Eurobarometer 2000 survey on behalf of the EUMC. Vienna.

Frankenberg, R. 1994. 'Whiteness and Americanness: Examining Constructions of Race, Culture, and Nation in White Women's Life Narratives'. *Race*. S. Gregory, and R. Sanjek eds. New Brunswick, New Jersey: Rutgers University Press, 62–77.

Gaasholt, Øystein and Togeby, L. 1995. *I syv sind. Danskernes holdninger til flygtninge og indvandrere*. Århus: Politica.

Gates, H.L., Jr. 1985. 'Writing "Race" and the Difference it makes'. *'Race', Writing, and Difference*. H.L.P. Gates ed. Chicago: Chicago University Press, 1–20.

Hage, G. 1998. *White Nation. Fantasies of White Supremacy in a Multicultural Society*. Australia, Comerford and Miller, U.K.: Pluto Press.

Handler, R. 1984. 'On Sociocultural Discontinuity: Nationalism and Cultural Objectification in Quebec'. *Current Anthropology*, 25, 1: 55–71.

Hastrup, K. 2001. 'Toleration: Making Room for Difference'. *Discriminatin and Toleration: New Perspectives*, K. Hastrup and G. Ulrich eds. International Studies in Human Rights, Vol. 68, Martinus Nijhoff Publishers.

Hervik, P. 1999. *Den generende forskellighed. Danske svar på den stigende multikulturalisme*. Copenhagen: H. Reitzels Forlag.

———— 2001. 'Danish Denials of Racism'. Paper presented at the 100th Annual Meeting of the American Anthropological Association, Washington, DC, Nov. 28–Dec. 2, 2001, in presidential session 'Initiating Cross-Atlantic Dialogues on Race and Class in Europe.'

———— 2002. *Mediernes muslimer. En antropologisk undesögelse af mediernes daekning af religioner I Denmark*. Copenhagen: Naevnet for Etnisk Ligestilling.

———— 2004a. 'Anthropological Perspectives on the New Racism in Europe'. *Ethnos* 69, 2: 149–55.

———— 2004b. 'The Danish Cultural World of Unbridgeable Differences'. *Ethnos* 69, 2: 247–67.

————— (forthcoming). 'The Emergence of Neo-Nationalism in Denmark, 1992–2001'. *Neo-Nationalism inside the EU: Anthropological Perspectives*. M. Banks and A. Gingrich eds.

Hervik, P. and Jørgensen, R.E. 2002. 'Danske benægtelser af racisme'. *Sosiologi idag* 32, 4: 83–102.

Kurtz, P. 1996. 'The Limits of Tolerance'. *Free Inquiry Magazine* 16, 1. Internetversion http://secularhumanism.org/library/fi/kurtz_16_1.2.html

Norman, K. 2002. 'Is There "Racism" in Gruvbo? Equality and Hostility in a Swedish Small Town'. *Racism without a Face: Anthropological Perspectives on New Racism in Europe*, M. Gullestad and P. Hervik eds. New York and London: Routledge.

Nyt fra Danmarks Statistik. 2002. Nr. 321, 13 August.

Stolcke, V. 1995. 'Talking Culture; New Boundaries, New Rhetorics of Exclusion in Europe'. *Current Anthropology* 36, 1: 1–24.

Togeby, L. 1997. 'Er vi ved at vænne "os" til "dem"? Ændringer i danskernes holdninger til flygtninge og indvandrere, 1993–96'. *Politica* 29, 1.

UNESCO. 1997. Declaration of Principles on Tolerance. 28th session. Paris, 1995.

Vanges, U.S. 2001. 'I tolerancens navn. En undersøgelse af forskellige diskurser om multikulturalisme i Australien'. Master's Thesis, University of Copenhagen.

Walzer, M. 1997. *On Toleration*. New Haven and London: Yale University Press.

Wellman, D. 1993. *Portraits of White Racism*. Cambridge: Cambridge University Press. 2nd edition.

Wodak, R. 1995. 'Others in Discourse: Racism and Anti-Semitism in Present-Day Austria'. *Research on Democracy and Society* 3: 275–96.

Newspapers

Berlingske Tidende
4 October 1997

Ekstra Bladet
19 September 1997
15 December 1999

Politiken
13 March 1997
23 May 1997

Weekend Nu
September 2001.

The Politics of 'Caste is Race': the Impact of Urbanisation

Dipankar Gupta

The arguments in this paper are presented in three stages. First, I will point out why caste should not be seen as another variant of 'race'. If this position is sustained then it follows that 'casteism' is not racism under a different name. In the second section, I hope to demonstrate the political consequences, some quite damaging, if caste were to be equated with 'race'. Finally, I will discuss why the politics of the 'caste is race' thesis is particularly attractive to urban Scheduled Caste activists.

For a long time anthropologists and sociologists felt that the 'caste is race' thesis was dead and buried. It is obvious that it was not given a decent enough burial, because it surfaced again in the context of the United Nations conference on racism held in Durban in August 2001. The heat and dust raised during the Durban conference necessitates a return to some of the points made much earlier in scholarly contributions on caste. This is why, on occasions, the professional academic might have a sense of *déjà vu* while reading this paper. However, the fact that the parallelisms between caste and 'race' are still compelling enough for many political activists demonstrates that something was obviously missing in previous presentations. In my view, the best way to nail down the 'caste is race' thesis is to logically show how this equation is politically misleading, if not, in fact, dangerous. It is ineluctable that the distinction between caste and 'race' be made more fulsomely than before, keeping in mind all the while that this exercise has clear political implications.

Why is caste so often mistaken as another kind of racism? There are two reasons for this. One is a misreading of Vedic texts inspired by the distinction made by early Indologists between fair Aryans and dark Dravidians. The other reason for equating caste with 'race' comes about because there are some similarities between the ways blacks were treated in Southern United States, or in South African apartheid, and the treatment meted out to so-called 'untouchables' in caste Hindu society.

There is no doubt that people known as the Aryans came to India around 1,500 BC in successive waves and settled along the Indo-Gangetic plains. However, there is no unambiguous evidence to suggest that these migrating Aryans were physically of a different sort from those who were already living in this region. What is clear, however, is that the Aryans who came across the mountains brought in a different language that was quite distinct from the families of languages that were spoken by the people who were earlier inhabitants in the landmass that we now identify as India. There also appears to be good reason to believe that Aryans met with some resistance from indigenous peoples of this region. It is, however, far from clear whether Aryans overcame such opposition by superior military might, by ideological warfare, or by hard-nosed diplomacy. The evidence seems to suggest a combination of all three.

Early European Indologists took a liking to the notion that fair Aryans conquered dark Dravidians in remote history – probably because it justified such a reenactment in colonial times in India. But what is really quite surprising is the alacrity with which Indian intellectuals internalised this position and began to draw racial lines of distinction within Hindu society. There is a well-worn sociological cliché, which says that the dominated people often appropriate aesthetic standards of the superior community. This seems to have happened in India as well. Thus, those from Punjab and the northern regions proudly took on the mantle of being Aryans and distanced themselves from the darker people of the southern provinces of India, as they considered them to be Dravidians. Even a staunch Hindu nationalist like Bankim Chandra felt a sense of pride in the belief that superior Aryan blood was flowing through his veins. Those from the south, not to be outdone by all this, began demonising Aryans and all those who claimed ancestry from them. This was how the Dravida Kazhagam and later Dravid Munnetra Kazhagam rationalised their demands for secession from the Indian union several decades ago. Therefore, the 'caste is race' thesis played a politically divisive role during the years of our nationalist struggle against colonialism. If left unattended it will continue to be divisive, though 'racial' opponents may be arraigned differently in different times. However, we are already jumping ahead of our presentation.

In terms of empirical detail, a lot more is required than has been provided so far if the theory of the racial origin of caste is to be made convincing. The factual evidence given in favour of this point of view is exceedingly exiguous. In fact, the manner in which dark skin and fair skin have been read into Vedic texts is itself highly disputable. What is interpreted as 'fair skin' in the Vedas could easily mean, and most probably did mean, 'light'; in which case it was not a matter of skin complexion, but of knowledge. The Aryans, then, distinguished themselves from others not by their complexion, but by their belief that they were in possession of superior knowledge and wisdom. They were the carriers of light, and that is how they dispelled the darkness and ignorance that reigned during pre-Aryan times.

Further, there is only one passage in the Vedas that purportedly depicts the Dravidians as being 'nose-less and bull-lipped'. The Sanskritist Hans Hock has convincingly demonstrated that this particular sentence in the Vedas has been translated and interpreted in a highly dubious fashion. The same word, viz., *anas*, can also mean a person of poor speech and not someone who is nose-less. If the Aryans indeed brought in a new language then it is only natural that they should emphasise proper speech and pronunciation (or, *uccharan*) to differentiate themselves from those over whom they ruled, or with whom they had an uneasy relationship. The term bull-lipped can also have a variety of meanings. Remember, the bull is not really looked down upon in India as it is in many European metaphors (see Hock 2000). The bull in Indian tradition is not seen as dumb and obdurate but as strong and determined. So the evidence from the Vedas is not conclusive at all. Moreover, what is most striking is that this description of Dravidians is to be found in only a single passage in the Vedas, and yet so much is being made of it.

It should also be noted in this connection that the term *varna* in the Vedas need not necessarily mean skin colour. *Varna* can also refer to order. Therefore, if there were four varnas, or two (as in the early Rig Veda), then it signified that the society was stratified along four orders, or two orders, as the case may be. Each order was supposed to have a colour pennant of its own, as they represented different phases of the sun's journey round the earth. The rising sun, the grandest of all, was red in colour, and this was the colour given to the ruling Kshatriyas. Brahmans were signified by the colour white because that was supposed to be the colour of the sun at noon. Vaishyas were yellow because that is the colour the sun took in the east, and finally Sudras were blue, for that was the hue of the setting sun. To extrapolate racial segregation from factual material of this order is indeed far-fetched. It will then also have to be admitted that even the Vedas concede that Kshatriyas are superior to Brahmans as they represent the rising sun. Further, from where does the colour yellow get any material substantiation? Why have yellow or red not received any attention at all from those who argue in favour of the racial origins of caste? Why also are many of us committed to a two-race theory and not a four-race one? Quite clearly, the thesis that caste originated from 'race' is flawed because it is based on very flimsy evidence.

The 'race' argument takes a further beating when we study gene distribution and racial measurements along caste lines. Once again, no clear pattern emerges between different castes on the basis of the distribution of heavy gamma chains and light kappa chains in their genetic makeup. It has also been pointed out in this context that the presence of African haplotype among some people of North India obviously means that the term 'African' is a misnomer (see Field, Surje and Ray 1988: 34). Much earlier, in 1960, Majumdar and Rao conducted a statistical study of so-called 'race' elements in Bengal and came to the interesting conclusion that there were overwhelming physical similarities between high and low caste within the same geographical region. However, between different regions the story was different. Upper castes in one area differed to a great degree from upper castes in a different geographical locale. The same held true between lower castes in different regions of the country (Majumdar and Rao 1960). In an influential paper published in 1990 in *Current Anthropology*, an international team of scholars undertook anthropometric exercises and found no differences between different castes. They took three important measurements, namely, head length, head breadth and bizygomatic breadth. After examining a wide range of material they concluded that all efforts 'at typological/racial' classification should be abandoned (Majumder et al. 1990).

Interestingly enough the various *smritis*, like the Yagnavalkyasmriti and the Manusmriti, strongly disapprove of marrying outside one's caste. Out of such cases of miscegenation, the *smritis* (i.e., the laws emanating from the oral tradition) argue, that new and despicable castes are formed. Thus, the Chamars were born out of the union of a Vaideha and a Nishada. In the case of the lowliest of the low caste, the Chandals, something much, much worse is said to have happened. A Brahman woman had sexual relations with a Sudra man and, not surprisingly, therefore, a monster in the shape of a Chandal was born (see Gupta 2000: 71–72). Note, no matter how fanciful and spiteful such origin tales might be, nowhere is it said that the child of such unions is half a Vaideha and half a Nishada, or half a Brahman and half a Sudra. The miscegenes of such highly despised unions belonged to a different breed altogether, to a completely different caste. Mixed marriages, in such cases, do not result in mixed offspring but in dangerous and impure outcastes.

This situation changes when we move from caste to 'race'. Children born out of interracial unions, however, are socially recognised as carrying the strains of both parents and are thus classified as hybrid, mulattos, octoroon, quadroons, etc. In many racist societies, mulattos and mestizos have greater privileges and occupy a higher rank than other blacks. We will have occasion to return to this in a little while when we discuss the differences between the politics of caste and the politics of 'race'.

It must also be mentioned in this connection that it was quite commonplace to have a black cook or wet nurse in white homes in the racially segregated antebellum Southern United States. While blacks were despised, they were not considered polluting. Imagine the horror that would be aroused in the home of a traditional privileged caste in India at the very suggestion of an untouchable cook in the kitchen. Thus, while racism at its height might consider blacks to be despicable, it did not regard them as polluting.

Additionally, in a racially segregated society one's sense of identity gets stronger as one moves from the particular to the more general level. In other words, it does not matter if the person is from Belgium or from Germany or from Holland, as long as the person is white. Any further subclassification is not necessary and may indeed take away from the power of racial consciousness. Likewise, to be considered black it is not at all important, or relevant, to know whether the person is from Botswana or from Nigeria. If the person is black, then that is enough regardless of where the person comes from. Caste identity works in a reverse direction. Caste loyalties gain in commitment the more localised and particularised they get. It is not enough to be a Brahman but to be a Brahman of a certain endogamous *jati*, such as the Kanyakubja Brahman or Chitpavan Brahman or Barendra Brahman. In many cases this may not be enough either, and further subdivisions are necessary. The same holds true for Rajputs, Jats and Kayasthas, and indeed for all other caste clusters as well.

This brings us to the crucial analytical difference between caste and 'race'. Strata based on 'race' are arranged along a continuum of colours. Whites occupy one end and blacks the other of this hierarchical ladder. The colours in between are positioned accordingly along this scale: this is why those who are one-eighth black are superior to those who are one-fourth black and so forth. In Washington, light-skinned blacks set up an organisation called the Bon-Ton Society in the 1930s. To be a member of this society was fairly prestigious for mulattos of various degrees, but they had to pass two qualifications tests. Their skin colour had to be lighter than the standard brown paper bag, and when a comb was run through the prospective candidate's hair, it was not supposed to meet with any resistance. In Nashville around the same time, there existed the Blue Vein Society. Light-skinned blacks too formed this, and they too wanted it to be quite an exclusive affair. The criterion in this case was that the fine blue criss-cross of veins on the applicant's wrist should be easily discernible (see Gupta 2000: 91–92).

In the Caribbean, in Latin America, and in the United States there are a range of terms to encompass those who are not black but not quite white either. Harry Hutchinson found eight terms in Brazil distinguishing different shades of black (Hutchinson 1957: 120). Charles H. Parrish listed 145 different terms to denote fine shades of colour distinction in the United States (Russel, Wilson and Hall 1992: 60). Malcolm X, the famous black Muslim leader, confessed in his autobiography that he was favoured over his siblings by his mother because he was lighter skinned. Melville Herskovitz studied successful black couples in Harlem and found that as many as 56.5 percent black men married light-skinned women (ibid. 116). The really successful black men like Quincy Jones, Justice Clarence Thomas, O.J. Simpson, James Earl Jones, and even the revered Frederick Douglass, all had white 'trophy' wives.

The colour continuum is in many senses objective and demonstrable. There is little point in a black person claiming to be white if the person's skin colour and features do not help to back this claim. On the other hand, there are a large number of light-skinned blacks who want to be taken for whites and often succeed in 'passing off' as such. This phenomenon of 'passing' has been widely noticed and commented upon in the United States. Journals such as *Ebony*, *Jet* and *Essence*, which have a predominantly black readership, devote pages to help black women solve their 'hair problem'. Straightening one's hair and cosmetically changing the colour of one's eyes are quite well known among black people in America (see ibid. 47). In other words, blacks accept white aesthetics and would like to be like them if it were possible. The only way this could happen is through intermarriage.

This is probably why blacks in America have a low sense of self-esteem; nor have they much use for their heritage. This is also evident in the politics of Louis Farrakan. Farrakan urges blacks to reform themselves, to be caring parents, and to be hard-working and diligent breadwinners. If Blacks were in a bad way, Farrakan would argue, the prevailing black way of life is certainly not going to help them come out of their misery. The 'Black is Beautiful' phase is now more or less over in the United States. As many as 72 percent blacks prefer to be called blacks and not Afro-Americans (ibid. 71; see also Gutman 1976: 309).

Caste based stratification displays very different characteristics. To begin with, it is impossible to construct a uniform hierarchy of caste based on the notion of purity and pollution. No caste would acquiesce to its placement among the so-called 'untouchables'. No caste would agree that members of other castes are made up of substances better than theirs (Gupta 2000: 72–85; see also Appadurai 1974). No caste would like their people to marry outside their community. No caste would like to merge their identity with any other caste. No caste accepts that it has originated from a shameful act of miscegenation. Any suggestion of being half-breed is dismissed haughtily across the board by all castes (see Gupta 2000).

It is true that castes try to elevate their social status through a process known as Sanskritisation (reusing ancient terms and customs). This term should be handled carefully for it can give rise to certain misinterpretations. It is not at all true that those castes that emulate the lifestyle of powerful Brahmans or Kshatriyas, or Baniyas want to merge their identity with these castes. The Viswakarma Brahmans have Sanskritised much of their lifestyle but do not want to marry Chitpavan or Saraswat or any other kind of Brahman. They want to stay separate but they would claim equality with, if not superiority over, other Brahmans and prosperous castes. Sanskritisation does not mean merger with other castes. On the contrary, it is a show of defiance and an extraversion of what the caste always believed in an introverted fashion all along. In the past, members of such Sanskritising castes dare not work out their ambitions, or express them in any way, for fear of being punished by wealthier and more powerful castes. But now with democracy and an open market economy such displays of self-assertion are gaining prominence. In Rajasthan until a few decades ago, Jats could not wear a turban, carry arms, or ride a horse (see Sharma 1998: 83). Jats today flout all these restrictions against them, but in the 1930s, they encountered stiff resistance from Rajputs. Although Jats now lead a lifestyle similar to Rajputs it does not mean that Jats want to merge with Rajputs, or 'pass off' as one.

While Sanskritisation may involve some amount of emulation of the powerful caste of the region, it is not as if the upwardly mobile Sanskritising caste is ready to jettison all its earlier beliefs and practices. Castes always differentiate themselves from other castes on multiple fronts: on how they get married, on how they conduct their funerary ceremonies, on the cuisine they cook and prefer, and even on the basis of Gods that each caste considers to be special to its members (Gupta 2000: 77–85). Each caste has a clear idea of which caste it considers to be below it and which ones roughly equal. Endogamy, or marrying within one's *jati*, is a strict rule that all castes hold dear. It is not at all true that poorer castes are less punctilious in observing their caste norms. Each caste inspires its own variety of caste patriotism, which is why *jati puranas*, or origin tales, are such an important aspect of their cultural legacy and heritage. All dominated castes explain their subjugation, not on the basis of purity and pollution, but on the basis of lost wars, chicanery and deceit by kinsmen and fairweather friends. Sometimes the Gods too are blamed for being fickle, inconstant and temperamental in bestowing their favours (ibid.: 73–78, 116–129).

Unlike the distinctions used to demarcate racial separation, there is no objective indication of which category is to be placed where in the caste hierarchy because no caste accepts that it is less pure than other castes, though it would easily grant that Brahmans are ritual specialists. There are probably as many hierarchies in practice as there are castes. In the past when the economy was controlled by rural oligarchs and petty potentates, the hierarchy on the ground was the one that was ordained by the superior caste of the region. Other castes had to acquiesce to this or face brutal consequences. They dared not express *their* version of the 'true' hierarchy. With the growth in commercialisation, urbanisation, and democracy, poorer castes are becoming bolder and now have the courage to openly express what they have always held dear, but dared not manifest in any form in the past.

The distinguishing characteristic of the caste order is the discrete character of its constituent units that resist being forced into a single hierarchical frame. As these castes are discrete and their separation is on multiple fronts, caste competition is built in at various levels. It is only by accepting the reality of multiple hierarchies that we can conceptually make room for the existence of caste politics. If one were to go by the traditional understanding of a single hierarchy of purity/pollution, with Brahmans at the top, then any evidence of caste conflict should have meant the dissolution of the caste order. Nor is it true that caste politics is a recent phenomenon. All through traditional and medieval India, castes have fought and slaughtered each other to gain worldly preeminence. Once a caste is politically and economically powerful, it can then live out its own belief in hierarchy. This is as true of the Gujara Pratihara and Rajput kingdoms in medieval India (Chattopadhyaya 1976: 59–82), as it is of Jat supremacy in Punjab several centuries later, and of Baniya ascendance in Rajasthan and Gujarat today (see Babb 1998: Shah and Shroff 1975). The difference between traditional and modern displays of caste politics is not that there were no power struggles between communities in the past, but that the format for such competition and strife has now changed. Democracy and commerce have created new avenues that were not available to caste antagonists even in early colonial India.

If one is to understand caste politics in its vivacity and depth, it is necessary to appreciate that in the caste situation there are multiple nodes. Jats are against Gujars, together they are against urban castes; Kolis are against Patidars; Thevars oppress Pallars or the Devendrakula Vellalas; the Vanniyars torment Adi Dravidas, even as many of them may be against, or for, Brahmans in their local settings (see Radhakrishnan 2001). Caste alliances such as the KHAM (Kshatriya, Harijan and Muslim) and AJGAR (Ahir, Jat, Gujar and Rajput) are made and then cast aside. New alliances come into being with quite different caste friends and enemies. Even as castes may enter into political alliances, however ephemeral, they do not drop the barriers of endogamy, though they may occasionally ease up on inter-dining restrictions.

'Race' politics gets its charge from the bipolar antagonism between blacks and whites. Half-breeds, mestizos, quadroons, etc., are of no consequence. They have to align themselves with one side or the other. They cannot form an independent front of their own. In America until about fifty years ago, the 'one drop' rule applied. This meant that if a person had as little as one sixty-fourth black blood, then the person was considered black. This is why many who would like to 'pass' as Whites cannot easily pull it off. As the Black Panthers put it in America: 'You are either part of the problem, or part of the solution.' There is no other alternative.

As castes operate based on separation into discrete categories, which then fashions multiple hierarchies, the single hierarchy principle of 'race' would be quite alien to it. Consequently, caste politics would be imbued with a logic quite different from what obtains in racist politics. It is because many members of India's literati did not quite appreciate this and, perhaps unconsciously, applied the 'race' model to caste politics that they let Mandal recommendations pass without too much opposition. In the view of these pro-Mandalites, caste politics in India is really between powerful Brahmans and the oppressed rest, just as in 'race' politics it is whites versus blacks. In fact, Brahmans do not always occupy the top spot in most hierarchies. Moreover, whenever Brahmans hold such a position it is because they have economic and political power to match. However, this would still be a very small and atypical part of the entire caste and politics scenario. If caste politics is seen only in terms of superior Brahman versus the suffering rest then the atrocities that Yadavas inflict on ex-untouchables, what Thevars do to Pallars, and what Rajputs did to the Jats, would be unnoticed and brushed aside. This would impoverish and distort our understanding of caste politics in India and would allow for the intellectual acceptance of dangerous and retrograde policies such as those recommended by the Mandal commission.

The distinctions between the politics of caste and 'race' can and should be made if one is interested in fighting casteism in a concrete and meaningful way. While a radical advocacy of some form of inverted racism may seem feasible to some in the United States, such a stance would make no sense in terms of caste politics in India. In caste politics there is casteism at multiple levels and inversions at one level would leave the rest quite untouched. This is why Dr B.R. Ambedkar saw no future in politics of this sort. He anticipated the limitations of using caste as a perennial political resource and fought instead to extirpate this cultural blot from our society. As there are multiple castes in India, and as many of these castes occupy, statistically at least, different positions in the economic structure, caste politics often passes off as democratic politics. I have heard it said that in India we have a caste democracy.

It is possible to overlook the inherent drawbacks of a caste democracy because there are so many castes occupying different occupational and income positions in society. There is no caste that is dominant in numerical terms, and if the plain game of numbers was to apply, then a semblance of democracy may well have arrived. However, at what cost? Caste would be a permanent feature of mobilisation, dividing the country on the basis of birth and ascription without giving citizenship a chance to establish itself. Caste then becomes an immutable category. The reality of caste is, however, very different. Not every Harijan is a leather worker, and not every Brahman is a Pandit. In contemporary Uttar Pradesh, Harijans are generally employed as agricultural labourers. They have given up their traditional occupation of skinning and tanning leather. Today many of them are also moving to cities and have jobs far removed from what their predecessors were forced to commit themselves to just a few generations back.

When an equation is made between caste and 'race' the suggestion often is that these caste categories are fixed and immutable. However, many once-upon-a-time low castes have become Kshatriyas, Sudras have become elite pen-pushers, and, if the tales of Doms and Mochis are to be believed, then those who were once in positions of power have now fallen upon really bad days. If the ignominies heaped on certain castes arise from the occupations they were forced to follow by tradition, then it can be safely said that such a state of affairs no longer holds everywhere with the same degree of consistency. It is very rare that one can correlate caste and occupation in contemporary India.

'Race' politics accepts that blacks and whites are immutable categories. In this situation, there are two options: inverted racism, or racial representation. In either case, one has to work within the framework of race. Black Panthers advocated inverted racism and it did not work. A small minority cannot overturn a majority. What remains problematic, however, is that in inverted racism, it is racism that is still triumphant, albeit of another kind. 'Race' representation, the other alternative, accepts that races are here to stay, since it is not possible to change the colour of one's skin. Hence, when there is a question of fairness, the tendency among liberal democrats is to push for a policy that would ensure some kind of proportionate representation in the job market and in educational institutions. In the caste order, how a caste is perceived depends to a very significant extent on what occupation members of that caste follow.

In India it is possible, and, indeed, feasible, to move from one kind of job to another in one's lifetime, and with greater facility over two to three generations. Over 13 percent of Grade A services in the government of India are today occupied by those whose predecessors were once considered untouchables. This percentage is bound to increase in the years to come. In that sense, those who are descendants of so-called untouchables are no longer untouchables today. For them, at least, their caste position has changed significantly.

Caste is, therefore, not as immutable a category as 'race' is. This is why the provisions for reservations in the Constitution could think in terms of extirpating caste altogether in the not too distant future. Reservations for Scheduled Castes and Tribes in India were never envisaged in terms of either compensation or retribution, as is the case with Affirmative Action in America. In racism, a person continues to be black no matter what position that person may occupy in terms of status and wealth. However, history has shown that though caste mobility may be much more pronounced today, it was not unknown in ancient and medieval India. The reservation policy for Scheduled Castes is based on giving this latent dynamic a greater filliup by unearthing and releasing talents that were hitherto hidden in these communities. In this process, it is not just that these historically underprivileged castes could improve their status, but that society as a whole would benefit from a wider pool of talents than is now available. As the question is not of compensation, but of a dynamic transformation of the caste order itself, the system of reservation eventually looks towards a state of affairs where it would make itself redundant.

In the 'race' scenario, it is quite different. Once a black, always a black. This fixity cannot be transposed to caste politics, without doing a lot of damage to empirical reality. Once a Chamar is not always a Chamar; once a scavenger is not always a scavenger; and so forth. The Vahivanca Barots of Gujarat earlier called themselves Kshatriyas, but now prefer to be known as Baniyas (Shah and Shroff 1975). Further, as we mentioned earlier, ex-untouchables have never ideologically acquiesced to their own degradation. This is why whenever they are able to improve their economic situation, they successfully shed their earlier caste status and move on.

Once we use the language of 'race' with the caste situation then the emphasis shifts from removing the scourge of caste from Indian society to making one's caste identity a fixed political resource. In which case, quite understandably, castes would tend to be viewed as permanent fixtures and caste identities as political assets. The task would then be not so much to eradicate castes but to give proportionate representation to different castes in educational institutions, in jobs, housing, and so on. This again closely resembles the Mandal formula. The current Raj Nath Singh government in Uttar Pradesh is making even finer distinctions among the Other Backward Castes (OBCs). According to his formulation, from the 27 percent reserved seats for OBCs, 5 percent should go to Yadavas, 9 percent to eight most Backward Castes such as Lodhs, Kurmis and Jats [sic], and the remaining 13 percent or so to the 70 other OBCs that remain (Bhambri 2001). Mandalism encourages this game of numbers and proportional representation. It does not employ reservations to uproot caste identities in public life, but rather to perpetuate it. Those Scheduled Caste activists, who want to see caste as a form of 'race', should then be prepared for this eventuality. Caste identities, in this case, would always be an important mainstay of public life in India. This is a self-defeating project for any self-respecting Scheduled Caste activist.

If caste is not 'race' then why is there this attraction among a certain section of the Scheduled Castes, or 'ex-untouchables', to see themselves as a distinct 'race'? What advantages do they think they can gain by adopting this strategy?

In answering this question it is important to take into account how urbanisation affects one's caste identity. In a village, because of its dense interactive nexus, it is difficult to break out of one's past (Marriot 1959). Not that there is prejudice just between the prosperous castes and the rest, there is a great degree of distance and alienation even between the poorer castes. It is not as if all the Scheduled Castes are on one side against the rest. The competition for caste status goes right down the order. While no member of the Scheduled Caste would accept the stigma of untouchability, many would, nevertheless, insist that other low castes deserve to be where they are. This is what led the famous anthropologist I.P. Desai to comment that 'there exists untouchability among untouchables' (Desai 1976). For example, in South India the Kurivikarans, or crow catchers, are considered to be untouchables by other so-called 'untouchables' (Rao 2001: 78; see also Guru 2001: 106).

In the cities, the situation is quite different. As there exists a certain amount of anonymity in urban surroundings, it is not interaction but one's attributes that matter most. In an urban environment one's education, style of life, taste in clothes, kind of dwelling, possession of motorised vehicles, all make a difference. This is why Scheduled Castes want to leave the village as soon as the urban world will have them. This explains why there are more

Scheduled Castes in urban India then is true for the rest of the population. At the all-India level, about 70 percent are rural, but when it comes to Scheduled Castes only 50.5 percent are rural (National Commission for Scheduled Castes and Scheduled Tribes: 13). In the urban world, the occupation that Scheduled Castes aspire to is a government job for which there is a quota. This quota, or reservation, is for Scheduled Castes in general, and not for this or that member of the Scheduled Castes. In the urban world, their identity as a Scheduled Caste is much stronger than it is in the village where the endogamous *jati* identity is still very strong. This does not allow for a larger pan-Scheduled Caste identity.

The reasons why Scheduled Castes want to leave the village are not hard to decipher. For one, the anonymity of the urban world allows them to live with a measure of self-respect that is impossible in the village. Secondly, if they get a government job, at whichever level, their standard of living improves dramatically. Thirdly, the prospects for upward mobility are much greater in towns and cities than in villages. Finally, and this is a corollary of the above, there are no jobs in the villages. Most families that earlier hired landless agricultural labourers are unable to do so now as their landholdings have shrunk due to subdivision of plots. This is why most cultivators employ family labour to the maximum and only use hired hands for some very critical days in the entire agricultural calendar. Obviously, there is a great push from the villages to the cities as well.

Unfortunately, India's rate of urbanisation slowed down in the 1990s. This must have had a very negative effect on Scheduled Castes for whom the city is an escape from the drudgery and the humiliation of the past. It is all the more important that the Scheduled Castes press for greater job opportunities in urban areas to meet their aspirations. Lieten and Srivastava have found that non-agricultural labour and migrant labour together outnumber agricultural labour. The largest number of wage labourers are employed not in the agricultural sector but in non-agricultural occupations (Lieten and Srivastava 1999: 168). In fact their fieldwork shows that the 'percentage of households reporting "cultivation" as the principal occupation is highest among the upper and intermediate castes and lowest among SCs' – or Scheduled Castes (ibid. 123). I interviewed members of the Bahujan Samaj Party in Delhi and found this to be an important concern for them. The Bahujan Samaj Party emerged in the 1990s as a Scheduled Caste party, but espouses today the cause of all marginalised peoples regardless of religion or caste. Consequently, they occasionally align with representatives of Muslim and Other Backward Caste groups. However, these alliances do not last very long, often only for the duration of the election. The members of the Scheduled Castes constitute their most dependable support base.

The leaders of Bahujan Samaj Party (BSP) are educated, urban people. The supreme head of that organisation is Mr Kanshi Ram, who began his career as a low-level government official in Maharashtra. Mr Kanshi Ram is a Scheduled Caste Sikh and was born in Punjab. Today his mass base is in Uttar Pradesh, though he has organised several very successful rallies in Punjab and Haryana. The leaders I met in Delhi were all educated people, who felt that the greatest need of the hour was to provide education to the Scheduled Castes so that they can leave the villages and find jobs in cities, in particular, government jobs. Education is their top priority, and understandably so. This shows in the great surge Scheduled Castes have made on the educational front. From a dismal 10.27 percent literacy in 1961, the figure has steadily climbed to stand at 37.41 percent (National Commission for Scheduled Castes and Scheduled Tribes: 12). This is a dramatic fivefold increase over thirty years. This figure is no doubt well below the national literacy rate, which hovered around 52 percent, but seen by itself the increase in Scheduled Caste literacy is quite impressive. Today, the Scheduled Caste representation in Grade A government jobs is up from a little over 1 percent to about 13 percent. The Scheduled Caste quota is approximately 17 percent, which is roughly their proportion of the population of India. In central government service, their numbers have also gone up five times (National Commission for Scheduled Castes and Scheduled Tribes: 14). The Scheduled Castes, however, are overrepresented in lower-category government jobs. Nevertheless, the fact that their numbers are steadily increasing in the upper echelons of state bureaucracy is indeed a very positive sign. Reservations work!

The urban tilt among Scheduled Castes is also discernible at other levels. Scheduled Caste mobilisations seem to depend on the extent to which their leaders get an urban background. Dr B.R. Ambedkar studied in America, and later became one of the principal architects of the Indian Constitution. Today, Ambedkar is revered by Scheduled Castes all over India, and in parts of Maharashtra as a near God. Ambedkar led many Scheduled Castes to embrace Buddhism in 1956. Admittedly, most of the converts came from his own caste, the Mahars, and from a particular region of Marathwada, but today the call of Ambedkar is resonant among Scheduled Castes in North India as well, even though they may not have all converted to Buddhism. Incidentally, the three districts in Marathwada, namely, Nanded, Bhid, and Parbhani, where the incidence of Scheduled Caste activism is highest, are also the areas where Scheduled Caste literacy rate is most impressive compared to the rest of the country.

It is therefore among such urbanised members of the Scheduled Castes that there is an awareness that as ex-untouchables their fortunes are linked together, which gives the idea of seeing caste as 'race' a certain legitimacy. There is another reason, which may be rather cynical, but needs also to be mentioned. The government of India's provisions on reservations for Scheduled Castes for jobs and educational placements only applies to Hindu, Neo Buddhists (Ambedkar's variety) and Sikhs. Those Muslims and Christians who were members of Scheduled Castes prior to their conversion, are not recognised as

Scheduled Castes by the government of India even though they may face all the handicaps that Hindu Scheduled Castes face. This certainly makes the job of Christian proselytisers very difficult. The Indian Council for Churches is therefore an interested party in viewing the Scheduled Caste as a 'race', in which religion would no longer be a factor in determining Scheduled Caste status. This would make it easier for Christian missionaries to convert Scheduled Caste Hindus. About 300 delegates were sponsored by the Indian Council of Churches to Durban to press for the claim that caste is equal to 'race'. The Catholic Bishops Conference of India is also solidly behind this move. Not surprisingly, some of the most articulate spokespeople in Durban for the Scheduled Caste cause were Christians. Of course, the Church does not want class to be the critical factor in determining social status, therefore, the only alternative left before it is to opt for the racist thesis.

Even though there are some sociological, and a few strategic, reasons why there is a certain attraction in some quarters to liken caste with 'race', it must be admitted that the two are quite distinct, and to merge them would have rather negative consequences for combating caste politics in India.

If caste were 'race' then caste politics would be salient only when Brahmans are pitted against the rest. Ahirs, Kurmis, Thevars, Vanniyars, Okkaligas, Rajputs and Jats, they do not matter as full-bodied entities. If caste were 'race', the reality and brutality of Yadavas marauding in the fields of Bihar would be a bloodless reality and would not have any symbolic energy at all. It has to be a Brahman plot, or a Brahman inspired one, nothing else is of any significance. Those who have felt the full wrath of non-Brahman superior castes, either in the North or in the South, will never accept such a characterisation of caste atrocities. Again, if caste were 'race', according to the project of the urban Scheduled Castes and their Christian supporters, this would not include the degradation that non-Scheduled Castes also face at the hands of the more powerful castes. For example, the 'caste is race' notion cannot take into account the insults that Jats face at the hands of Rajputs, or Kolis at the hands of Anavils. Finally, if caste were 'race', then one's caste identity is fixed, both internally and externally.

We must also remember in all of this that the majority of people still live in villages where the fight against caste is not quite the same as it is in the cities. This is probably why leaders of the 'caste is race' thesis have little to say about undermining caste in rural India. It is true that the most favoured way out is through education and urban employment, but this is still a distant dream for many.

There is one similarity, however, between the fight against caste and the fight against 'race.' Ultimately, the battle has to be fought and won by those who are victims of such stratified social orders. It is only by empowering the Scheduled Castes and blacks that casteist and racist prejudices, respectively, are not given the scope to manifest themselves in practice in everyday relations. No amount of consciousness raising can do this job adequately. Only when those that have been hitherto denied privileges obtain the power and the wherewithal to fight back, will sectarian prejudice be halted in its tracks.

References

Appadurai, A. 1974. 'Right and Left Hand Castes in South India'. *Indian Social and Economic History Review* 11: 216–60.

Babb, L.A. 1998. 'Rejecting Violence: Sacrifice and the Social Identity of Trading Communities'. *Contributions to Indian Sociology* (N.S.) 32: 387–407.

Bhambri, C.P. 2001. 'Caste Aside'. *Pioneer* (3 October 2001).

Chattopadhyaya, B.D. 1976. 'The Origin of Rajputs , The Political, Economic and Social Processes in Early Medieval India'. *Indian Historical Review* 3: 59–82.

Desai, I.P. 1976.*Untouchability in Rural Gujarat*. Bombay: Popular Prakashan.

Field, L., Surje, S. and Ray, A.K. 1988. 'Immunoglobin (GM and KM) Allotypes in the Sikh Population of India'. *American Journal of Physical Anthropology* 75: 31–35.

Gupta, D. 2000. *Interrogating Caste: Understanding Hierarchy and Difference in Indian Society*. New Delhi: Penguin Books.

Guru, G. 2001. 'The Language of Dalit-Bahujan Political Discourse'. *Dalit Identity and Politics: Cultural Subordination and the Dalit Challenge*, G. Shah ed. vol.2, New Delhi: Sage.

Gutman, H.G. 1976. *The Black Family in Slavery and Freedom, 1750–1925*. New York: Pantheon Press.

Hock, H.H. 2000 'Philology and Historical Interpretation of the Vedic Texts'. This paper was presented at the meeting of the World Association for Vedic Studies, held in Hoboken, New Jersey, U.S.A. in July 2000.

Hutchinson, H.1957. *Village and Plantation Life*. Seattle: University of Washington Press.

Lieten, G.K. and Srivastava, R. 1999. *Unequal Partners: Power Relations, Devolution and Development in Uttar Pradesh*. Sage: New Delhi.

Majumdar, D.N. and Rao, C.R. 1960. *Race Elements in Bengal: A Quantitative Study*. Calcutta: Asia Publishing House and Statistical Publishing Society.

Majumder, P.N. and Shanker, B. Uma et al. 1990. 'Anthropometric Variation in India: A Statistical Appraisal'. *Current Anthropology* 31: 94–103.

Marriot, McKim. 1959. 'Interactional and Attributional Theory of Caste Ranking'. *Man In India* 39: 92–107.

National Commission for Scheduled Castes and Scheduled Tribes, (Fourth Report, 1996–97 and 1997–98) 1.

Radhakrishnan, P. 2001. 'The Politics of Perdition'. *The Hindu*, 21 September 2001.

Rao, N.S. 2001. 'The Structure of South Indian Untouchable Castes'. *Dalit Identity and Politics: Cultural Subordination and the Dalit Challenge*, G. Shah ed. vol.2, New Delhi: Sage.

Russel, K., Wilson, M. and Hall, R. 1992. *The Colour Complex: The Politics of Skin Colour among African Americans*. New York: Anchor Books, Doubleday.

Shah, A.M. and Shroff, G. 1975. 'The Vahivanca Barots of Gujarat: A Caste of Genealogists and Mythographers'. In *Traditional India: Structure and Change*, M. Singer ed., Jaipur: Rawat.

Sharma, K.L. 1998. *Caste, Feudalism and Peasantry: Social Formation of Shekhawati*, Delhi: Manohar Books.

PLAYING THE MEDIA:
THE DURBAN CASE

Guy Poppe

Not being familiar with the caste system in India, my response to Professor Dipankar Gupta's chapter, 'The Politics of "Caste is Race": the Impact of Urbanisation', will be of an indirect nature. Not being a scholar either, my comments will thus not have a thoroughly scientifically underpinned argumentation. In my response, I will stick to the approach of a journalist with twenty-five years of experience in his field, having covered events on the African continent on many occasions during that period, and will specifically be referring to what I have experienced in Durban (South Africa), in September 2001, at the World Conference against Racism, Racial Discrimination and Intolerance.

A striking phenomenon at the conference, and especially on secondary platforms (e.g., at the NGO forum, at the opening session thereof, in and around the media building, and in the streets surrounding the conference hall) was the way Palestinians advocated their cause. They made sure that decision makers, other participants at the conference and – last but not least – media people could not overlook their presence. They looked omnipresent, waving flags and banners, showing posters and shouting slogans, but were also actively lobbying on all levels, marginalising those who were defending pro-Israel positions.

Coming a very good second in being present all over the conference, and succeeding in advocating their cause, were Dalit people from India (some of us might be more familiar with terms like 'casteless' or 'untouchables'). At first sight the Dalit were using the same methods as the Palestinians to get as much attention as possible from participants and journalists, but in addition some of them organised a hunger strike in front of the main entrance of the conference hall in order to be sure nobody would miss the point they wanted to make.

A casual observer might thus have concluded that the Dalit case was by far one of the most important issues in the field of racial discrimination that the Durban conference had to tackle. Nevertheless it did strike my attention – although it is of course quite absurd to try to arrive at some sort of a ranking of problems of racism and intolerance throughout the world – that some themes were almost completely absent from the conference, as if they were banned in some way. Some examples:

- The war in the Great Lakes region in Central Africa. Of course, it is widely known that one of the reasons for the continuation of this war is the economic yields it provides for some of the countries involved in it – if not all of them. And of course, as in almost any war, there is huge power struggle going on between Central African states. But it is also true that the warfare in the Eastern Congo is at least partially ethnically motivated and is – if you look at it with a long-term perspective – a consequence of the genocide that took place in Rwanda in 1994, the biggest in human history since the Holocaust. How can a world conference, being preoccupied with racism, leave this war aside as it did?
- The intolerance of the Taliban regime in Afghanistan. It destroyed centuries-old Buddha statues, in the region of Bamiyan, in the spring of 2001, considered by Unesco to be part of the cultural heritage of the world. Was this operation not the most striking example of many years of religious (cultural and social) intolerance? Not to mention the treatment Afghan women underwent under the Taliban regime. What a coincidence that a world conference being preoccupied with intolerance did not go into this topic, just days before the September 11 terrorist attacks in the U.S.

How can we explain the fact that the Durban conference did not tackle the war in the Great Lakes region or the wrongdoings of the Taliban, and that the Dalit issue – at least in the media – did receive a degree of attention that by most standards can be qualified as out of proportion? There is only one possible answer to this question: the Dalit present in Durban – like the Palestinians, for that matter – were advocating their cause in a very efficient and media-friendly way.

This might lead us to the conclusion that if you want your message to be heard by the whole world, you have to devote lots of time and most of your energy to the question of how it is perceived. Positioning yourself as an active lobbying group, grasping for the media, being well organised and taking care of the necessary funding or sponsoring, will get you a lot farther than patiently explaining a maybe just cause to a casual passer-by – as I saw two shy Congolese doing, who were not even fluent in the conference main working language, English.

Conclusion

Let me include Professor Dipankar Gupta's reply to my response on his contribution. Thanks to his final intervention at the Ghent venue, it became clear to me how it was that the Dalit were able to invest such tremendous efforts in using the platform of the Durban conference to advocate their cause, a question that had remained unanswered at the time. The one point – one could call it the official version – is that the Dalit of India found the stand of their government unacceptable – the government was unwilling to wash its dirty linen in public. It refused to discuss the issue of caste in Indian society at the Durban conference, stating that such a debate would not be helpful and that on the contrary it should be discussed at home.

A second point Professor Gupta made – one could call it the hidden agenda – was of another nature. Most of the Dalit (more than 90 percent) being Christians, the Catholic Bishop Conference of India decided to fund 300 of them to stay. The Dalit were convinced Durban would be a good place to network. If, through their lobbying operations, they were able to persuade the world conference to accept that caste is a form of racial discrimination, this would open new economic opportunities to them. In India only Hindu Dalits are entitled to what is called 'reservations', i.e., affirmative action for victims of discrimination on caste basis. Christian Dalits are not. But on racial grounds they could become part of the quota system.

The example of Durban shows that if an organisation or campaign group looks for empowerment, gets organised and funded, its message will be heard more loudly and clearly than that of those who do not understand the media game.

THE RELEVANCE OF THE LANGUAGE OF RACE IN SOUTH ASIAN CONFLICTS

Sumit Sarkar

During the world conference against racism in Durban, Dalit activists and sympathisers (speaking on behalf of the lowest and most oppressed stratum of Brahmannical Hindu society, traditionally considered 'untouchable') argued that the question of caste discrimination had sufficient affinity with racism to be worthy of inclusion in the agenda. The Indian government, at present dominated by an extreme right-wing and chauvinist, predominantly high-caste Hindu, political formation, objected vehemently – and successfully – to any such inclusion, claiming that questions of race were irrelevant within India, and that their discussion at an international forum would be an insult to national 'honour'. Indian academic opinion was also revealed to be sharply divided about the contemporary relevance of 'race'.

Several implications that can be teased out from this controversy may help to introduce my subject. There can be little doubt, in the first place, that the language of race is very much less obviously present in postcolonial South Asia, than in many Western countries, which have seen large-scale immigration of non-white groups in recent decades. Academic discussions of race remain uncommon in India, and, where the theme is put forward, tend to get located fairly firmly in the colonial past, when imperial white racism was often undeniably evident.[1] Yet it is difficult to deny the existence of what may be called 'race-like' situations and conflicts, if we mean by 'race', roughly, a combination of three characteristics: widespread essentialisation of an Other, its inferiorisation, and – above all – the ascription (and sometimes effective interpellation) of qualities assumed to be inherent, ineluctably hereditary, in a word, biological. In 1992–93, to take one particularly notorious Indian instance, the Muslim minority was frequently denounced for being 'descendents of Babar' (a sixteenth century Muslim conqueror and ruler), in a manner quite reminiscent of anti-Semitism of the worst kind. The campaign culminated with the destruction of an ancient mosque at Ayodhya, the slaughter of more than 2,000 in cities like Mumbai, and eventually the rise to power of the present ruling combination. Yet the Hindu/Muslim distinction is of course fundamentally religious, not ethnic or racial: a reminder, if one is needed, that racial conflict and/or the language of race often does not exist in isolation, but is intermixed with tensions of many different kinds. Thus the kind of conflict I have just referred to would normally be termed in India, in a peculiar usage of Indian English, 'communal' – which does not mean that in some contexts, and in relation to the kind of questions being explored, an attention to race-like aspects would be necessarily irrelevant or unproductive.

The deployment, as well as the avoidance (or indignant rejection, as in the Durban case) of a language of race is clearly related, not just to specific conflicts, but often to the location of an individual, group, or putative community in such conflict. Here interesting divergences sometimes become apparent. Those situated at or near positions of superiority in a hierarchy, whether of social status, class, gender, age, colonial authority, or race, might well be less aware of the associated iniquities, or certainly averse to expressing it verbally – except in conditions of great self-confidence, imminent danger, or self-critical doubt. To take another recent Indian example: around 1990 a move to extend 'reservations' (the Indian term which is the rough equivalent for the U.S. 'affirmative action') in central government services to grossly under-represented 'backward castes' led to a hysterical upper-caste backlash in some areas. Many of our high-caste students in Delhi declared, at times maybe quite sincerely, that they had not been 'aware' of caste before: the reservation proposal, and the enthusiastic support it was getting from subordinate castes, meant that the latter were 'casteist', while they themselves were fighting for the cause of 'merit-based equality'. The backlash certainly contributed to the growth of the Ayodhya movement I referred to above, and elements still linger on of a discourse of merit which forgets that examination-determined 'merit' cannot be abstracted totally from inherited social and family conditions in a highly unequal and hierarchical society like that in India.[2]

I intend in this paper to examine three South Asian conflict-situations where racial, or race-like, languages, can be discerned: colonial domination (the most obvious, and the most explored), caste, and religion-based identity-politics (the two latter often run into each other, as the concordance between the anti-reservation and Ayodhya campaigns will have indicated already). My effort throughout will be to historicise, to try to distinguish changes and variations, for there does exist a tendency in some contemporary oppositional, antiracist discourses to take over in inverted forms the essentialisms so evident in all racist stereotyping and homogenisation.[3] I must add that, despite the title of this seminar, a distinctive focus on metropolitan or urban manifestations of racism will not figure much in my paper. In the contemporary West, the more-or-less recent immigration of visibly distinct, mostly non-white groups has been most obvious in towns and metropolitan areas, and racist phenomena are consequently most visible there. Modernity as manifested in significant part through urbanisation has certainly had a major impact in South Asian race or race-like distinctions too, and will be touched upon on occasion: but none of the conflicts I intend to examine have been purely urban.

For fairly obvious reasons, the racism so often associated with Western colonial domination was not quite so evident in India as it was in settler-colonies. Europeans always remained too thin on the ground to even think of attempting the massive extermination that happened in large parts of the 'New World', nor did racial discrimination ever attain the systemic level of South African apartheid. Yet there was no lack of racist everyday behaviour and formal or tacit double standards, and these, intensifying through the latter part of the nineteenth century in the wake of the bloody suppression of the military-cum-popular rebellion of 1857, ultimately became a major stimulus for emergent anticolonial nationalism.[4] There were frequent instances of racist behaviour aboard trains or steamers, considerable spatial segregation through distinct European cantonments or quarters in towns, and many shooting 'accidents' when the 'sahib' out on his favourite 'manly' pursuit of hunting got a 'native' by mistake, and then was most often let off with only token punishment by British Indian justice. Eighty one such accidents were recorded between 1880 and 1900, and incidents like these could unite, at least momentarily, the most privileged with the most humble in a society otherwise deeply divided by hierarchies of class, caste, and gender.[5]

Racism also had deeper and more structural dimensions: in British-ruled India, as elsewhere, it was not just an unfortunate aberration. The leading economic historian Amiya Bagchi has illuminated the many ways in which it helped to consolidate what he calls the 'collective monopoly' of European businessmen that was a striking feature of much of the industrial and commercial life of particularly the eastern part of the Indian Empire. As late as 1944, just three years before independence, an Indian manufacturers' association was complaining about 'the silent sympathy from the mystic bond of racial affinity with the rulers of the land, which procures them [British businessmen] invisible, but not the less effective, advantages in their competition with their indigenous rivals'.[6] The other crucial area was constituted by the army and administration, where every effort was made, despite many assurances to the contrary, to ensure that the really key and senior posts remained a British preserve. There were also the courts, and the ticklish question as to whether Indians could be trusted to sit in judgement over whites. The violent backlash when the Ilbert Bill in the early 1880s tried to take a small step in that direction became a major input into the emergence of middle-class Indian nationalism. Recently a feminist historian has explored the multiple ramifications of that moment of extreme racism, highlighting in particular the interconnections between processes of gender, class and ethnic stereotyping both in British-ruled India, and within Britain. Thus, a British Indian official argued that Indians (more particularly Bengalese, since a few members of that linguistic-cum-ethnic community would have benefited immediately from the Ilbert proposal) were as a race too 'effeminate'; being no hunters, they would be unable to understand what he described with much affection as 'the thoughtless schoolboy spirit', which was all that lay behind the shooting of natives by mistake. The Indian male was simultaneously accused of gross patriarchal oppression – with much justice – but what was happening, clearly, was an appropriation in the cause of colonial domination which would enable the Englishman (and Englishwomen, too) appear to others, and themselves, as benevolent guardians of Indian womanhood. An additional gain was that the 1880s were also a time of incipient feministic activity within Britain, the energies of some of whom could be neatly diverted into channels of what some have called 'maternal imperialism'.[7] And the role of racist-imperialist ideologies in halting the revival of labour militancy in Britain and elsewhere in Europe during the years of the long post-1873 depression has of course been much studied by historians.

Work like Mrinalini Sinha's indicates the value of firmly historicising the specific deployments of race sentiment and language, and not treating it as a kind of constant across the colonial era, if not indeed a characterological essence. Even the Aryan myth, so rightly discredited as racist by its centrality for Nazi ideology and the Holocaust, did have a complicated earlier history, for it originated, with late-eighteenth century Orientalist scholars like William Jones, as a theory of linguistic, and not primarily racial, affinity. It could at times even be a bit of an embarrassment for the more extreme white supremacists, since it seemed to suggest that the English and their 'native' subjects had important things in common: a problem tackled eventually by theories of racial degeneration, through miscegenation with other, 'non-Aryan' or 'Dravidian' races, or life in a hot climate. There was also a significant difference between what has been termed the 'Mosaic ethnology' of William Jones – where, following the biblical account of the origin of languages, the central image had been that of a branching tree springing from an ultimate beginning with Adam father of all peoples, and hence a kind of basic equality – and later assumptions of a 'staircase-like ascent' from primitive to civilised of some – not all – biologically distinct races.[8] A late-eighteenth century initial phase of considerable Orientalist admiration for Indian achievements (mostly relegated, though, to a distant ancient past) was followed by the much more aggressive assertion of Western cultural superiority, taking the distinct but often not entirely unrelated forms of Christian-Evangelical missionary arrogance and Utilitarian-Liberal self-confident reformism. This has been termed 'cultural' racism, as distinct from (and somewhat more open than) the post-1850s 'biological' assumption of irremediable inferiority. It was associated with an ideal of paternalistic 'assimilation', whereas the latter would emphasise the inevitability of difference.[9] Biological racism, of course, derived some sustenance from certain readings of the *Origin of Species* (1859), and culminated in the 'Social Darwinism' that became such an influential ideology in the late-nineteenth and early twentieth centuries.

A major advantage of the deployment of the category of race in the analysis of South Asian situations is that it can suggest important interconnections that might otherwise be missed. Some recent very interesting work on the development of what has been termed the 'Atlantic economy', linking up Britain, West Africa, and the West Indian and Southern U.S. plantations through the immensely profitable horrors of the slave trade, suggests that the sharpening of racism was often associated precisely with an intermittent, yet recurrent fear of alternative multiethnic solidarities of the dispossessed and exploited men and women whose labour helped to build up the prosperity of the modern West.[10] Intensifications of white racism in colonial India were often closely related to extra-South Asian developments, and many of the more extreme racist discourses of leading late-nineteenth – early twentieth century British Indian administrators and/or scholars were directed in significant part towards Western audiences.[11]

It was probably not a coincidence, for instance, that one of the sharpest early manifestations of cultural racism, Charles Grant's *Observations*, was written in 1792 and published in 1797. This was precisely during the years of intense panic in British ruling-class circles caused by the French Revolution, the Jacobin abolition of slavery, and the subsequent slave rebellion and 'Black Jacobinism' in San Domingo (Haiti). The development of more biological forms of racism – often in association with the 'science' of anthropometry – had a major root in justifications of Afro-American slavery in the antebellum South. Along with notions of 'polygenesis'(as contrasted to 'monogenetic' theories of common origin in Adam of all humanity), this was expounded, for instance, by the Philadelphia doctor Samuel George Morton in the 1830s. Morton was described by a Charleston newspaper in an obituary in 1851 as one who had aided the South 'most materially' by 'giving to the Negro his true position as an inferior race'. (Morton claimed to have proved by skull measurement a hierarchy in mental capacity of white/American Indian/Hindu/Negro). Subsequent events in the European-cum-Atlantic world – the brief revolutionary 'springtime of peoples' in 1848, above all, but also the revolt of ex-slaves in Jamaica in 1865, the brutal British suppression of which provoked an intense controversy among leading metropolitan intellectuals, and the run-up to the 1867 extension of the franchise – were associated with an immense sharpening of biological-racist theories and values. During the Jamaica controversy, liberal thinkers like John Stuart Mill came under attack from an emerging brand of advocates of 'race-science' for holding on to a false 'day-dream of racial equality'. Such attitudes fitted in very well, of course, with the intensified racism in British thinking about India after the 1857 Rebellion. Anthropometry came into great prominence in the work of leading Census officials of British India, most famously H.H. Risley, head of the 1901 Census and then Home Member in Lord Curzon's viceroyalty. Risley's writings were peppered with references to the leading contemporary authorities of race science in the West, men like Paul Broca or Paul Topinard. It may be interesting to note in passing that the biological determinism of such scholars was not confined to inferiorisation by race alone. For instance, a student of Broca 'discovered' in 1879 that the brains of Paris women were 'closer in size to those of gorillas than to the most developed male brains'.[12]

Racist discrimination often breeds types of identity politics that can veer towards counter-racism, and elements of that were not entirely absent at some moments of anti-colonial nationalism in India. The Orientalist theory of Indo-

European or Aryan common origin, naturally enough, became the subject of a variety of Indian/Hindu appropriations, which could range from modest affirmations of self-esteem against Western denigration, to aggressive claims that ancient Hindu culture had been the point of origin for most achievements of world civilisation. There was a premium on claims of the latter kind during what in Indian historiography has been generally termed an 'Extremist' phase, roughly around the time of the nineteenth-early twentieth century, when there was a brief convergence between conservative or revivalist forms of Hinduism and nationalist militancy. In 1903, to cite one instance, the Extremist leader Tilak hailed the 'superiority of the Aryan races, as disclosed by their conquest, by extermination or assimilation, of the non-Aryan races ...'[13] British repression, along with a general failure of such middle-class nationalists to develop effective links with broader masses, then pushed some of them into methods of individual terrorism. What remains very significant is that such chauvinistic trends were overcome from within anticolonialism itself, precisely in proportion that it became more effective, and developed under Gandhi to become one of the biggest mass movements of the early twentieth century world. Claims to 'Aryan' (in effect, high-caste or Brahmannical Hindu) superiority were hardly conducive to such mass mobilisation, which had to try to reach out to lower castes, untouchables and Muslims, groups which Aryan race theory would despise as 'non-Aryan'.

The subjects of colonial-cum-racial domination also normally require allies and ideological resources from metropolitan countries. Their need to know their masters is much greater than their overlords' need to know them. Not total rejection of the West on the basis of assertions of cultural 'authenticity', but selective appropriation of ideas and methods (from ideologies of liberal and then socialistic hues, notably), consequently was on the whole much more evident. (Even theorists of Indian, Hindu or Oriental authenticity often borrowed heavily from guilt-ridden and/or romantic internal critics of the West, in a pattern that of course remains quite common). The three most outstanding Indian thinkers of the late colonial era, Tagore, Gandhi and Nehru, all in different ways rejected total repudiations, and repeatedly condemned narrow forms of nationalism. Despite much misreading to the contrary, Gandhi's rejection of industrial modernity cannot really be understood in terms of any neat West/East divide. He never denied his indebtedness to Emerson, Thoreau, Ruskin or Tolstoy, and for him an industrial society dominated by non-white peoples was as unacceptable as the contemporary West. Perhaps the sharpest condemnation of chauvinistic nationalism, whether of the West, or Japanese or Indian, came from Rabindranath Tagore, who in 1916–17 denounced what he called the 'endless bull-fight' between nation-states and incipient nationalisms, in which the 'unfit must go to the wall'.[14] This was a total repudiation of Social Darwinistic values. As his near-contemporary novel *Home and the World* indicates, a principal element in this critique was precisely a very sharp rejection of Indian Extremist–nationalist attitudes and values that he, too, had briefly shared.[15]

Racism then was a rather minor and evanescent element in effective anticolonial Indian nationalism. However, the latter was by no means the sole claimant to late-colonial South Asian sociopolitical or cultural space. Much recent historical work has explored the ways through which, from the latter part of the nineteenth century onwards, tightening levels of communicational, economic and political integration combined with colonial institutions and policies to stimulate numerous kinds of more crystallised community-formations. These developed along very varied, often mutually conflicting, lines of difference and identity: all Indian, regional, ethnic or 'tribal', religious, caste, class, gender. In addition, in such formations and conflicts race-like language or theories did come into occasional use, notably in contexts of caste, and Hindu–Muslim difference.

The literal meaning of *varna*, the indigenous term for 'caste' in its simplest and theoretically basic sense of a fourfold hierarchised classification, is 'colour'. It does seem likely that assumptions of some kind of superiority of fair over darker skins, along with a degree of correlation of such difference with distinctions of higher and lower castes, far preceded the coming of white-complexioned European conquerors. But nineteenth century European notions of 'Aryan' linguistic and then racial common origin, and associated assumptions of Aryan conquest-cum-civilising assimilation of non-Aryan or 'Dravidian' peoples (another linguistic concept expanded into a race-category), certainly systematised and vastly extended the earlier notions. These came to be appropriated widely by dominant high-caste elements, which, overall, had benefited greatly from many aspects of early colonial rule, but were coming under pressure from around the beginning of the twentieth century as demands for equality came to be raised by or on behalf of some lower-caste groups.[16] The basic thrust of high-caste deployment of race-language, however, has been towards what Christophe Jaffrelot has termed hierarchised 'domination', rather than total exclusion or 'exterminism'. Lower-caste and Dalit groups, many possibly originating as outsiders or impure 'mlecchas', need to be kept or incorporated within Hindu society, but in suitable and strictly hierarchised slots – not driven out of it, in classic biologically racist manner.[17]

The modified but still recognisable racism of high-caste deployments of the Aryan myth stimulated an occasional counter-racism of subordinated groups, which made effective use of inverted versions of that same schema. In the 1870s Jyotiba Phule, an intermediate caste leader and ideologue of Maharashtra (Western India), developed a sustained and powerful critique of Brahmannical domination of that region in terms of a North Indian/Aryan conquest by force and fraud of an indigenous Marathi peasant-warrior people, presented as once living in idyllic conditions. The assumption of racial division-cum-conquest as underlying caste oppression acquired a sharper edge further south, where the notions of a distinct 'Dravidian' language-group-cum-race developed by British scholar-missionaries like Caldwell acquired great potency, notably in Tamilnadu. In one phase of the strongly anti-Brahmannical Self-Respect or Dravidian movement led by E.V.R. Naicker ('Periyar'), a Dravidian unity of race was emphasised in an effort to unite South Indian lower castes, both within and outside Tamilnadu, against the alleged Brahman invaders from the North – who could not be part of this projected unity even if they were linguistically

Tamil. However, this proved to be a rather brief phase, mostly confined to the 1940s, for the Periyar tradition then evolved mainly in a Tamil-nationalist direction, retaining some of the anti-caste rhetoric but toning it down in practice as identity was sought more in terms of Tamil language and culture.[18] More generally, as already noted with regard to anticolonial projects, movements of subordinate groups do seem to have a rather limited capacity to sustain aggressive counter-racist ideologies or practices. A variety of lower-caste claims to pedigrees more ancient than the Aryan, and allegedly conquered unjustly by the latter, did briefly emerge in many parts of the subcontinent during the early decades of the twentieth century. One of the best explored of these is the Ad-Dharma movement in the Punjab region, which claimed continuity with the vanished Harappan civilisation soon after excavations in the early 1920s had revealed its existence.[19] But none of these have had a sustained career, and it is surely important to note that B.R. Ambedkar, by far the most outstanding Dalit leader and a principal maker of India's present secular and democratic constitution, strongly repudiated theories of origin of untouchability in any kind of innate racial distinction.[20] Towards the end of his life, Ambedkar led a large number of Dalits into a mass conversion to Buddhism, which he interpreted as a religious tradition marked by a profound stress on human equality and this-worldly social justice and welfare. Tendencies towards narrow forms of identity politics remain strong among many Dalits and other subordinated caste-formations, which do often seem to get absorbed into what sometimes becomes a mutually divisive concentration on reservations of jobs alone. However, there do exist alternative pulls and ideologies within what is nowadays sometimes termed 'Dalit consciousness', and 'race' does not seem to be a particularly relevant category for understanding this increasingly vital dimension of contemporary Indian society and politics.

The relevance of racist language has been considerably greater in late- and post-colonial South Asian religious, predominantly Hindu/Muslim, conflicts – though here too it has seldom been more than a partial affinity or appropriation. Historical research in this area – flourishing, for obvious reasons, over the last decade or so – has increasingly highlighted the ways in which 'internal' divisions within religious communities (notably, caste, or more precisely, lower-caste affirmations among Hindus) have been sought to be overcome, in the main by dominant groups, through the development of powerful enemy-images of one or several Others.[21] And here a language veering towards race and race-hatred has been found to be helpful, particularly in the interwar years before Nazi genocide made it widely disreputable – but sometimes, as I indicated at the beginning through a reference to the Ayodhya campaign, even nowadays.

In Muslim identity politics, self-projections as a 'race' – distinct from and superior to Hindus – were not uncommon during the run-up to the formation of Pakistan as a partitioned subcontinent in 1947. However, there remained a problem in combining such emphasis with notions of ecumenical Islam as an umma that needs to rise above all notions of racial difference. Even the thinking of Muhammad Iqbal, the poet and ideologue who is supposed to have first formulated the notion of Pakistan as a Muslim nation-state, often suffered from such a tension, as has been pointed out in a recent article.[22] And actually the most devout and orthodox section of Indian Muslims, the theologians trained in the Deoband seminary, had little difficulty in cooperating with the nationalist Congress movement despite the preponderance of Hindus among the latter's ranks and leaders.

That a racial slant found easier entrance into Hindu-chauvinist ideology, is perhaps indicated by what can be considered the founding text of that movement, V.D. Savarkar's *Hindutva /Who Is A Hindu?* (1923). The author had been an extremist revolutionary, deported for many years by the British to their penal settlement of the Andamans. Yet the tract is strangely silent about British rule, repression or anticolonial nationalism, for by 1923 Savarkar had switched targets, and become convinced that only Hindus could really claim to belong to the holy land of Bharat. Central to his argument was a key prioritisation of cultural-religious authenticity determined by origin. Only for Hindus was the 'fatherland' (*pitribhumi*) also the holy land (*punyabhumi*) – while for Muslims, Christians, all groups whose ideals originated from countries beyond the Indus, the 'holy land' could never be India. This was a strange argument, of course, since by this logic no Christian, outside the small number of them living in Palestine, could ever be genuinely patriotic. Nevertheless, it did serve the purpose of latching an aggressive Hindu-chauvinism firmly on to a central emotive element in much patriotic rhetoric ('the sacred love of the fatherland', in the language of the Marseillaise), while directing it entirely against other Indian communities and not the British rulers. (The latter had never claimed India to be their fatherland, and so the entire argument passed them by.) The text was replete with references to 'our Hindu race', and emphasised the commonality of 'fatherland', 'blood', 'our Hindu culture ... Common laws and rites... feasts and festivals'.[23]

The racist language gathered strength over the next decade and not without some affinities and even direct connections with the dominant ideologies of Fascist Italy and Nazi Germany, as recent historical research is discovering. The diary of B.S. Moonje, an old associate of Tilak who became the mentor of Hedgewar, founder of the RSS, as well as some archival material, indicates that through a visit to Italy and a warm reception from Mussolini in 1931, he, and through him the RSS, became quite enamoured of Fascist methods of youth indoctrination and organisation. Italy, Moonje and his RSS colleagues felt, had progressed from a phase of social anarchy and near-revolution to discipline and proper hierarchical order under Il Duce.[24] The second supremo of the RSS, M.S. Golwalkar, went a step further in 1938, precisely around the time of Kristallnacht in Germany:

> German race-pride has now become the topic of the day. To keep up the purity of the Race and its culture, Germany shocked the world by her purging the country of the semitic races ... the Jews. Race pride at its highest has been manifested here. Germany has also shown how well-nigh impossible it is for Races and cultures, having differences going to the roots, to be assimilated into one united whole, a good lesson for us in Hindustan to learn and profit by.[25]

Other Indians had also tried to develop connections with the Axis powers, most notably Subhas Bose, but in their case, the primary motivation had clearly been anti-British nationalism, the assumption that England's enemies could be of help in the Indian struggle for independence. With Savarkar, as well as with Golwalkar and the RSS, the affinity seems to have been much more ideological, for the Hindutva groups kept firmly away from all phases of anticolonial struggle with total consistency.

The real connection, Jaffrelot suggests, was not so much biological racism, but the appeal of what appeared to be ideologies of hierarchy, order, discipline – very appropriate for a refurbished Brahmannical social ideal. With this, is combined a deep distrust of democracy, and a strong attraction for notions of dictatorial leadership. The RSS has always followed the organisational principle of what it calls '*ek chalak anuvartita*' (obedience to one leader), and certainly some of the speeches of Golwalkar during the war years, as reported by British Intelligence, have an ominous ring: 'Hindus are the only Nationals of Hindustan. One ideal, one way, one heart, one expression, and all at the disposal of one leader.'

Today, with a BJP-led coalition ruling in New Delhi, openly racist language is less in evidence, except at extreme moments of near-genocidal violence as in 1992–93. But the social ideals remain unchanged, as well as the oft-repeated argument of cultural-religious 'authenticity', which nowadays takes the form of abuse of a so-called Trinity of 'Marx, Macaulay, and the Mullas'. A very recent instance is the deletion of all critical references to the varna system from a high-school history textbook, on the ground that this might hurt sentiments – obviously, high-caste ones. Moreover, on a scale far more dangerous than during the brief Extremist phase a hundred years ago, chauvinistic cultural nationalism is being combined with near-abject surrender to multinationals and Western, more precisely U.S., political hegemony.

Notes

1. Thus Peter Robb, ed., The *Concept of Race in South Asia* (Delhi: Oxford India Paperbacks, 1995), one of the very few works on modern Indian history directly bearing on the theme of race, consists of eleven essays all focusing primarily on colonial South Asia.

2. For a recent, and to me a most surprising instance, since it comes from a very well-known and deservedly respected economist, see Pranab Bardhan (2001: 233).

3. The critique of 'Orientalism', so influential among many radical intellectuals since Edward Said's book of that title, has occasionally suffered from such homogeneisations. I have written extensively elsewhere about this: see, for instance, my 'Orientalism Revisited: Saidian Frameworks in the Writing of Modern Indian History', as well as *Writing Social History* (1997), passim.

4. For a brief account of the importance of racism in late-colonial India, see Sarkar (1983: 22–24).

5. Europeans, of course, tended to be more physically visible in urban areas, where were located also the government and commercial offices where white bosses often directly faced 'native' clerical and worker subordinates. Yet, as the instance of shooting 'accidents' indicate, there was little specifically urban or 'metropolitan ' about manifestations of colonial racism. Forced indigo cultivation in the Bengal countryside, and then tea plantations located in far-off Assam hills, provided probably the worst examples, and became staples of much nationalist critique.

6. Bagchi (1972: 166, and passim).
7. Sinha (1998: Chapter I); see also Burton (1994).
8. Trautmann (1997: Chapters I, II, and passim).
9. I am borrowing this formulation from Hall (1992: Chapters 9, 10).
10. See, particularly, Linebaugh and Rediker (2000).
11. A point elaborated very effectively by two contributors to the above-cited volume edited by Peter Robb (note 1 above): Susan Bayly, 'Caste and "Race" in the Colonial Ethnography of India', and Crispin Bates, 'Race, Caste, and Tribe in Central India: The Early Origins of Indian Anthropology'.
12. Robb (1995: 179, 227, and passim). The Jamaica controversy is discussed in detail in Hall (1992: Chapter 10).
13. Balgangadhar Tilak, *Arctic Home of the Vedas* (1903), cited by Leopold (1970).
14. Tagore (1917: 44–45).
15. For more details, see my 'Nationalism and "Stri-Swadhinata": The Contexts and Meanings of Rabindranath's *Ghare-Baire*', in Sumit Sarkar (2003).
16. High-caste Hindus had got a head start over others in the new structures of Western education, which became the basic qualification for jobs in the services and 'modern' professions, while many Brahmannical notions were incorporated – and, indeed, made much more systematic – in the 'Anglo-Hindu' system of family law. A historian has even described the nineteenth as the most 'Brahmannical' of Indian centuries, and has gone on to suggest that this helped to make the twentieth century the most anti-Brahmannical. Washbrook (1981).
17. Jaffrelot (1995).
18. Hellman-Rajanarayan (1995).
19. Juergensmeyer (1982).
20. Ambedkar (1948).
21. To take one example: the aggressively-Hindu political-ideological formation that currently dominates the Indian political scene emerged in the mid-1920s in the Nagpur region of Maharashtra, where the Rashtriya Swyam Sevak Sangh (RSS) was founded in 1925. It claimed to be a Hindu defence organisation to meet a terrible threat from Muslims – yet Muslims were and are very thin on the ground here. The RSS (of which the present ruling party in New Delhi, the Bharatiya Janata Party or BJP is an affiliate) was, and remains, an overwhelmingly high caste group – and the Nagpur area already by the early 1920s had become a major centre of Dalit activity. For more details about the RSS as the core of today's 'Hindutva' formation, see Basu et al. (1993), and Jaffrelot (1996).
22. Majeed (1995).
23. Savarkar (1923: 4, 91–2, and passim).
24. Casolari (2000).
25. Golwalkar (1945) . The Preface mentions that the manuscript was ready 'as early as the first week of November 1938' – an exact concordance with *Kristallnacht* in Germany.

References

Ambedkar, B.R. 1948. *The Untouchables: Who Were They and Why They Became Untouchables*. Delhi: Oxford University Press.

Bagchi, A. 1972. *Private Investment in India 1900–1939*. Cambridge: Cambridge University Press.

Bardhan, P. 2001. ' Sharing the Spoils: Group Equity, Development and Democracy'. *The Success of India's Democracy*. Atul Kohli, ed. Cambridge: Cambridge University Press.

Basu, T. et al. 1993. *Khaki Shorts and Saffron Flags: A Critique of the Hindu Right*. Delhi: Orient Longman.

Bates, C. 1995. 'Race, Caste, and Tribe in Central India: The Early Origins of Indian Anthropology'. *The Concept of Race in South Asia*. P. Robb, ed. Delhi: Oxford India Paperbacks.

Bayly, S. 1995. 'Caste and "Race" in the Colonial Ethnography of India'. *The Concept of Race in South Asia.* P. Robb, ed. Delhi: Oxford India Paperbacks.

Burton, A. 1994. *Burdens of History: British Feminists, Indian Women, and Imperial Culture, 1865–1915.* Chapel Hill: University of North Carolina Press .

Casolari, M. 2000. 'Hindutva's Foreign Tie-up in the 1930s: Archival Evidence'. *Economic and Political Weekly* 35: 4.

Golwalkar, S. 1945. *We, or Our Nationhood Defined,* 3rd edition, Nagpur: Oxford University Press.

Hall, C. 1992. *White, Male, and Middle-Class: Explorations in Feminism and History.* London: Polity Press.

Hellman-Rajanarayan, D. 1995. 'Is There a Tamil race?' *The Concept of Race in South Asia.* P. Robb, ed. Delhi: Oxford India Paperbacks.

Jaffrelot, C. 1995. 'The Idea of the Hindu Race in the Writings of Hindu Nationalist Ideologues in 1920s and 1930s – A Concept between Two Cultures'. *The Concept of Race in South Asia.* P. Robb, ed. Delhi: Oxford India Paperbacks.

———— 1996. *The Hindu Nationalist Movement in Politics, 1925 to the 1990s.* Dehli: Penguin India.

Juergensmeyer, M. 1982. *Religion as Social Vision: The Movement against Untouchability in Twentieth Century Punjab.* Berkeley: California University Press.

Leopold, J. 1970. 'The Aryan Theory of Race'. *Indian Economic and Social History Review* 7.

Linebaugh, P. and M. Rediker. 2000. *The Many-Headed Hydra: Sailors, Slaves, Commoners, and the Hidden History of the Revolutionary Atlantic.* London: Verso.

Majeed, J. 'Pan-Islam and "Deracialization" in the Thought of Muhammad Iqbal'. *The concept of Race in South Asia.* P. Robb, ed. Delhi: Oxford India Paperbacks.

Robb, P. (ed.). 1995. *The Concept of Race in South Asia.* Delhi: Oxford India Paperbacks.

Sarkar, S. 1994. 'Orientalism Revisited: Saidian Frameworks in the Writing of Modern Indian History'. *Oxford Literary Review* 16.

———— 1997. *Writing Social History.* Delhi: Oxford University Press.

———— 1983. *Modern India 1885–1947.* Delhi: Oxford University Press.

———— 2003. *Beyond Nationalist Frames.* Delhi: Permanent Black.

Savarkar, V.D. 1923. *Hindutva / Who Is A Hindu?* Delhi: Oxford University Press.

Sinha, M. 1998. *Colonial Masculinity: the 'Manly' English and the 'Effeminate' Bengali in the late 19th century.* Manchester: Manchester University Press.

Tagore. 1917. *Nationalism.* New York: Macmillan.

Trautmann, T.R. 1997. *Aryans and British India.* Berkeley: California University Press.

Washbrook, D. 1981. 'Law, State and Society in Colonial India'. *Power, Profit, and Politics.* Baker, Johnson and Seal, eds. Cambridge: Cambridge University Press.

THE FREMMEDE AND THE DALIT ARE SILENT: DANISH AND INDIAN CULTURAL WORLDS

Donald Robotham

The chapters on which I am going to comment – those by Peter Hervik and Dipankar Gupta – form an interesting pair in so far as they seem to share similar assumptions about the inevitable primacy of 'difference' – 'socially constructed' in one case, 'primordial' in the other – which in quite different contexts – Denmark and India – are drawn on by large sections of nations for the purpose of excluding other human beings within their borders. Interestingly enough, both papers discuss difference but the victims of difference make no direct appearance even in reply, let alone in their own right. One wonders what the fremmede (i.e., the foreigners) and the Dalit would make of the claims in these papers. There is a strange silencing here.

Reading these two papers, one comes away with the feeling that it is only 'natural' for human beings to react negatively to 'a social experience of cultural difference' and that the acceptance of this cognitive 'fact' is the beginning of scholarly wisdom. In this sense, both papers leave one with a rather pessimistic feeling about the possibility of getting beyond difference, whether in Europe or the Third World, to what we all have in common as human beings and making that commonality primary. But is this pessimism justified?

Hervik's is a very clear empirical account of the 'unbridgeable' differences which his research indicates a large majority in the Danish population see between themselves and immigrants from the Third and Islamic World (apparently especially Somalis, but including Turks). The approach is to attempt to develop 'cognitive schemas' of popular consciousness and to detail these schemas through various quotations from respondents. In his view these schemas reveal a strong 'neoracism' rather than plain old racism as such.

Gupta's is a rather orthodox account of the 'hierarchy and difference' of the Indian caste system, as it appears from its upper reaches. No mention is made of exploitation and oppression of lower castes by higher, although this is clearly a major issue, in parts of the Indian countryside in particular. Much reliance is placed on the highly intellectualised and abstract analyses of Dumont whose entire methodology would certainly be rejected by many anthropologists today. As in the Hervik paper, major issues of methodology arise for this paper. At the same time, a number of assertions are made about anti-black racism in the United States by way of sharply distinguishing it from the caste system in India. These assertions are open to question, to say the least, especially the extraordinary one that 'in a society organised around race, there is no disputing the hierarchy'.[1] I comment mainly on Hervik's paper although I think many of the points, suitably adjusted, would apply to the Indian situation as well.

Hervik gives many and varied convincing examples of this rather selective sense of cultural difference in a part of the Danish population relative to such immigrants (not white Christians from North America or Australia)! The predominant view seems to be that such immigrants must change their cultural ways and adopt informants' ideas of what constitutes the principal characteristics of Danish 'culture'. Even were they to do this, however, Hervik makes clear, it would be to little avail: there would still be a perception of lack of belonging. A majority in Denmark seems to regard the differences between themselves and such immigrants as so deep as to be ineradicable.

Yet this is not the view of all Danes, a point that Hervik confines to elsewhere. This note reads: 'I do not deny that alternative cultural understandings exist, but I claim that the cultural world of unbridgeable [sic] dominates Danish perception to an overwhelming degree.'[2] In other words, there are Danes, however small in number and however isolated from mainstream Danish society who seem to be able to bridge the 'unbridgeable'. Hervik's account, however, sheds no light on this miracle, the understanding of which is of the greatest possible importance for this Conference, for Denmark, Europe and indeed, for the whole world. This merits much more than a footnote!

Hervik could rightly respond that 'unbridgers' woefully outnumber 'bridgers' and that any interpretation of Danish 'culture' must necessarily present the dominant view. This is undoubtedly true and is a problem inherent in the methodology of cognitive or cultural anthropology, especially of the Geertzian variety. As Barth and others never tire of pointing out (see the important Barth-Borofsky debate in *American Anthropologist*[3]), the culturalist approach always privileges those ideas and viewpoints that are most widely 'shared', forthwith baptising these as 'the culture'. The analysis then proceeds in terms of this dominant alone. Even when the variations in this dominant are presented – in other words, a nuanced dominant, as Borofsky demands – this does not resolve the difficulty. The issue is not one of the variation of 'shared' ideas, but the out-and-out contradiction between different set of ideas (and their proponents) contending with each other in the same society on the same issues. Nuanced 'culture' still homogenises.

Hervik's cognitive account is thus useful as far as it goes. He certainly paints a disturbingly detailed and, I have no doubt, truthful picture (as far as it goes), of the extent to which racist ideas are abroad in large sections of the Copenhagen population across a range of social strata. His descriptions are clear and convincing, but in the end remain descriptions. There is surprisingly little analysis of nuances in the Borofsky manner, let alone of contradictions, even though at least one informant shows some sign of self-doubt (Yes, they have to learn to eat pork and drink beer! Well, no, it depends on what we mean by saying that they need to learn to adjust) and a number of other excerpts read awfully like persons arguing with their own conscience – possibly to preserve their sense of self-righteousness.[4] However, the rather straightforward picture of Danish cultural homogeneity and boundedness presented conveys little sense of self-doubt and contradiction and no sense at all of the roles of power and money. These are common failings and critiques of a culturalist methodology. For these and other reasons this kind of anthropology fell into disrepute in the 1980s, at least in some parts of the United States.

I was also surprised that Hervik did not raise the question of Danish Lutheranism, especially at what one may call the popular level (the reactions and actions of the very powerful established Danish Church is another matter), since so many of the issues with immigrants have to do with Danish reactions to Islam. I am no expert, but the little I have read tells me that Denmark is a society very deeply imbued with a particular brand of Lutheranism, which has played and probably continues to play a decisive role in the society, secularisation notwithstanding.[5] It is possible that the historical triumph of the doctrines of this particular version of the Protestant ethic at the popular level, at least after 1849 and probably long before,[6] has been crucial in justifying and reinforcing a particular kind of dominant Danish identity.

This dominant identity seems to be composed of a strong sense of individual rights and therefore of tolerance of the rights of others (historically, limited to other Christians); a rather sharp business sense; an almost religious duty to disciplined labour (the notorious 'calling'); submission to authority; conformity to the ways of the majority (not upsetting anyone or not 'integrating')[7]; a strong sense of the dangers and attractions of 'sin' combined with a deep abhorrence of those who seem to lack these Lutheran virtues, and an associated tendency to moralise (what the English call 'cant'). There are no Levellers or Diggers here, although I am sure that Danish political and social history must have generated (and still generates) its own popular dissenters and nonconformists from these self-serving principles of the bourgeois gentry. Eat pork and drink beer!

From this viewpoint, the experience of England is of some comparative importance. There we have a northern European society also with strong Protestant traditions in which a much more differentiated reaction to cultural difference – much more positive at the popular level – seems to have developed. As scholars such as Christopher Hill have pointed out,[8] northern European Protestantism was and is a diverse, tumultuous and contradictory creature, with the often bawdy Protestant 'difference' of the ranting masses perpetually scandalising the good bourgeois gentry (although not the 'degenerate' aristocracy).

Of course, this gentry did not hesitate to use force to make their version of the Protestant ethic 'dominant'. One result in a place like England – which may make it very different from Denmark (and the United States) – is the notoriously vast social and 'cultural' gulf between the white English aristocratic-bourgeois-upper professional elite and the white English working classes. The relative weakness of social solidarity across this English gulf, one-nation Tories notwithstanding, is striking, not to mention the conflicts with Wales, Scotland and Ireland. Here, a healthy appreciation of the hypocrisy of the top, especially the religious top, has long pervaded popular life at the bottom. This is not to say that exhortations against difference emanating from the top are not widespread and that they do not also fall on much fertile soil at the bottom. Nevertheless, in general, atheism, nonconformity and cynicism to the moralising of the top are commonsensical and commonplace. This creates a large space for solidarity with or at least indifference to 'difference' rather than knee-jerk hostility to it, since historically the charge of intolerable 'difference' (glossed as 'heathenish behaviour' or 'Satan') has been so frequently a class tool of the top to bring the bottom into line. In this sense – in the relatively weak penetration of popular consciousness by the bourgeois Protestant ethic – England may be less of a bourgeois society than Denmark.

In fact, one of the historical ironies of the present situation in Europe is that, having laboured in the vineyard long and hard to convince the people to internalise an austere Protestant ethic (even in Catholic areas), the cosmopolitan elite, intent on globalisation, now find this cultivated narrowness of the old bourgeois order rather bothersome to their new-found political and especially economic ambitions in current conditions. The same could be said of the attitude of sections of the Mumbai bourgeoisie to the communal fanaticism of Shiv Senna, which in another context, they may themselves share and encourage. Hervik alludes to these manoeuvres of the European bourgeoisie, which we see not only in Denmark, but also in Austria, Germany, Switzerland, Italy, Spain, France, Britain and the United States, and to the skill with which the right-wing newspapers demagogically play upon the (quite instrumental and conditional) support of the more globalised sections of the bourgeoisie for selective immigration and a certain amount of cosmopolitanism.[9]

Because the methodology is ahistorical, cognitive anthropology fails to emphasise (or even recognise) the fact that though such ideas may be dominant for a considerable period of time in a given society, in fact these triumphantly 'shared' ideas themselves began life in the minds of a few isolated individuals. These ideas, or more accurately their proponents, had to fight to win and to retain dominance against many contradictory and tenacious contenders. The importance of mobilising social and political forces around one's ideas – the understanding that one is in a battle of ideas – is fully appreciated by the Danish right-wing parties and newspapers, according to Hervik's own account. They certainly leave nothing to chance or to 'culture'. On the contrary, they are consumed with a sense that other contradictory ideas have appeal and in fact contend fiercely with theirs and that they have to fight with all their might in order to win out. Why does the right fight so hard, if there is nothing to contend against, if it is simply a matter of 'second nature' – read 'culture'? For that matter, why did as many as 49 percent vote in favour of Maastricht in 1991? The right seems to understand that one cannot rely on 'culture' for victory. Ideas become 'shared' after a hard-fought struggle for hearts and minds. Even when they win out, in few societies do these 'shared' ideas ever have the field entirely to themselves. They rarely go unchallenged by some group or the other at some time in that very same society, often when one is least expecting it.

This is why it is so vital to present the range of contradictory ideas which always exist in any society and not to be overly impressed with one particular set of dominant perceptions (declaring this to be the 'culture'), even if 90 percent of people share it. The 'dominant' and the 'subdominant' need to be presented not only side by side, but in relation to each other, since they shape and even arise out of each other and are not really comprehensible outside of this context of mutual struggle. In particular, the viewpoints of the victims of exclusion – Somalis and Dalits – need to be made to speak for themselves, to directly answer the dominant views, if we are truly to understand either set of viewpoints. This is because, as has been already pointed out, these views arise and take shape in response to each other and not in the abstract. However, in both papers, the fremmede and the Dalits are silenced.

This is not primarily a matter of fair-mindedness or correct academic methodology. It is also a highly important political matter. For it should be clear by now that if racism is to be defeated anywhere, this will require the full mobilising of all antiracist ideas, persons and movements.

This omission is a particularly strange occurrence in the case of India, given the enormous impact which Dalits had on the Durban Conference against Racism. A number of accounts suggest that, after the Palestinian and Slavery-Reparation issues, the issue of racism against Dalits in India was the most salient issue. A number of African American scholars, who attended this conference, came away deeply impressed with the struggle of the Dalits and an appreciation for their plight which was entirely new.[10] Whatever Gupta may or may not think, clearly large sections of the Dalits regard their treatment in India as racist and even if one rejects this claim one must at least mention and give space to these views from the victims themselves.

Indeed, one of the most interesting features of the Durban Conference was the way in which it highlighted a variety of racisms, and not just the traditional and well-known anti-black racism in the United States and the West. Without decentring the struggle against anti-black racism which is clearly the alpha and omega, Durban effectively ended the political and intellectual holiday enjoyed by these 'lesser' racisms and exposed them to the light of day. There is no sign of this process in Gupta's paper.

In other words, dominant or no, these 'cognitive schemas' remain simply hotly contested ideas, which have a history, which wax and wane with the vigorous actions of individuals, social forces and social movements, according to certain historical conditions. These are incomprehensible without understanding the particular economic and political challenges that various groups of people confront at a given moment of time in a particular set of countries. This is another problem with Hervik's account.

Despite repeated statements to the effect that these ideas are 'social constructions'[11] Hervik's cognitive approach fails to discuss the social, economic and political forces that are operating in the Danish situation (and indeed, in the world as a whole) to generate frustration and anxiety among specific sectors of the Danish population. Such forces, if they are analysed at all, remain firmly in the background, which is exceedingly odd, since a number of informants hint at just such issues. More than one excerpt refers to the frustration that large sections of the Danish people are experiencing with the political establishment, and points to the fact that part of the turn to the right-wing parties is as a result of this frustration. But Hervik does not seem to pursue that line of inquiry with his respondents.

Yet there is much to suggest in this paper and others that globalisation has created a severe crisis of the postwar political, economic and social contract of the welfare state all over Europe, and that this has placed the entire political class – and social democrats in particular – with seemingly little other choice except neoliberalism or some form of 'third wayism'. This political and economic crisis is not mentioned in the paper, yet it is clearly the background against which the insecurity of the Danes arises, especially in relation to financing the welfare state. Not too far in the background also is the generalised and well-founded fear of the social and economic implications for Danish society of globalization and of integration into the European Union. This is not mentioned for India either, even though here too a central political and economic issue which Indian society has faced in recent years is precisely this question of the breakdown of the old postcolonial Congress consensus: how India is to reconfigure itself in the light of the new globalised world which it faces, what sort of changes inside and outside this may or may not require, what interests are threatened and what is to be done about it and by whom.

The role that social constructivism seems to play in this paper is to sustain the argument that popular prejudice against immigrants in Denmark is somehow 'natural'. It arises out of 'peoples' social experience of cultural difference'.[12] In other words, people in Denmark are reacting to actual cultural differences, which they experience, say on the street or in the media as a kind of 'social fact'. But this argument only works if one assumes that reactions *against* difference are somehow 'natural,' or are 'common-sense understandings that cultural differences, are disturbing,'[13] especially since immigrants are only 8 percent of the Danish population and the vast majority of Danes have had no direct social experience of cultural difference. This brand of experiential social constructivism may in fact be only a polite form of primordialism. It is in fact not so far from the views of Gupta that, 'That human kind everywhere demonstrates actively this propensity to differentiate ...'[14] Of course, what is in question is not 'the propensity to differentiate' but the reactions to this 'propensity'.

Why isn't it equally 'natural' and common-sensical to react with delight, appreciation or even indifference to the 'social experience of cultural difference'? It goes without saying that negative or positive reactions (or elements of both) are all possible for commonsense from a 'social experience of difference'. To hold otherwise would be to mystify difference. To say therefore that a cultural category is 'socially constructed' without explaining the social, economic and political interests which do the constructing, why and against what, in fact tells us little or nothing about what is taking place and why, who and to whom. The apparent uniformity of negative reaction needed to be problematised in this paper and it is not. In the end, social constructivism looks suspiciously like a form of what one may call social primordialism.

What both these papers reveal, interestingly, is that there is as much a need for changes by academics in the developed, as in the Third World. Exclusion, exploitation and oppression must be contested not only in Europe but also everywhere on the globe, if it is to be contested effectively. Clearly, new kinds of studies, research strategies and methodologies are urgently required. In such approaches, no assumptions of social or natural primordialism should be made and the contested terrain of ideas and the actors who develop and propagate them in their manifold inter-relationships and contradictions must be depicted with a greater historical sense. A greater appreciation and study of the vital importance of agency is urgently needed. Much more careful attention must be paid to the complex and quite real threats of globalisation to the interests of specific social strata, documenting these in detail. Above all, the voices of the victims must speak for themselves in research. Such approaches require not only changes of methodology but also changes in society and in academia itself.

Acknowledgement

It is a great privilege to be accorded the opportunity to participate in this extremely important publication, if only by proxy. I would like to thank the sponsors and organisers of the original conference and especially Ms Ellen Preckler and Professor Rik Pinxten for making possible this important academic, indeed political, initiative. In the times in which we live, one cannot emphasise too much how important it is to have such forums for the exchange of views on critical issues that divide peoples within and between societies. Here it may be said that it is now clear (for reasons which themselves bear pondering) that the people of a small state, Belgium, seem to be playing an extraordinarily important role in helping others in the world to grapple with these difficult issues. This is a great credit to Belgian society.

Notes

1. *Abstract: Caste and Race: A Comparative Study of Ascriptive Mobilizations*: 1.
2. Hervik (2001: 4–5).
3. Borofsky, R. and Barth, F. (2001: 432–46).
4. Hervik (2001: 22). See also excerpts at 20–21.
5. Official statistics claim that Denmark is as much as 91 percent Lutheran.
6. Where, when and how these doctrines originated, how they changed as they developed, whose interests they represented and why and how they triumphed against other doctrines, are another set of matters entirely.
7. Hervik (2001: 21).
8. Hill (1982).

9. Hervik (2001: 5). See the discussion of the anti-Maastricht campaign of the rightwing newspaper *Ekstra Bladet* and their commentaries against 'the upper class, sometimes epitomized as the extravagant bourgeoisie'.
10. Personal discussions with Professor Leith Mullings.
11. Hervik (2001: 25).
12. Hervik (2001: 8).
13. Hervik (2001: 6).
14. Gupta (1998: 3).

References

Borofsky, R. and Barth, F. 2001. 'WHEN: A Conversation about Culture'. *American Anthropologist* 103, 2: 432–46.

Gupta, D. 1998. *Hierarchy and Difference: An Introduction*. Oxford: Oxford University Press.

Hervik, P. 2001. *The Danish Cultural World of Unbridgeable Differences*. Department of Social Anthropology, University of Oslo.

Hervik, P. in press. 'The Emergence of Neo-Nationalism in Denmark: 1992–2001'. *Neo-Nationalism inside the EU: Anthropological Pespectives*, M. Banks and A. Gingrich, eds.

Hill, C. 1982. *The World Turned Upside Down: Radical Ideas in the English Revolution*. Harmondsworth: Penguin Books.

Approaching Racism: Attitudes, Actions and Social Structure

Robert A. Rubinstein

Introduction

In December 2002 the leader of the Republican Caucus in the United States Senate, Trent Lott, resigned his post in response to the uproar caused by remarks he made that signalled to many his private approval of segregation in the United States and of the racist legacy that such approval entails. According to Human Rights Watch, anti-Muslim crimes in the United States increased between 2000 and 2001 by about 1,658 percent (Singh 2002: 16). These crimes included murders, assaults, arson and attacks on places of worship. In 1995 in the United States, one in three African American men between the ages of 20 and 29 was involved with the criminal justice system. They were in jail or in prison, on parole or on probation (Mauer and Huling 1995). Do these facts have something in common with the youth unemployment described by Duster (this volume), the increase in racial disturbances in the North of England reported by Seward (this volume), or the remarkable ability of Danes to view themselves simultaneously as both tolerant and racist (Hervik, this volume)? The papers in this book contain rich empirical and theoretical materials for exploring the interplay of the factors that contribute to discriminatory practices. My view is that these social facts are all connected to one another. To understand how, we need to look beyond their apparent similarities and differences. In this paper I sketch some of the prerequisites for adequately understanding and hence responding to racism that I think emerge from a consideration of the papers presented at the Ghent conference on 'Racism in Metropolitan Areas'.[1]

Multiple Levels of Organisation

If we want to understand the social reality of discrimination, we must start by recognising that we are speaking about a social phenomenon that is complex. It follows that our theoretical accounts of what is happening also need to be complex lest they confound rather than facilitate sound understanding (Quine 1963).

Part of the complexity is that the phenomena take place at many levels of organisation, from the intra-personal, through the inter-personal and small group, to the macro-social. In general, accounting for complex social phenomena requires that we adopt a multilevel approach (Rubinstein et al. 1984: 90). Racism has manifestations at all levels of organisation, and these manifestations are not discrete from one another. The race-based violence in Bradford was most certainly a mass process. It involved a (relatively large) group and it must be understood through an understanding of group process. Researchers would better their understanding of the violence by tracing the dynamics of how word was spread by youths using cell phones that a conflagration was unfolding, for instance. Seward's description that 'Word quickly spread by mobile telephone that a racial fight was going on and a large number of Asian (Pakistani) youths hurried to the scene,' is remarkable for its similarity to Roy's (1994) description of how conflict intensified in the Hindu-Muslim communal riot she studied in Bangladesh. I suspect that it would also parallel the intensification of caste violence in Gujarat mentioned by Gupta. Those who wished to intervene might be prepared to identify the networks of communication involved so that they can act to disrupt them.

The disturbances were also energised by material concerns. The distribution of economic and other opportunities plays a role. The fact and the perception that these opportunities are available to some but not others also create the social conditions for conflict. Such material concerns seem to be common to the situation of growing structurally based decreases in employment opportunities considered by Duster, and to the mobilisation of caste identities described by Gupta. It is clear that access to or exclusion from various kinds of resources have real effects on the lives of groups. Gee (2002), for example, showed that discrimination in relation to individual and institutional resources leads to poorer health outcomes for those discriminated against.

The Bradford disturbance also involved individual motivations. Participants in the disturbance responded as they did in part because their motivational state disposed them to act violently rather than in a cooperative manner (Apter 2001). I will return to the question of motivational state later when I discuss the interaction of attitudes and actions in encounters with diversity.

Some sense of the motivational component of racism can be gained from attention to language, which is why, as Sarkar points out, questions of language use are important. Additionally, language use (and the use of other symbols) helps to frame the discourse through which people contest the legitimacy of social action (Lane and Rubinstein 1996). This also helps to account for the force of the response that led to Senator Lott's resignation as majority leader.[2]

Not only is racism manifest at various levels of organisation, actions at each of these levels interact with the others to establish a 'dispositional field' within which understandings and actions are formed. A multilevel approach is as essential for calculating ways to combat racism as it is for forming an adequate understanding of it.

Racism as a Special Case of Ethnocentrism

It is worth recalling the enumeration of the characteristics of the 'universal syndrome of ethnocentrism' as identified by LeVine and Campbell (1972) (see Table 1). In this enumeration we can see that both the in-group and the out-group hold attitudes and condone actions that stigmatise and may harm the

Table 1 *LeVine and Campbell's Twenty-three Facets of the Universal Syndrome of Ethnocentrism*

Attitudes and Behaviours Toward In-group	Attitudes and Behaviours Toward Out-group
See selves as virtuous and superior	See out-group as contemptible, immoral and inferior
See own standards of value as universal, intrinsically true.	See own customs as original, centrally human
See selves as strong	See out-groups as weak Social distance Out-group hate
Sanctions against in-group theft	Sanctions for out-group theft, or absence of sanctions against
Sanctions against in-group murder	Sanctions for out-group murder or absence of sanctions against out-group murder
Cooperative relations with in-group's members	Absence of cooperation with out-group members
Obedience to in-group authorities	Absences of obedience to out-group authorities
Willingness to remain an in-group member	Absence of conversion to out-group membership
Willingness to fight and die for in-group	Absence of willingness to fight and die for out-groups Virtue in killing out-group members in warfare Use of out-groups as bad examples in the training of children Blaming of out-groups for in-group troubles Distrust and fear of the out-group

Source: LeVine and Campbell (1972: 12)

Other. Hervik argues that 'tolerance/toleration' is an inadequate basis upon which to build an equitable society because it involves the giving of permission by the more powerful group to less powerful groups. Hervik is correct, I think, to distinguish between the attitude of 'tolerance' and the act of 'toleration'. Further, these affect one another and both involve accepting a discourse in which one group is unmarked while others are marked. I think Hervik is only partially correct when he points out that tolerance/toleration always implies broad, stable power asymmetries.

Tolerance/toleration involves power, but it is not a stable unidirectional power. Rather, power is local and dynamic, increasing and decreasing in its scope of application depending upon a number of structural and other variables. Tolerance implies willingness to 'put up with' the Other. Yet, as LeVine and Campbell (1972) showed, ethnocentrism, of which racism is a special case, is a universal phenomenon. Not only do Danes as the 'host' society put up with immigrant groups but within their own communities immigrant groups put up with aspects of Danish society and culture that they do not seek to adopt or of which they do not approve. In communities where these groups become the majority (that is, are structurally more powerful than their hosts) they may well stop putting up with those despised aspects of their host's society. Examples of this are efforts in some Muslim-American communities to close liquor stores and movie rental shops in their communities.[3]

Racism is a special case of the 'universal syndrome of ethnocentrism', in that it depends upon a specific biologically based understanding of the Other, as Sarkar points out. The result is a kind of strong stereotype that depends upon essentialising a group of people to a set of presumed biological characteristics. Certainly, the extensions of this essentialisation depend upon specific cultural logics.

For this reason I cannot agree with Gupta's argument against the politics of 'caste is race', even though I appreciate the ethnographic details upon which he relies. Gupta makes a strong case that the logic of caste is different from the logic of American race-based systems. Especially strong, I think, is his analysis of racial identity, which becomes stronger at general levels of society while caste identity becomes weaker at higher levels.

He argues as well that racially segregated societies are different from caste-segregated societies in that the latter incorporate ideas of purity and pollution while the former have no such ideas. I think this is a less strong argument than his arguments about the relationship between societal level and strength and importance of identity. It is clear that in Hindu society there are clearly articulated cultural models relating to purity and pollution. In mainstream American society, there are no such explicitly articulated models of purity and pollution. Yet, in examining the literature and discourse of segregationist groups, it is clear that there is an unarticulated notion that 'race mixing' is in some sense a pollution of the white race.[4]

While both of the foregoing observations are ethnographically astute, I do not think that they support Gupta's view that caste is not race. Rather, they describe the operation of distinct cultural logics in American and Hindu society.

There is no reason to suppose that the operation of racism is the same in all contexts. Quite the contrary, one would expect variations in the way that culturally distinct societies construct and express racism. The key to denying the 'caste is race' claim would be to show that caste is a form of ethnocentrism that does not depend upon the biological for its force.

Gupta argues against the biological essentialisation of caste by citing two very interesting kinds of ethnographic evidence. The first is the evidence that no low-caste person accepts the claim that their biological essence is inferior to that of other castes, except as a kind of false acceptance of this claim when power differentials make it unwise or unsafe to contest it. Likewise, the second ethnographic claim Gupta offers against the 'caste is race' construction is that in their own narratives members of low castes offer stories to suggest that in fact they, not the other castes, are made of superior essence.

These two interesting ethnographic details argue against the case that Gupta tries to make. Rather than undercutting the 'caste is race formula', in my view they make the case. The dominant discourse in both cases remains biological.[5]

Further, in comparison with American racism, there is ample evidence to suggest that analogous processes are at work, though they engage different cultural logics. As with members of lower castes, no black person would accept that they are biologically inferior to whites, except as a kind of false acceptance of this proposition when power differentials make it unwise or unsafe to contest it. Indeed, within African American culture this situation is explicitly recognised in the named and institutionalised communicative form of shucking and jiving, which identifies the situation in which an individual deceives by pretending to be respectful and perhaps simple-minded (Kochman 1972, McArthur 1992).

Caste in India and race in the United States do indeed differ. They differ in the manner in which people express the twenty-three facets of the universal syndrome of ethnocentrism. Nevertheless, at a deeper level they do not differ in their ascription of group differences to biological, hereditary attributes.

Attitudes and Action

In addition to acknowledging that racism has manifestations on many levels of organization, and that its particular expression will vary in the context of different cultural logics, in my opinion, it is also important to engage the fact that those manifestations are expressed in a variety of ways. I think it is helpful to distinguish between attitudes and actions in considering racism. Of course, attitudes and actions interact and mutually shape one another.

Figure 1 shows an idealised model of the relationship of attitudes and actions in discriminatory practices. The actions range along a continuum from direct violence to equality, with structural violence falling between the extremes. Attitudes range from racism to genuine acceptance.

The attitudes dimension of this model shows the range of sensibilities that one group may display towards others. Racism involves the open despising of

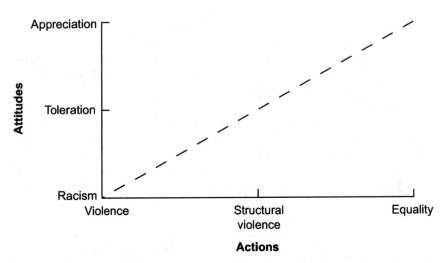

Figure 1 *Conceptual Relationships among Attitudes and Actions in Encounters with Diversity*

the Other. In this situation the racist adopts a biologised view of the differences between their group and other peoples, very much like in-group–out-group differences described by LeVine and Campbell. Tolerance in this model is much the same as the description that Hervik offers when he sees tolerance as the willingness to put up with various characteristics of other groups that are alien to one's own group. Appreciation implies an explicit valuing of different ways of viewing and interacting with the social and physical world.

The actions dimension of this model is intended to display the variety of ways in which groups may interact with one another. Equality is a condition in which others are treated in the same ways that members of one's in-group are treated; everyone is extended the same rights and respect. At the other behavioural extreme a condition of violence denotes actions that are intended to harm members of the other group by hurting them physically or by destroying their property, or by defacing symbols that they hold dear. Subtler, but no less destructive, is the condition of structural violence. As first described by Galtung (1969) and elaborated by others (Barash and Webel 2002; Weigert 1999), structural violence denotes actions that systematically harm groups of people by denying them access to resources like jobs, education, health care and other rights. The results of structural violence, of which 'institutional racism' is a special case, can be clearly seen in the lives of people. Yet because the discriminatory practices are embedded in the structures of society they cannot be traced to individuals; no one and everyone is responsible for the discriminatory action.

I suggest that the actions and attitudes are systematically related. As Figure 1 suggests, violence is related to racism as defined above. The confluence of racism and violence results in phenomena like the Bradford racial disturbances, the post-

11 September 2001 anti-Muslim hate crimes in the United States, and caste violence in India. Structural violence occurs in the presence of tolerance in which there is a tension between in-group and out-group for the ability to define what can be 'put up with'. Appreciation entails the action of equality, the extension to all persons of the same rights and access to material and normative resources.

The model is, of course, an idealised representation of these relationships. It is evident that in reality people and groups do not always display racism, tolerance or appreciation, but rather move among them. What causes this movement? My suggestion is that discriminatory practices take place in a dispositional field. The dispositional field has three components: motivational states, structural aspects and symbolic meaning systems.

Based on considerable empirical research, Apter (2001: 6) suggests that individuals' motivational states can be described by four dispositional states. These describe how a person (1) relates to their goals-are they goal directed? (2) whether they are inclined to follow rules; (3) whether they display sympathy towards or a desire to achieve mastery over others; and (4) whether they are self – or other-centred in their relationships. Motivational states are evanescent; a person moves among the possible states as a result of internal and external stimuli.

In this regard, the structural aspects of a social context may initiate movement among the various motivational states. Social structures may incline an individual towards one motivational state or another. Language, symbolism and ritual then move these motivations and structural opportunities for discrimination to a more macrolevel.

I propose that discriminatory practices depend on a motivational field that merges the individual motivational states of mastery and a self-centred orientation towards relationships with social structures that encourage these states, and symbols that give them exclusionist meanings. Social scientists approaching racism need to acknowledge that adequate understanding of discriminatory practices requires appreciating the similarities and the differences in particular instances of racism, like those offered in this volume. Meeting this challenge of elaborating a complex rather than simplifying view of racism qua social phenomena offers two challenges. The first is to identify in individual cases the functioning of these mechanisms. The second is to articulate ways of interrupting and reversing the discriminatory motivational field.

Notes

1. The contributions that I considered especially were those by Duster, Gupta, Hervik, Poppe, Sarkar and Seward.
2. The segregationist nature of the comment was not the only factor leading to Lott's resignation. Many analysts believe that a contributing factor was the desire on the part of the Bush administration to consolidate its power. Lott was not closely aligned with Bush and received little assistance from the administration in his attempts to remain majority leader.
3. The ceasing to put up with aspects of the host society's culture that are disapproved of by immigrants need not depend upon their achieving structural power in an area. Rather, they

may invoke a normative power to assert their desired practice, as when parents of Muslim school girls assert their claims for their children to wear headscarves, or when some immigrant communities maintain their practice of female genital surgeries (Lane and Rubinstein 1996).

4. This claim is based on a casual, rather than exhaustive, review of the pamphlets and speeches of segregationist and white supremacist groups in the United States.

5. Gupta's argument that caste hierarchies' supposing that the salient dimension of biological difference is light skin versus dark skin rests on a misreading of the Vedic texts seems reasonable to me. But accepting such a misreading does not mean, therefore, that no claim of biological essence is invoked in relation to distinguishing among castes.

References

Apter, M. ed. 2001. *Motivational Styles in Everyday Life: A Guide to Reversal Theory.* Washington, DC: American Psychological Association.

Barash, D. and Webel, C. 2002. *Peace and Conflict Studies.* Thousand Oaks, CA: Sage Publications.

Galtung, J. 1969. 'Violence, Peace, and Peace Research'. *Journal of Peace Research* 6: 167–91.

Gee, C.G. 2002. 'A Multilevel Analysis of the Relationship between Institutional Racial Discrimination and Health Status'. *American Journal of Public Health* 92: 615–23.

Kochman, T., ed. 1972. *Rappin' and Stylin' Out: Communication in Urban Black America.* Urbana, IL: University of Illinois Press.

Lane, S.D. and Rubinstein, R.A. 1996. *Judging the Other: Responding to Traditional Genital Surgeries.* Hastings Center Report 26: 31–41.

LeVine, R.A. and Campbell, D.T. 1972. *Ethnocentrism: Theories of Conflict, Ethnic Attitudes and Group Behavior.* New York: John Wiley and Sons.

Mauer, M. and Huling, T. 1995. *Young Black American and the Criminal Justice System: Five Years Later.* Washington DC: The Sentencing Project.

McArthur, T. ed. 1992. *The Oxford Companion to the English Language.* Oxford: Oxford University Press.

Quine, W. 1963. 'On Simple Theories of a Complex World'. *Synthese* 15: 103–6.

Roy, B. 1994. *Some Trouble with Cows: Making Sense of Social Conflict.* Berkeley, CA: University of California Press.

Rubinstein, R.A., Laughlin, C.D. and McManus, J. 1984. *Science as Cognitive Process: Toward and Empirical Philosophy of Science.* Philadelphia, PA: University of Pennsylvania Press.

Singh, A. 2002. '"We are not the enemy." Hate Crimes against Arabs, Muslims, and Those Perceived to be Arab or Muslim after September 11'. *Human Rights Watch* 14: 1–40.

Weigert, K.M. 1999. 'Structural violence'. In *Encyclopedia of Violence, Peace, and Conflict.* New York: Academic Press, Vol. 3: 431–40.

PART TWO

EMPOWERING TO COMBAT RACISM

The Paradox of Secondary Ethnicity

Emanuel Marx

We tend to believe that immigrants to cities gradually adapt to the new environment and in the process lose much of their ethnic heritage. This seems to be true in the early stages of adaptation, when the immigrants try to establish a foothold, to find work, lodgings, and schools for their children. They seek to develop a network of social relationships to answer their various needs. This network often includes many former countrymen, some of whom may be the kin and friends who facilitated their immigration in the first place. These persons sustained the immigrants during their first days in the new country, found them accommodation in their own ethnic neighbourhood, and introduced them to their social networks, usually to persons who could communicate with the immigrants in their mother tongue and could cater to their various needs. Gradually the immigrants find their own way in the new environment and develop their social networks without further assistance. While some of them may stay with their compatriots all their lives, and never become familiar with the country's official language, others seek to enter the wider society. If the extent and the diversity of social networks are the ultimate test of assimilation, then both types of immigrant adapt very successfully. Yet the immigrants themselves applaud especially those who learn the new language and compete successfully with the veteran citizens. Although in practice these successful men and women tend to move out of the ethnic neighbourhood and drop some of their old friends, their fellow-immigrants are proud of them and hold them up as shining examples of success. Thomas and Znaniecki (1918) were the first sociologists to describe these early stages of the immigrants' adaptation – in their case, Polish immigrants in Chicago.

Do people then shed their ethnicity and become fully absorbed in the new country? It appears that sooner or later they reach a point where further progress towards full assimilation is checked. Hard as they might try, they are never fully accepted by the old-timers. Ironically, the immigrant who is told by the official representatives of the new society that only if he or she conforms to its ways can he hope for full acceptance now finds that, in the end, he always remains an outsider. He meets one rejection after another. He is not invited to the homes of people whom he considers his equals, and is not elected to exclusive social clubs and professional bodies. His career does not reflect his real achievements and his children are not admitted to the right schools. He is, in short, treated as an ethnic and thus as a second-class citizen.

How can one explain this apparent contradiction? It seems to be connected to the essence of life in cities. In the city, people meet an infinite number of others. They can cope with this endless stream of experiences only by summing up persons in the basic categories of sex, age and ethnicity. This shorthand is applied not only to strangers but also, in some measure, to superficial acquaintances and even to friends. Official bodies also emulate it, for every authority wishes to assign its clients to a limited number of clear-cut categories. Once a person is tagged, she becomes part of an imaginary group that can be treated uniformly. Ethnic stereotypes play a central role in this mostly unconscious categorisation. For instance, the officials who dealt with the Ethiopian immigrants who arrived in Israel during the 1970s tacitly assumed that they were illiterate villagers who had never been in touch with bureaucratic bodies. This assumption allowed them to treat all the immigrants in the same manner, and to send all of them to holding camps, which they called Absorption Centres (Hertzog 1999). They did not bother to enquire more deeply into their educational and occupational qualifications. A random enquiry I made in one particular camp, however, revealed that the immigrants' qualifications differed widely: one of the persons interviewed was an English teacher, the next was a merchant, a third was a commercial pilot, a fourth was a farmer, and so forth.

A very effective and empowering response to ethnic labelling is for the immigrants to make a virtue out of necessity, and to become once again ethnic. They may set up an ethnic organisation in order to combat ethnic discrimination. Their imputed ethnicity turns into the organising principle of an ethnic group. It begins life as a response to discrimination, and may eventually become a vehicle for empowerment, and a source of pride in belonging to a successful group. The group may set up all the institutions to which its members were formerly denied access, such as social clubs and sports centres. This process is contagious and may, in the long run, lead to a situation where every citizen must belong to an ethnic group in order to participate in the larger society. This seems to be happening in the United States, where it is becoming harder and harder for people to become simply Americans. Access to the large American society is mediated by their membership of ethnic associations. Members of these groups consider themselves to be full-fledged Americans, and it is as Americans that they cultivate their ethnic affiliation. Needless to say, their devotion to the old homeland and its culture, such as their pride in Italian cooking and Polish music, are as American as can be. And so are their ties to the former homeland, even when they culminate in the project of buying a piece of property there. The links with the home country serve chiefly as the focus of the ethnic association in the new country. Frequently the people back home are set up as the moral arbiters of the members of the immigrants' association. The fear that any improper behaviour may be reported to the people back home keeps many individuals to the straight and narrow path. This type of behaviour can be called secondary ethnicity, because it concerns people who have become naturalised in the new environment, but are forced by the need for empowerment to organise on an ethnic basis.

The ethnic association may also become a proper foundation for business relations. Thus, Pakistani immigrants in Britain managed to corner the textile trade because they could trust the word of their fellow-Pakistani trade partners. They could arrange transactions by word of mouth and on the phone, without resorting to lengthy legal or bureaucratic procedures (Werbner 1990). They knew that their Pakistani business partners could be trusted, because the people back home, a somewhat nebulous community, were watching their conduct.

Racial or ethnic stereotypes thus are part of our social repertoire; they may sometimes favour our interests and at other times work against us. They are 'bits of knowledge' about people and thus facilitate initial contacts between strangers. I would argue that they are no different from most of our knowledge. For all the bits of knowledge (as distinct from connected bodies of knowledge) we use are stereotyped, to the extent that we accept them unconditionally as true. Ethnic or racial stereotypes are then a normal and necessary aspect of social life. They are particularly important in the cities, where we encounter many new faces and must make quick assessments of how to deal with each person. Racial stereotypes become dangerous only when they are taken up by the state and other bureaucratic organisations and serve as the basis of social policies, or when racialist organisations attack people they define as belonging to other racial categories. Thus, some former East Germans have organised violent gangs to combat foreigners who, they believe, endanger their livelihood (Peck 1995). Here, as elsewhere, the weak organise to attack even weaker sectors of the population, instead of organising against the real culprits, the large economic organisations and the agencies of the state. Recent immigrants are especially vulnerable to racial discrimination and criminal assaults, as they are relatively powerless and disorganised. Once the immigrants are integrated in the new country, and especially after they have set up secondary ethnic organisations, they are less liable to be attacked. A country that has opted for cultural pluralism, like the United States, can therefore overcome the paradox of the apparent resurgence of ethnicity among its long-established citizens. Most European countries are still pursuing various more or less unsuccessful policies with regard to their immigrants. In many countries the second- and third-generation descendants of the erstwhile immigrants have become citizens of the State and yet remain unwanted strangers. Even their ethnic associations, all of which have developed secondary ethnicity, are sometimes still frowned upon.

References

Hertzog, E. 1999. *Immigrants and Bureaucrats: Ethiopians in an Israeli Absorption Center*. New York: Berghahn.

Peck, J.M. 1995. 'Refugees as Foreigners: the Problem of Becoming German and Finding Home'. *Mistrusting Refugees*. E.V. Daniel and J.C. Knudsen, eds. Berkeley: University of California Press: 102–25.

Thomas, W.I. and Znaniecki, F. 1918. The *Polish Peasant in Europe and America,* Chicago: University of Chicago Press.

Werbner, P. 1990. *The Migration Process: Capital, Gifts and Offerings among British Pakistanis*. Oxford: Berg.

Is Harmony Possible in a Multiracial Society? The Case of Singapore

Mary Judd

Introduction

Modernisation and globalisation have brought many benefits to the world including a higher standard of living, a longer life expectancy, rising literacy and education, and an increasing economic interdependence and social complexity. Boundaries between countries have become more porous, allowing for easier access to information, communication and transportation. This accelerated change, however, has also brought with it increasing socioeconomic disparities and a widening of the gap between rich and poor, and heightened ethnic, religious and cultural differences. The increasing reality of these social problems has prompted development agencies to convene a policy discussion on the issues of social cohesion, conflict, and the management of diversity (e.g., by the World Bank in 2001).

Social cohesion can be defined as 'the glue that bonds society together, promoting harmony, a sense of community, and a degree of commitment to promoting the common good' (Colletta et al. 2001: 2). It is argued that it is the interplay of horizontal social capital (crosscutting, networked relations among diverse communal groups) with vertical social capital (that, is, the responsiveness of the state to its citizenry) that shapes social relations and social cohesion which is the foundation for managing conflict (ibid.). Too often, it is only the horizontal social capital at work where community groups, civil society and non-government groups are working tirelessly to promote harmony. The other critical component of the vertical capital of the state is either missing or there is very little of it.

The role of the state in promoting multiracial harmony cannot be overemphasised. The next few pages looks at one state, Singapore, which does not take harmony for granted but has introduced legislation and development programmes to manage conflict and to ensure multiracial harmony. The objective of the case study is to bring some perspectives on these issues, bearing in mind the dangers of extrapolating from the experiences of a single country, and a very small one at that.

Singapore and Its Make-up

Singapore is located at the narrow point of the Straits of Malacca off the southern tip of the Malay Peninsula in Southeast Asia. It has a land area of 636 square kilometres, consisting of one main island and fifty-eight islets. The main island is 42 kilometres long and 23 kilometres wide, with a coastline of 138 kilometres. The country has a population of 3 million people, which represent a mix of multiracial, multiethnic, multilingual and multireligious groups. There are 75 percent Chinese, 15 percent Malays, 7 percent Indians and 3 percent other. Buddhism, Taoism, Christianity, Islam, Hinduism, and other beliefs including secularism represent the diversity in religion. The population is highly educated and enjoys a high standard of living. Once a British colony, Singapore gained independence in 1959, briefly joined Malaysia in 1963, and has been a sovereign, democratic, independent nation since 1965.

Important Economic Centre

The country's strategic location has made it an important crossroads for trading between east and west. It is also the world's busiest port with excellent telecommunication facilities. The economy is one of free enterprise and it is home to 4,000 multinational corporations. Its extensive banking system makes it one of the world's key financial centres. The national airlines are profitable and are rated among the top airlines in the world. On any average day, about 190 foreign newspapers circulate in Singapore. The country is also noted among the international business community for its clean and transparent government.

It is to Singapore's benefit that it projects a clean, well-run and peaceful country with modern facilities and a highly skilled labour force. The country has no – or very few – natural resources of its own. Its survival depends on its human resources and on international businesses that make Singapore a base of operations. The leaders of Singapore realised early on that they had to ensure racial harmony in order to achieve peace and prosperity for the country.

Multiracial Vision

The national pledge of Singapore is as follows:

> We, the citizens of Singapore
> Pledge ourselves, as one united people
> Regardless of race, language, or religion

> To build a democratic society
> Based on justice and equality
> So as to achieve happiness
> Prosperity and progress for our nation.

The Deputy Prime Minister Lee Hsien Loong envisions Singapore as 'a multi-racial society comprising overlapping circles. Each community would retain its cultural space and distinct identity. But over time, the areas of overlap should gradually widen and our common Singapore identity should strengthen' (*The Straits Times*, 25 September 2001).

Other officials, who say that the country has a vision that wants to turn diversity into strength and create a common identity while respecting differences (Foo, 2001), echo this. The country's stated 'core values' reflect this vision: (1) Nation before community and society before self; (2) family as the basic unit of society; (3) community support and respect for the individual; (4) consensus, not conflict; and (5) racial and religious harmony.

Multiracial Strategies

Singapore based its multiracial vision on three key pillars: common aspirations; clear rules of engagement; and strong institutions. The government held extensive consultations with its people and based its national development plans on the common hopes and aspirations of the people. These are universal aspirations of ordinary citizens all over the world – to live in a safe and secure country, to lead a better life, to provide for one's children, and to plan for a better future. The government also realised that it needed clear rules of engagement when people from different cultural backgrounds interact. It had to be firm but at the same time fair and even-handed. It could not promote one religion over another. Therefore, it had to be a secular state and allow space for groups to practise their own religion. Singapore also strengthened its national institutions and used them to promote social integration and build social cohesion, the glue that bonds society together. In order to increase its vertical social capital (i.e., the state's responsiveness to its citizens), it focused on three key institutions – public housing, education and national service.

The Housing Development Board (HDB) of Singapore is one of the more progressive public housing institutions in the world. In the early years of the island's statehood, ethnic residential concentration was the norm (Chew 1987: 30). The HDB implemented a public housing programme, which allocated low-cost government-built apartments to Singapore citizens on a 'first come, first served' basis without regard to ethnic group membership (ibid.). This move gradually diminished the ethnic enclave settlement pattern and physically integrated the various ethnic groups. Eventually, it developed a quota system (1989) to ensure that the housing estates continue to be racially mixed. The apartment buildings were also designed with an eye for promoting cultural integration. There are no ground-floor dwelling units in most of the public housing. The space is left open so that the tenants could use it for social events, such as community meetings, weddings, children's parties, funerals, playgrounds, etc.

Singapore has a national school system with English as the main medium of instruction. The government provides opportunities for each ethnic group to study in their own language. While primary education is free for everyone, the government offers free higher education for the poorer groups. Through a systematic National Education programme, the country reminds its children about the multiracial and multireligious character of Singapore, and the importance of harmony. Each year, on 21 July, all schools commemorate Racial Harmony Day, as a reminder that racial harmony cannot be taken for granted (the day was selected because of race riots in Singapore in 1964 which the country does not ever want to see happen again).

All young Singaporean males have to participate in national service. They come together for two and a half years of military and other training. This is an opportunity for them to learn to live and work together and it forms a lasting bond as only a deeply formative experience can.

In addition to the three key pillars above, the government has also introduced legislation to promote harmony. Such is the Maintenance of Religious Harmony Act (1990), which was introduced to deal with possible religious disharmony and to deal more efficiently with those who incite feelings of religious animosity. The government's rationale for the legislation was based on both internal and external conditions. The internal conditions were the government's perception of a 'shift in religious sentiment from "tolerant co-existence" to "fervently held beliefs"' (Sinha 2001: 13). The external conditions were examples in other countries that had been plagued by communal – ethnic and religious – tensions and violence, most noticeably India, Sri Lanka, Fiji, Lebanon, Northern Ireland, Philippines, Iran, Iraq, Armenia and Azerbaijan (ibid.).

The State's Role in Nurturing

Singapore is seen by many as a model for race relations (Fuller 1998: 5). However, the leaders of Singapore are the first to admit that multiracial harmony cannot be taken for granted and has to be seen as an ongoing achievement. The government has to be nurturing and constantly work at maintaining racial and religious harmony. The 1997 post-election speech of Mr Goh Chok Tong, Prime Minister of Singapore, reflects this sentiment clearly:

> This election has again shown that the deep fault lines in our society over race, language, culture and religion will not go away... Singapore is a multi-racial, multi-lingual and multi-religious society. It requires a fine balance to keep every community at ease. Every community has an equal place in Singapore... Our approach is fair to all: of an open, level playing field for all Singaporeans with English as the common language, plus separate playing fields for each community. (*The Straits Times*, 7 January 1997)

Another official has said that 'even if a policy or an institution has been successful in increasing dialogue and understanding, it is up against very strong centrifugal forces which tend to pull communities apart' (Foo 2001). This means that there can be no complacency but continuous vigilance to manage tensions that lead to conflict.The government has taken many steps and made strong communication efforts to prevent conflict and to ensure racial harmony in order to achieve peace and prosperity for the country.

Conclusion

Singapore has been criticised by the West as flexing too much control over society. Its first Prime Minister, Mr Lee Kuan Yew, has been described as running an iron-handed government. The dominant Chinese population has the upper hand in economic, political and social power over the other ethnic groups. 'The rhetoric of equality pervades the multi-cultural discourse in Singapore, particularly in official public domains' (Sinha 2001: 8). However, at everyday-life level, one does hear the language of majority–minority group dynamics, and note the presence of racial prejudices and discriminatory acts, the sense of specific groups being culturally, ideologically, politically and economically dominant (ibid.).

In hindsight, especially after the events of September 11 2001, when Muslim terrorists destroyed the World Trade Center in New York City, Singapore's actions do not appear to be so extreme after all. In fact, other countries are introducing legislation to deal with terrorism, which in many ways are infringing on the rights of citizens. Perhaps, one could say that Singapore had the foresight to see what was needed for nation building in a multiracial society.

There is a strong link between political stability, racial and religious tolerance and moderation. The state has an obvious and pragmatic interest in ensuring that racial and religious differences do not lead to conflict – something it sees as counterproductive to socioeconomic and political security.

Yes, harmony is possible in a multiracial society as illustrated by the case of Singapore. However, as demonstrated by Singapore, the harmony has to be promoted and nurtured by the state. The horizontal social capital of communal action by citizen groups and non-government organisations alone is necessary but not sufficient to sustain multiracial harmony. The degree of interplay between horizontal social capital of communal action and the vertical social capital of state action has to be high with strong and lasting commitment from the state.

References

Chew, S.F. 1987. *Ethnicity and Nationality in Singapore*. Athens, OH: Ohio University Center for International Studies.

Colletta, N.J., Lim, T.G. and Kelles-Viitanen, A., eds. 2001. *Social Cohesion and Conflict Prevention in Asia*. The World Bank, Washington, DC.

Fuller, L.K. 1998. 'The Role of Dominant Ethnicity in Racism: Reportage on Chinese Rule in Multi-Racial Singapore'. *The Edge: The E-Journal of Intercultural Relations* 1, 3.

Foo, C.C. 2001. Opening speech by the Permanent Secretary of Education at the conference on Asian Inter-Faith Dialogue: Perspectives on Religion, Education and Social Cohesion.

Sinha, V. 2001. *Scrutinizing the Themes of 'Sameness' and 'Difference' in the Discourse on Multi-Religiosity and Religious Encounters in Singapore*. Paper presented at the conference on Asian Inter-Faith Dialogue: Perspectives on Religion, Education and Social Cohesion.

The Straits Times, 7 January 1997; 25 September 2001.

RACISM AND INTERCULTURAL ISSUES IN URBAN EUROPE

Jagdish S. Gundara

Statecraft, Governance and Interculturalism

The fact that the conference, at which this chapter was originally delivered, was being held in Ghent and Belgium, where dramatic changes in the socioeconomic and political environments have taken place, is particularly appropriate for the theme of racism in European cities. However, the challenge for Belgian cities in dealing with racism is an issue of wider international concern where racism, xenophobia and chauvinism are multiplying. At the preparatory seminar for the United Nations Durban Conference on Racism (September 2001), a range of societal sector issues were discussed (see Appendix I). This chapter will discuss the issue of governance, diversity and racism in European cities. One of the intercultural problems that currently impinges on the urban European context is the rise of Islamophobia. Groups who are visibly different become vulnerable not just because of racism but because of their religion. In Britain Sikhs, who wear turbans and have beards, have been as vulnerable to violence as Muslims with beards and turbans.

Tackling racism and implementing interculturalism in European cities raises issues for the state in articulating policies at the national level to ensure that the multicultural nature of European societies and therefore of the cities is recognised. This involves a statecraft which ensures that all citizens, immigrants and refugees have legal protection from racism and also have rights and responsibilities in the polity. To avoid ethnic Armageddon in the cities it is necessary that the state at the central level ensures national resolution of racial conflict and inequity in all areas of public and social life.

National and European Union policies would then ensure that democratic solutions in complex societies are based on inclusive value systems and on shared and common understandings in the public domain. National policies to bridge ethnic, religious, linguistic and racial cleavages would obviate the rise of extreme forms of xenophobia. It is partly the failure of statecraft that is responsible for the rise in xenophobia and racism because such phenomena are not natural to groups in society, and preventative policies are preferable to reactive strategies. The stress on *jus sanguinis* (based on blood) and *jus soli* (on soil) notions of citizenship in societies and the privileging of the ties of blood and soil undermine not only the civic concept of the national societies. They also exacerbate tensions in urban areas, particularly in the way in which urban territories become contestable spaces because nonbelongingness of certain groups is emphasised. Notions of public safety and policies to defend human rights and the plural social environments in societies are of fundamental importance to the civil state (*état de droit*) so that the school as an educational institution has a formative role in developing an inclusive ethos amongst all young people and ensuring that all children in European cities stand together as they grow together.

The transnationalisation of the economic process raises further questions of governance and regulatory processes to ensure that the polity retains enough control over its political economy to obviate inequality; breakdown of communities, high levels of unemployment and the development of a disaffected and disenfranchised underclass. Economic liberalisation and subsequent economic decline has increasingly taken away the safety net provided by the social policy provisions in society. As Castells states, the 'globalisation of power flows and the tribalisation of local communities' become increasingly juxtaposed (Castells 1989: 350). The doctrinal hegemony of the market has fragmented groups and increased tensions in mixed urban communities. Refugees and asylum seekers created by political and economic devastations are caught in 'Catch-22' situations both in countries of origin and in receiving countries. Neither provides a safe haven, yet paradoxically borders remain permeable and the issues are not purely those for cities but for the polities as a whole. In a climate of scarce resources, the refugees become the new victims of exclusion and violence at the lower strata of city life.

The basic issue of political representation and active participation in national and city politics is a prerequisite for ensuring that rights, responsibilities and civic values are indispensable and that all voices are heard. It also raises the question of how to devise integrative public policies. For instance, in order to provide access to social institutions should the underlying policy be based on social class or on the presumed 'racial' identity of excluded groups to avoid their being labelled as special beneficiaries? Hence, policies to bring about equity in education ought not to privilege one group against another. This is a difficult issue because in an urban sprawl, as opposed to the city, there are ghettos and *bidon-villes* which include single nationalities or marginalised immigrant groups.

This Third Worldisation of so-called First World cities has a yet darker version of neighbourhoods where poverty, uncertainty and displacement represent new forms of neighbourhoods. These urban slums, refugee camps, prisons and ghettos are also sites of wide-ranging sociocultural interactions, and represents sites for futurist forms of conflicts and wars. These 'translocalities' in diasporic forms represents another issue of social diversity which remains largely underresearched. The governance of these communities may also necessitate new and different forms of EU cooperation.

The Kerner Report in the U.S.A. and the Scarman Report in Britain clearly shifted the analysis of urban unrest towards issues of disadvantage, which was exacerbated by cultural differences. Social policy planning and improved community relations are of great importance in avoiding the emergence of no-go areas and exclusive consciousness. The exclusions of groups from social and economic life would lead, as the Archbishop of Canterbury's Report *Faith in the City*, states to 'separate territories outside mainstream life'. As Peter Hall in *Cities of Tomorrow* (1998: 399) writes:

> Here then is the final irony: in the mid 1980's the problem of the urban underclass was still as stubbornly rooted in the world's cities, and in the consciousness of its more sensitive citizens, as in the mid 1880's, when it provided the vital stimulus to the birth of modern city planning.

While the cities have on the one hand generated sophisticated knowledge, complex physical landscapes as well as sociotechnical and political innovations of great splendour, they also remain a 'site of squalid human failure' (D. Harvey 1990: 229). The impact of individualism and market-oriented government policies do not square with governments' policies of family virtues (Harvey Ibid.: 238).

The 'hidden hand of history' continues to play a role in the life of the city. The inability of schools to devise strategies and policies to combat xenophobia and racism can lead to grave uncertainty and to pupils 'Learning in Terror' (CRE Report 1988). At another level it raises issues of even more dangerous levels of conflict based on ethnicisation of youth gangs and the division of young people on religious and narrow nationalistic identities. This could then negate the educative purposes of school and the development of a critical consciousness and ethos, and may lead to a secular morality amongst the youth. School policies to combat xenophobia and racism may combat behaviours but not the imagination of children, and yet unless a school has effective policies and strategies to combat racism, teachers cannot do effective work with children's imagination.

Diversity and the City as an Entity

Professor Colin Holmes, in writing about London states that refugees and immigrants have been driven to this city for 'temporary or permanent shelter from the well founded fears of persecution, which haunted and pursued them in other countries' (Holmes 1990: viii). The onus of the multicultural nature of London is therefore left to those who came from 'other countries'. Yet, it is the movement from within the polity that fundamentally makes London a multicultural city, and not just those from other countries who have migrated to it. This partly derives from how issues are defined and on the taxonomy of what constitutes elements of a multicultural city or society. If categories of language, religion, social class and nationality are part of this taxonomy, then London has been multicultural since medieval times when the French language was spoken, and traders from diverse backgrounds and Latin Christendom arrived here. Nationals of Scotland, Wales, Ireland and other parts of England brought diversities of various kinds, which contribute to London's multicultural character. Professor Holmes also stresses the notion of 'push' and 'pull' as the vehicle for migration across frontiers. Yet, urbanisation in London or other large European cities should not necessarily be seen as a consequence of 'push' and 'pull' factors, thus confusing migration with urbanisation. The assumption being made by him is that humanity is basically sedentary and society a static organism and that certain factors (economic, persecution etc.) 'push' people into migrating; and that they are 'pulled' into migrating, to certain places. However, people have continued to move and settle (as a universal and human phenomenon) from time immemorial for hunting, gathering, economic, political, travel, spiritual, pilgrimage, slavery, climatic and other reasons. Hence, the development of many other cities as diverse entities is itself part of this larger process of the human dynamic of movement and settlement. In terms of dealing with the ways in which the 'othering' of groups takes place, this raises important questions for how the social sciences should analyse the notions of belongingness, movement and of exclusion of a group in a locality.

The issue at the level of cities is about the belongingness of all groups in European cities. This presents problems because certain dominant nationalities see these cities as being 'theirs' which are encroached upon by 'others' who are aliens and not regarded as belonging. There are obviously specificities of different localities, communities, families and groups, which provide a different colour, texture and hue to different parts of many European cities. There are also differences of local politics, economies and histories – as well as how these interact with national, European and global contexts – which constitute differences in urban areas. Hence, for instance, an urban school in one European country may have more in common with an urban school in another country than schools in smaller towns or rural areas in the country in which it is located. In some cases a cross-national and European Union initiative is required to tackle common issues in large cities.

Urban Communities and Identities

One of the issues in analysing racism is that the minority groups are ascribed essentialist and ethnicised identities – although the realities of these presences are more complex. This sharing of spaces by the dominant and the subordinate, the coloniser and the colonised, the rich and poor, comes together in a city in a way which makes the city what it is and contributes to how it functions, as well as distinctions in all its aspects, and in its production. This production includes: political, economic, literary and cultural as well as media output. The 'other' is no longer out there but here, and there is an intersection of 'histories, memories and experiences' (Chambers 1994: 6).

One of the issues requiring analysis in relation to antiracist and intercultural agenda is the establishment of the basis of belongingness of diverse groups within an urban area or a polity. This ought to be based on a notion of inclusiveness of all groups. Hence, research in this field needs to be contextualised within a more intercultural framework, which has both historical and contemporary dimensions. In establishing such a context, the past and current exclusions would be put to rights. This therefore makes it possible to initiate a dialogue between the various groups of those who live in our cities. The past and present exclusivities, interaction and intersection of the histories, cultures and languages enables the construction of a more realistic understanding of cities, which may in turn inform us about constructing a less biased and a more meaningful future.

Communities that constitute populations in cities are not only situated within their localities but also have other identities, both at national and supranational levels. This lends an enormous range of heterogeneity to the city and its life. The complexity of all this activity defies a simplistic definition by either a dominant or a subaltern culture.

Yet, the sense of a mainstream imposed by the dominant group does not hold sway because the marginalised subaltern cultures no longer accept a subordinate status or triumphalist narratives. Hence, a reappraisal of both these narratives within European cities is necessary. This requires a re-understanding of the collated histories of what cities are, and which are seen to be more inclusive of 'other' histories, languages, knowledge and are not merely a dominant understanding of cities. One aspect of re-understanding cities is to examine the cultural production of the minority communities (in literature, films, dance, theatre, music, visual arts), when it becomes clear that such a presence cannot be stereotyped in a simplistic 'ethnic' basis. Yet, the ethnicisation of cultures as commodities mitigates against a genuine and syncretic development of such urbanised cultures.

The creation of stereotypes and caricatures is not halted by mass marketing of ethnicities, and the real lives of the various groups and communities are very distant from the world of fashionable ethnicity. The realities of the lives, struggles and the substantive concerns lose their meaning through this commodification. Those who are citizens face racial discrimination and devaluation of many aspects of their culture. Those who are refugees, asylum seekers or who do not have citizenship rights face even greater privations and are continually undermined by oppressive lives here, as well as, concerns about home, whether it is Somalia, a Kurdish village or Bosnia. There is also the loneliness of women, who are disadvantaged and powerless and of whom many have appallingly disadvantaged lives. Escape from political tyranny at home, does not improve the quality of life in many of the poor parts of European cities. A better and safe life remains a chimera.

Imagined Urban Ownerships

Such communities are trapped between the imagined pasts of home, and the alienation experienced as a result of the dominant European groups asserting notions of the 'imagined ownership' of 'their' cities in 'their nations', thus reinforcing the exclusion of already marginalised groups.

Many of the minority communities in European cities live as siege communities, whether it is women and young children who are harassed, or whether it is young men and women and the elderly who are beaten up and even murdered. These victims become symbols of retrieving what Phil Cohen (1991) has called their 'lost inheritances'.

Cities as such embody notions both of belongingness and of alienation. They have features both of a universalistic nature as well as particularisms and local differences. Yet, non-confederal localisms can become parochial, racist, insular, stagnant and authoritarian. There are thick and textured layers of political, social and economic contexts, which intersect with histories, cultures and languages. Cities therefore provide possibilities and prospects of an infinite nature, and yet can also be lonely and confining. The confederal nature of cities requires that integrative thinking and structures link individual groups and localities.

The differences between neighbourhoods and parts of the city mask the myriads of ways in which there are criss-crossings, which make the distinctions between localities quite bewildering. While for some this suggests immense possibilities, for others it presents a foreclosing of options. To some, like those who came from Barbados to London, Harkis to Amiens (*The Independent*, 16 November 1994) or Pied Noir to Marseilles, it was like coming home; to others it is an exile. For some new identities are formed, and syncretism is the order of the day; for others there is an activation of 'siege mentality' within siege communities. Such developments can reinforce patriarchies and allow fundamentalisms to take root.

Community Education

While identities of adults are already formed those of children are in the process of being formed. Hence, the issues of belongingness and of exclusion should be part of an educational process that enables students to transcend narrow definitions of identity.

Children are able to construct a broader understanding of life based on their own personal concerns and experiences. These understandings underpin what may emerge as multidimensional identities. Children grow up and develop different identities, as they begin to get involved in different types of collectivities, ranging from family, peer group, schoolwork and other socialising influences, including the media. Yet, unless parents and adults are also part of the educational process, racism and the narrow ethnicised identities are likely to be reinforced. This is true for both the dominant and the subordinate groups. Chauvinistic parents and adults can undo the work of the school and unless schools have strong community links, negative spillovers can undermine their work.

In the journey from childhood to adulthood the symbols of what is important in early life change at a later period in life. The important issue to explore may be what the educational system can do in the early years of school and in higher education, to broaden the choice of identities to which young people have access.

Youth and Territory

Such questions become a major issue in modern urban contexts where youth from a diverse range of backgrounds inhabit the same territory. Youth from one particular rooted neighbourhood may feel that the emergence of 'outsiders' and other groups is occupying what they see as their locality. This feeling of displacement in their neighbourhood may be heightened because of the lack of secure identity, skills, knowledge and an ability to see the world in complex ways. The loss of the skills of the older generation heightens the dangers of this type of alienation for the younger generations. The uniqueness of being English or Belgian ought not to be so exclusive as to exclude identification with other nationalities. The school curriculum can be one site where in the history, personal and social curriculum areas, issues of nationalities and identities, including those at the local level, can be constructively explored.

The major problem facing the younger generation in poorer urban areas is their lack of educational attainments and skills. The lack of any certainty may further mar their ability to operate in complex societies. It is obviously the case that children do have a range of survival and street skills that are not recognised by formal institutions like the school, and only have currency as a subculture. One of the questions is, how can the school build constructively on the knowledge about survival and street cultures which are part of the lives of urban youth?

Much of the industrial growth in Europe in the postwar period was brought about by rural immigrants, whose skills were utilised in the development of industries in devastated economies. This was certainly true of the post-war industrialisation of Italy. Yet, as this generation of immigrants retire from work and their children are now in a position to join the working life there are various dilemmas. While the parents came from rural backgrounds and had skills related to rural areas, the younger generation who are products of the urban and industrial civilisation belong to neither, largely because of the failure of schooling to take both the educational as well as the work-skill aspects of their lives seriously. There are now young adults in European cities who have little security, education or technical skills to function as fully fledged citizens. Any intercultural education which is not fundamentally integrated into the mainstream education system or even within the main social policy provision can be counterproductive and in fact have negative i.e., xenophobic or racist, consequences.

The nature of cities and their complex population, which include the skilled working class and those working in trades and industries, has changed dramatically. Not only have many traditional trades disappeared but the movement of many industries from the large cities to new towns or to other parts of the world has removed the practices that apprenticed young men to those skills and masculine cultures. As Phil Cohen states:

> The disintegration of this material apparatus and its replacement by 'post-fordist' systems of training and work has not had the effect of dismantling its symbolic structures – these continue to reproduce racism and ageism in working class cultures; but it has altered their modes of operation and anchored them to racist practice in a new way. (Cohen 1991: 11)

Confederal Identities

There seems to be a danger of constructing a singular identity in cities not only in Europe but also in other parts of the world. There are, however, not many people (apart from a few isolated communities) who have the distinction of claiming that they are firmly located within pure communities. As Murray Bookchin states:

> The city is the historic arena in which – and as a result of which – biological affinities are transformed to social affinities. It constituted the single most important factor which changed an ethnic folk into a universal civitas where, in time the 'stranger' or 'outsider' could become a member of the community without having to satisfy any requirement of real or mythic blood ties to a common ancestor. (Bookchin 1992: xvi)

Urban culture would therefore be a realised signifying system and not merely a way of life.

If there are fears in European cities of the local identities being swamped by an immigrant minority then there must be something wrong with constructing a notion of the dominant nation, which is timeless and perhaps quaintly archaic. It also detracts from developing political relationships based on humanitas and reinforces continuing kinship ties based on clan or tribe. In fact, the vibrancy of being Belgian, French, Dutch or English in cities has a greater chance of being actualised and remaining dynamic if it is seen as being multilayered, vivacious and interactive. An interactiveness has the possibility of developing understandings which are shared and allow for change and dynamism to propel a more inclusive notion of citizenship and belongingness within the city. The education system has an important and creative role to play in developing such understandings, particularly in broadening the area of commonalities and democratic culture based on shared values.

Where diversity in many cities may have initially been based on the minority nationalities from within the larger nations, it may now be enhanced by those who come from other countries. The young black British generation or children from a Moroccan background predominantly socialised in Belgium, for example, are now losing the memory of their countries of origin and feel they belong more to the cities in Europe where they are socialised. They may also have a complex reading of cities like London or Ghent as well as British or Belgian society in general. Both the older and younger generations have complex, positive, negative and indifferent readings of these polities. They are not and cannot be converted back to subservient coolies, slaves, plantation workers, migrants, Gastarbeiter, squires or sahibs in brown skin.

To develop such an understanding requires a rational mind based on a rational system. Yet, an insecure national or city elite which has not had the courage and openness to deal with this critical issue has made things worse. It may be a problem of political failure because generally politicians have ignored the positive dimensions of social diversities in European cities. Through a sleight of hand, the deep social changes and inequalities that affect the belongingness of various groups are ignored, and problems in cities are blamed on market forces, or on the alienness and otherness of groups, based on real, or perceived, differences.

Construction of the Rural by Urban Elites

The importance of a shared belongingness in cities is necessitated by the ways in which images of green and pleasant, civilised European lands with their villages and towns are seen in essence as being part of English, Belgian or French national identities. Enoch Powell's reference to an 'alien wedge' is seen as being an intrusion into notions of Englishness, which lead to a confrontation with the English yeomen. This imagery is evoked in films and literature, and is also used by politicians like Schoenhuber and Le Pen.

As the uncertainties in the polity grow and the economy is decimated, the conurbations encroach, and the rural becomes the haven, in particular, for the upper middle class, patriots, and refuge seekers. The construction of this safe ruralism by those who are themselves thoroughly urban, hark back to the purities and certainties of the past. The values of being English, like those of the German 'Volk', emanate from the close connections between blood and soil. The village and the rural area therefore is not just a haven, but a construction related to the English or other national identity, which excludes 'the other'. As Alex Potts suggests about nationalist ideology in the interwar period:

> Theory of racial identity was transferred to the inanimate landscape, a kind of reification in which the people still living and working in the countryside were assimilated, not just pictorially and aesthetically, but also ideologically to the landscape. (Potts 1989: 189)

At one level, the construction of a viable British polity lies in reinventing a notion of the urban as well as the countryside, which is non-exclusive. In areas where there is urban and rural poverty, obviously the construction of a secure national haven raises a difficulty. To do this as Potts states would view 'England as an epicentre of dynamic change rather than England as a refuge from the more violent and thrusting tendencies of the modern world' (ibid.: 166). The establishment of a symbolic relationship as well as one of parity may obviate the changes of the narrow nationalistic construction of the city and the countryside.

The State and Identities

At the national level, there is a major issue in relation to such a shift. This is exacerbated by the stridency of subsequent governments. At another level there is the issue which Edward Said refers to as 'the idea of a nation, of a national-cultural community as a sovereign entity and place, set against other places' which separates 'us' from 'them' through boundaries. He suggests that this idea of place does not cover nuances, which is a cultural issue: 'It is in culture that we can seek out the range of meanings and ideas conveyed by the phrases belonging to or in a place, being at home in a place' (Said 1983: 8). Young men from dominant communities are themselves subject to being portrayed differently at different times. For instance, as young soldiers in the Falklands, they are seen as loyal patriots, sons of the soil and yeomen. In another context, they are constructed as football hooligans, whether at home or abroad, and they become an uncivilised and bestial mob. This was the case with English football supporters in Belgium during the World Cup in 2000.

The consequent rise of local or neighbourhood nationalisms can be seen as defensive attempts at ownership of local communities. However, while such groups might feel that they belong to certain neighbourhoods in cities, these neighbourhoods may themselves belong to a totally different set of agencies.

These realisations are personified by Canary Wharf in London, about which Stuart Hall in a lecture stated:

> The brutal reality was that a local community was expunged and expelled and an area flattened to give rise to that monument to Thatcherism – Canary Wharf. This Fetishistic token which can't even rent itself! In one small area a completely abandoned white population was left. Then into this cauldron were dropped some Bangladeshis. It should be no surprise that someone was able to knit these bits together ... It brings them together. It distils them. It requires a simple story and there is always at least one political group infinitesimal it may be, which will tell the story. (Hall 1998: 211)

The rise of neo-fascist activity and electoral strength in many cities is one obvious result of this. Rumour and misrecognition have added to constructing this 'other' who is amidst us and can never be one of us. 'The Other' can be identified as a source of 'our alienation'. The creation of such imagined communities to replace the disintegrated real communities attempts an instant retrieval of lost inheritances. Part of this retrieval is a retrieval of a territory. This is reflected in the 1936 March of the Mosleyites through the East End in London, when many Eastenders joined in stopping the march into what was seen as 'our area'. They yelled, 'they may be yids, but they are our yids'.

Cities are enriched by various communities such as the Italian, German, Jewish and Irish, who have made vast contributions to all aspects of life of a city like London. However, during periods of war and national tensions, those constructed as alien enemies have paid a supreme price. Peppino Leoni, the owner of the Quo Vadis restaurant in London during the Second World War, was arrested after Mussolini joined the war:

As I walked down the corridor towards the cells I felt a sudden hatred for the police, for the British Government which had issued instructions for my internment, and for all forms of authority. I have slaved for years, in fact 33 years, because I first came to England in 1907, to establish my restaurant, and a man of my own nationality had destroyed everything in an instant ... I deeply resented the fact that after 33 years in England with no political blemish on my record, I'd been scooped up without proper consideration.

Leoni was not alone in being treated like this. Others who did manual and skilled labour, worked in professions as well as made contributions to literary and cultural life were also interned.

The architecture in cities respects a complex story. For example, in London, the Jama Masjid at the corner of Fourier Street and Brick Lane started its life as a Huguenot Church in 1744; fifty years later it was a Wesleyan Chapel; then from 1898 to 1975 it was the Spitalfields Great Synagogue, when it was sold to the East End Bengalis. The Tower of London was used in the thirteenth century as a sanctuary for Jews from rioting mobs. Later it was used by the constabulary as a prison for Jews. The Tower therefore acquired different meanings at different times because of its different functions. In the same way, cities therefore have different meanings not just in architectural terms but because of the complex identities of people living in them. The city can be a very poignant tool for learning and teaching, a site for understanding the complex architectural and material histories of a polity.

Secular City and Education

The schools as secular institutions function in what have become largely secular cities. This in effect means that different groups can coexist in the city. The school as an institution has an obligation to provide a safe environment in which the educational process is not hampered by extremist racist or religious groups; although in many conurbations, racially discriminated communities not only live in terror but also have to learn in terror.

The right of all children to good quality education is a basic citizenship right, which the European Union and national governments should protect. The idea of a good intercultural education that is by definition opposed to racism and fundamentalisms ought to be based on a school ethos that is inclusive of the good values of urban communities. The best of these values are necessary in being represented in the school to ensure that all students are not only seen to belong, but do, in fact, belong to the school. This ought, in turn, to ensure individual and group rights as well as responsibilities.

A Eurocentric curriculum would unleash a reaction from groups who feel that their knowledge, histories and languages are excluded from the mainstream discourse of the school. Such a Eurocentric curriculum would not only disadvantage marginalised groups further but lead to 'politics of recognition' and separatist demands by subordinated groups. The 'curriculum of recognition' by such groups would also be based on demands for separate curricula, which would negate intercultural learning. The demand for and growth of separate religious schools in England shows this is happening.

Europe not only has a reservoir of universal knowledge but also a vast range of languages spoken in its cities. Optimum policies to draw together the vast linguistic knowledge would ensure that children with other first languages can acquire second languages more systematically but also have an integrated access to the curriculum as an entitlement.

To avoid an increase in xenophobic and racist activities taking root within the schools, a strategy at the European Union level needs to be developed which ensures that there are strong school/community links in major European cities. The use of the concept of life-long learning by young people and adults within the framework of community education ought to ensure that adults are not able to negate the good intercultural work done by schools. This life-long learning ought to have two faces. Firstly, it should be seen as a way of valuing education in its own right; and secondly it should be maintained through partnerships with training institutions and employers to provide appropriate skills and training as well as jobs. Tackling racism and bullying in schools requires a multi-agency approach because the school alone cannot deal with these issues.

The Department of Education and Skills in England completed a survey of access and achievement in urban education and reported that the standard and quality of teaching was 'very disappointing'. A situation like this in European cities can lead to dismal levels of failure as well as low educational performances, which spiral downwards, particularly for immigrant and other poor children. Unless concerted European Union-level policies are activated such groups would be blamed for their failures, as victims of the wider social exclusion.

A European-wide network of good antiracist and intercultural school practices in the inner-city areas also ought to include a consideration of good intercultural teacher education. Unless there are good interculturally educated teachers, the process of a narrow schooling will continue to alienate children and lead to greater inequalities and low educational outcomes.

Good intercultural teacher education (not training) is one of the greatest challenges we face in the European Union. This is the case because European cities have resources and are reservoirs of Europe's multicultural historic past. The negation in the eighteenth and nineteenth centuries of this syncretic history of learnings and borrowings by Greece from Phoenicians and Egyptians because of the rise of Eurocentrism can only be undertaken by interculturally competent teacher educators because they are multipliers of knowledge and attitudes. Only well educated professional teachers working in urban schools can teach children of the European polis with the Greek notion of paidea to develop good intercultural values and ethics. The German notion of Bildung which 'combines meanings of character development, growth, enculturation, and a well-rounded education in knowledge and skills' (Bookchin 1992: 59) is possible in the European city of the twenty first century, if we all work towards that future.

APPENDIX I

Durban International Seminar Preparatory Meeting on Mainstreaming Minority Rights in Development Assistance (London, United Kingdom 26–27 July 2001)

Recommendations of the Working Groups

Working Group A: Social Sector Development

- Governments should ensure that everyone under their jurisdiction including minorities and indigenous peoples has equal access to the provision of social services in law and in reality.
- Statutory bodies should develop inclusive and intercultural educational provisions and curricula that are culturally and linguistically appropriate which ensures that all groups have an understanding of their multicultural society and that there are shared and common values in the public domain which evolve through democratic consultation.
- Statutory bodies and donors should give full support to all groups and peoples, including women, the elderly, the disabled, children and those living with HIV/AIDS within those groups, assessing and analysing their own perception of rights and developmental situations and subsequent actions should reflect the outcome.
- Governments should take urgent steps to eradicate the widespread discrimination and persecution of minorities and indigenous peoples by:
  (a) implementing national public and social policies;
  (b) having regard to any history, particularly recent history of oppression or displacement of minority and indigenous peoples both by appropriate compensation and by remedial policies
- The recognition of social and cultural differences should be viewed as an asset and not a deficit. Groups such as the Roma and pastoralists' languages, lifestyles and livelihoods should be protected.
- All statutory bodies, donors and NGOs who fund initiatives in social service provision at various levels should ensure that minority issues are incorporated within the project management cycle, including monitoring and evaluation to ensure sustainability.
- The right to information and access to information technology should apply to all minority and indigenous peoples. Institutional networks aiming to promote and develop the minority and indigenous peoples' cultural heritage should be supported and developed.

References

Archbishop of Canterbury's Commission on Urban Priority Areas. 1985. *Faith in City. A call for action by church and nation.* London: Church Publishing House.

Bookchin M. 1992. *Urbanisation without Cities:The Rise and Decline of Citizenship.* Montreal: Black Rose Books.

Castells, M. 1989. *The Informational City*, Oxford: Blackwell.

Chambers, I. 1994. *Migrancy, Culture and Identity*. London: Routledge.

Cohen, P. 1991. 'Monstrous Images, Perverse Reasons' Working Paper 11, London: Institute of Education: International Centre for Intercultural Studies.

Commission for Racial Equality Report. 1988. *Learning in Terror*. London: CRE.

Hall, P. 1990. *Cities of Tomorrow*. Oxford: Blackwell.

Hall, S. 1998. *Postmodernity.* Oxford: Blackwell.

Harvey, D. 1990. *On Cities*. Oxford: Oxford University Press.

Holmes, C. 1990. 'Foreword'. *The Peopling of London: Fifteen Hundred Years of Settlement from Overseas.* N. Merriman, ed. London: the Museum of London.

Leoni, Y. 1990. 'Italians in London.' *The Peopling of London: Fifteen Hundred Years of Settlement from Overseas.* N. Merriman, ed. London: the Museum of London: 134–35.

Potts, A. 1989. 'Constable Countries between the Wars'. *Patriotism the Making and Unmaking of the British National Identity*, Vol. III. Samuel, R., Ed. London: Routledge.

Said, E. 1983. *The World, the Text and the Critic*, Cambridge, MA: Harvard.

Independent 16 November 1994.

Antiracist Empowerment through Culture and Legislation

Johan Leman

Introduction

The examples underlying our way of thinking are taken from Brussels, but may retain their relevance for other metropolitan areas at a comparable moment in their emigrational histories. Undoubtedly, many comparable cases can be cited for every example described. In Brussels, migration started at the end of the 1950s, when heavy industry (coal, iron and steel) was lost in other areas of the country and the economic relaunch was centred in and around a number of large cities (ports or cities confronted with massive new infrastructural works).

In the first instance, a number of ex-miners and their families, mainly Italians, came over to Brussels from the Walloon mining areas. It was an ageing first and ascending second generation. In the late 1950s, they were joined by Spaniards, and in the early 1960s quickly by a 'new' first generation of migrants from Morocco and Turkey, who arrived directly from their countries of origin. This new migration gained pace until 1974 (official end of migration in most countries of Western Europe), after which these communities tended to increase demographically by forming families and having children.

In the 1980s, the main increase was in the number of asylum seekers, which led to the first notable presence of communities from sub-Saharan Africa. This ran parallel with an increasing presence of undocumented migrants (Eastern Europe, Latin America and Asia). At the start of the year 2000, this led to a large-scale regularisation campaign. To interpret the figures adequately we should bear in mind that they are based on nationality, as recorded in the Belgian statistics. We should also be aware that Belgium operates a very liberal nationality legislation, which led to a great many migrants, particularly non-EU citizens, acquiring nationality in the 1990s. It is possible to hold dual nationality. This implies, for example, that the number of Moroccan inhabitants in Brussels would be twice as high if we used the Moroccan statistics as opposed to the Belgian figures.

According to Belgian statistics, 54,980 Moroccans and 15,799 Turks live in Brussels, and double that amount according to statistics of the countries of origin. Furthermore, there are 35,811 people with French nationality, 28,771 with the Italian and 21,019 with Spanish nationality of the approximately 1,000,000 people living in Brussels. There are 262,771 people with a foreign nationality, of which 121,383 are from outside of the European Union, but especially for these last groups the numbers supplied by the countries of origin are significantly higher (National Institute of Statistics, 1 January 2001).

In our discussion of the issue of antiracist empowerment, we will start by briefly covering the possibilities afforded by an antiracism legislation, as it might apply to the situation in Brussels. We will then discuss a number of cases of culturalist empowerment, which are of relevance to the first, second and third generations. What form do the culturalist strategies take? And is it really about empowerment?

Antiracism and Empowerment

In the first instance, the Belgian antiracism legislation (of 30 July 1981) makes it possible for individuals to enforce their rights. Between 1980 and 2002, it was a matter of criminal law, and it has been supplemented by a civil law since end 2002.

The law allows the individual to defend himself against discrimination on the grounds of race, skincolour, descent or national or ethnic origin. By the end of 2002, as the result of new legislation, ethnic minorities became able to do the same on the basis of religion. Used in coordination, both laws will ensure that ethnic communities have recourse to the law to defend their group interests. Brussels people from sub-Saharan Africa can use the reference to skin colour and origin as a means of improving their position on the labour and housing market, by turning to situation testing and by a shift of the onus of proof to the defendant. People with Islamic beliefs should also find it easier to enforce equal treatment of their religion. This is a transgenerational phenomenon, as distinct from culturalist strategies, which can be partly generational, with a basic distinction between first and later generations.

Culturalist Empowerment in a First Generation

Several types of communities are imaginable. Even though 'thin', 'superficial' relations are probably the most characteristic of our society, they are interwoven with relations that go together with professional categories (e.g., earlier networks and loyalties between miners in the traditional mining areas were well known), relations in residential areas of the 'parochial' type, or more superficial face recognition (depending on how well people know each other through their local social lives or the supermarket), and ethnic-based relations (expressed through an ethno-religious fabric, or in ethnic shopping).

It is in this complex cluster of fabrics that initiatives can be taken by more active ethnic leaders of the first generation to promote self-esteem and social life through elements thought to belong to the better aspects of the culture of provenance. They often search for continuity through their heritage of songs and musicality, or other artistic forms of expression from the area of origin.

In the 1970s and early 1980s Italians living in Brussels, the former CASI-UO (Centro di Azione Sociale Italiano – Università Operaia), circulated songs of Sicilian heritage or resistance during the Second World War within their own Brussels and mainly South Italian community, under the motto *Uniti si vince* ('together we will win'). At the same time they directed theatrical pieces that focused on the rights to be fought for, such as the political vote. This went in tandem with the development of leadership in the community, helped by others who had been affiliated to the unions, and with lobbying and the development of loyalties in the Brussels political scene. When the second generation became more involved in the movement, the ethnocultural and artistic-cultural component in the group became diluted. The former leadership sought and found its way to the official Brussels policy on minorities, outside of the original ethnocultural association.

In the second half of the 1990s people from the Kasai, an area in the Southwest Congo, under the name of Sangalay, drew on songs from their own area of origin, and started promoting a message in their community, with a view to preserving its continuity, memories of the earlier oppression in Congo, and, particularly, contact with and integration of the youth – the second generation. It is actually a common trend in all kinds of sub-Saharan African associations to mobilise and emphasise self-respect through song and work towards valuation in society.

We note among Italians and sub-Saharan Africans of the first generation, over a difference of twenty years, a dual cultural path: one elitist, an artistically minded path issuing from an intellectual ethnic leadership, and the other a popular religious path, through which efforts are made to develop an allochthonous religious network (Leman 1999). The first generation of Moroccan and Turkish migration is usually strictly 'immigrant religious'. In Brussels this was the case, not because of Islam, but because the first generation lacked an intellectual elite with an interest in developing laic community life.

Culturalist Empowerment in Second, Third and Further Generations

The voluntary redress of a limited, culturally and politically motivated first-generation ethnic leadership can never shift a community's position in the socioethnic stratification to the extent that the sense of discrimination it activates among its own grass roots can be removed. Indeed, this is almost always a work urging two full generations to become successful, which is emotionally not acceptable for the second generation.

At this point the first culturalist movements run aground due to a shortage of input from the inside out, and through a breakdown of the internal framework (disappearance through ageing, or through individuals gradually stepping over to the broader framework offered by a union or political party). In the meantime the immigrant 'religious factories, lead their own lives.

A younger generation, which is less fascinated by the ethnocultural and artistic history of the former leadership, takes its place and in turn tries to make its way, this time within the most popular channels of communication in the urban environment. All kinds of associations see the light of day, and try to spread their ideas through private radio stations, musical events and sports clubs. These instruments are also used as forums for political debate and the claiming of social rights. Brussels has an abundance of Moroccan associations and three 'Arabic' private radio stations.

Under the sports initiatives it is football in particular that plays a group-forming role. Football clubs are a place of emotional and competitive group identity. For years the 'Atlas' football club was a household name among Moroccans in Brussels (and *Etoile Marocaine* also), but proper infrastructure and management are manifestly lacking.

District Interculturalism

In the meantime, schools and districts are confronted with the trend of community mixing and cultural hybridising. Initiatives have been developed in both areas: interculturalism in education and a few 'multi-coloured actions' with a festive character at district level. To date the most successful event in Brussels is the *Zinneke Parade*, promoted as a biennial, large-scale parade, in which children from all districts of the city take part in a collective procession. In the mission statement of the *Zinneke Parade* (in which *zinneke* – dialect for 'a small dog' – is the word used to refer to the authentic inhabitant of Brussels, born and bred), we read that this is a party for all Brussels people. It is called a party 'of all districts', 'of freedom', 'of artistic, contemporary and multicoloured creation', that brings people together, a party 'of the future', 'a huge folk festival'. (info@zinneke.org)

Every two years this parade, a tail end of the European cultural capitals programme, through which Brussels could call itself one of Europe's cultural capitals in 2000, attracts a considerable, principally Brussels public to the centre of the city to follow the procession of the various districts. It is mainly children (from schools and youth centres), dressed up against the backdrop of scenes developed by all kinds of artists, that make it the creative spectacle that it is. The media takes a huge interest in the parade.

This type of intercultural action reveals a third, again rather artistic, form of culturalist empowerment, this time not referring to the cultures of origin, but to a proposed current, multicoloured beauty, which is hoped to have the power of mobilisation. The borders of the ethnic community are extended to the interethnic district in which one lives, and at the same time updated, independently of migration. The city as an artistic melting pot is at the top of the agenda.

Pluri-lingual Cities

We have just referred to education and its concern for intercultural encounters and the support of mutual respect. Sociolinguistically and culturally, Brussels is a 'divided' city (McAndrew 2002). To put this positively, we can identify the very same social reality as a plural linguistic city. The multilingualism is a part of the interculturalism.

At the start of the mission statement of the 'Zinneke Parade' Brussels is introduced as 'capital of Europe, capital of the French-speaking community, capital of the Flemish community, capital of the bande dessinée'. Every inhabitant knows that in certain places and on certain occasions, in view of the European function of Brussels, English is a major social and working language, and that in addition, the languages of German, Italian and Spanish are not simply the languages of marginal ethnic communities. This is what is meant by a Brussels multilingual normative framework.

For twenty years educational initiatives have been put in place and have attempted successfully to take advantage of that plural language environment (not specifically Brussels; see for other, similar large cities: Lamarre 2002), the most typical and most educational of which appear to be Foyer's multilingual, bicultural educational programmes (Byram and Leman 1990; Leman 1991, 2002). This multilingual educational programme is interesting for more than one reason. It shows that in educational matters the survival of minority-group language depends on sufficient transgenerational interest in this language within the community, supported, however, by interest from the majority group. Perhaps this also holds true for the survival chances of any product from an ethnocultural migrant community in the urban melting pot?

Assessment of the Elements and Phases of Empowerment

In any discussion of culturalist empowerment in a hybrid plural-ethnic urban setting, we note that there are several possible snapshots that can be traced back to two dynamics in particular: those of successive generations (Leman 1998) and those of developments in internal urban (dis)integration.

In the beginning, newly emerging communities have a need for internal reorganisation, which also positions the community within a social-ethnic urban stratification. This is a phase in which antiracism legislation can play a protective role in a discriminating environment. Immigrant religious fabrics tend to stand for a stirring of emotional self-esteem. A budding intellectual, ethnic leadership sets out the first markers for sociopolitical emancipation, in which elements of the culture of origin tend to be used.

That first movement of ethnocultural empowerment usually runs aground because the discourse finds insufficient grounding in the living world of younger generations and social promotion of the community, as promised by the leadership, is not successful enough. It seems then that a first, highly promising emancipation movement will come to a dead end. However, this is only partly true. In fact, a new movement of cultural empowerment begins, and it focuses on popularising and updating the base of support.

However, the asset from the culture of origin is no longer used to the same degree. For that matter, it can take some time before an artistic level comparable with that of the earlier, first generation can be reached. The discourse becomes more direct and focuses almost exclusively on social and political rights. Any means of communication available to the urban culture (private radio stations, concerts, club life), as well as the media, are used maximally within the possibilities to hand.

There is usually an internal struggle for the leadership and for 'the correct learning', the correct description of what the community is. At the political level, however, this is channelled by existing political parties who determine the political life in the urban area, so that there is little room left for an ethnic party (which usually doesn't get off the ground). The various movements described above can be found side by side in the present urban areas of Europe.

It is probably too early yet to map out the complex and surprising, multifaceted whole of initiatives within plural multiethnic urban areas of this type. Insofar as the Brussels urban area may be held to be representative, it seems that the basic rule is: from culture of origin, borne by monoethnic leadership (a); through trivial urbane culture, borne by pluri-ethnic leadership (b); to intercultural hybridism, borne by an abundance of political, social and cultural players (c).

We can reach a number of further conclusions:

1. Elements from the culture of origin earmarked for retention in the new whole have to be borne transgenerationally within the community, and if possible evoke the interest of the broader social environment;
2. After a phase of internal ethnocultural streamlining every community goes through an internal struggle for ideological dominance, which can sometimes engender resistance among people outside of the community. Not only do the borders between the different communities become blurred – except in situations where ghettos are created – but finally, and moreover, the pluralism of the external environment penetrates each community, or what is retained of it, to the full.

Does It Empower Antiracism?

If antiracism means that individuals from immigrant communities should be able to express themselves for what they are, and not be hindered by pressure from the majority among whom they live, or by their own leaders, who seek to keep them in an ethnic straight-jacket on the basis of supposed group characteristics of origin, then the developments that characterise cultural strategies, and an adequately enforced antiracism legislation, can be an effective instrument in the pursuit of emancipation, equality and internal pluralism. They guarantee a number of elements that can be considered essential:

achieving sufficient affiliation with the mainstream in an urban society, which should prevent any self-marginalisation on an ethnic or religious basis; the guarantee of sufficient internal pluralism, which promotes the personal freedom of the individual; opportunities for sufficient members of the community to profile their community more favourably within the ethnosocial urban stratification; and particularly, helping to stop individuals and groups from the majority group stigmatising and helping people from the minority to diversify on the basis of their true diversity.

References

Byram, M. and Leman, J., eds. 1990. *Bicultural and Trilingual Education.* Clevedon, OH: Multilingual Matters.

Info@zinneke.org

Lamarre, P. 2002. *Plurilingualism and Pluriculturalism: An Approach from the Canadian Perspective,* Brussels: KOLOR, 33–45.

Leman, J., ed. 1991. *Intégrité, intégration. Innovation pédagogique et pluralité culturelle.* Brussels:De Boeck University.

Leman, J. 1998. *The Dynamics of Emerging Ethnicities,* Frankfurt am Main: Peter Lang, 21–34.

—— 1999. 'Religions, Modulators in Pluri-ethnic Cities: an Anthropological Analysis of the Relative Shift from Ethnic to Supra-ethnic and Meta-ethnic Faith Communities in Brussels'. *Journal of Contemporary Religion* 14, 2: 217–31.

—— 2002. *Mutual Fertilization between Citizenship Education, Multilingual, Intercultural and Peace Education,* Brussels: KOLOR, 91–96.

McAndrew, M. 2002. *Ethnic Relations and Education in Divided Societies: Belgium, Catalonia, Northern Ireland, Quebec.* Brussels: KOLOR, 5–19.

Racism in Large Cities: the Means to Empower/Disempower Groups and Communities

Glyn Ford

Since the Dreux by-election in December 1983, when the French *Front National* had its first significant electoral breakthrough, we have witnessed the continued rise of fascist and extreme right parties in Europe. In the European elections of 2000, twenty-six MEPs from seven neo-Nazi, extreme right-wing parties, and their fellow travellers, were elected to the European Parliament.

Today, the Community states of France, Italy, Belgium, Austria and Denmark all have racist far-right groups entrenched in their mainstream party systems, and other European Union (EU) states are seeing similar trends. In many cities within the EU, extreme right-wing parties such as the Vlaams Blok in Antwerp, the Front National (FN) led by Jean-Marie Le Pen in Orange, and its splinter, Bruno Megret's Mouvement National Républican (MNR) in Marignane and Vitrolles (Bouches-du-Rhône), and the 'post-fascist' Alleanza Nazionale in the region of Lazio, are extremely popular.[1]

In Britain, we have the British National Party (BNP), the National Front, the National Democratic Party, and Combat 18, with the Nationalist Socialist Alliance acting as an umbrella under which these groups from time to time jointly organise. Meanwhile, the former leader of the U.K. Independence Party complains that it is being taken over by people with good things to say about the neo-fascist BNP. Yet all these parties have been small beer. However, in the June 2001 General Election, the BNP performed spectacularly well in Oldham with 16.4 percent, in Burnley (11.3 percent) – both in North West England – and well in East London. They gained their first seat in municipal office in May 2002's local elections, with three BNP Councillors being elected with 15 percent, 14.9 percent and 12.9 percent of the vote. Nevertheless, the real problems were seen to be – and still are – on the Continent where the extreme right is already a force to be reckoned with.

In France, Le Pen's politics can be summed up simply. He believes that the Holocaust, the death of six million Jews, was 'a point of detail in history', and that the Americans built the gas chambers in Buchenwald after the war. Despite this, Le Pen's FN had turned itself from what was in 1983–84 a refuge for protest votes, into a party that consistently gained the votes of one in six and one in five French men and women respectively. More recently, however, it has found itself in trouble. The split between Le Pen and his erstwhile Deputy, Bruno Megret, led to a decline in support and a haemorrhaging of seats. Between 1994 and 1999 in the European Election, there was a slippage in votes, down from 10.5 percent to 5.69 percent and a slump in seats from eleven to five, as the weaker half of the FN's fission narrowly failed to pass the 5 percent barrier. However, in April of 2001 in the first round of the French Presidential elections, it was 19.20 percent and 5.47 million votes for Le Pen and Megret combined.

In Belgium the Vlaams Blok, violently anti-Semitic and the most popular single party in Antwerp, Belgium's second city, has had representatives in the European Parliament since 1994. It is also beginning, exceptionally in this linguistically divided country, to make some headway in the French-speaking capital Brussels now that the Front National (Belge), the country's francophone equivalent of the FN, has seemingly imploded.

Austria's Freiheitliche Partei Osterreichs (FPÖ) (Freedom Party) won 26.9 percent of the vote and fifty-two seats in the 1999 general elections, overtaking the Die Österreichische Volkspartei (ÖVP) (Austrian People's Party). The Austrian Christian Democrats formed a coalition, in full knowledge that this would institutionalise and give the party much-desired credibility. This coalition has since collapsed.

In Italy in 1995, the Movimento Sociale Italiano (MSI) at the urging of its leader, Gianfranco Fini, was dissolved into the only marginally wider Alleanza Nazionale (AN). The AN was set up as a front organisation to fight the Italian General Election of 1994 in a pact with Silvio Berlusconi's Forza Italia; neo-fascists combined with desperate former Christian Democrats seeking a home following the virtual annihilation of their former party by the Tangentopoli scandals. Despite the current post-fascist rhetoric of Mr Fini, it was only months before the 1994 European Parliament election that he was making common cause with Le Pen's Group of the European Right in their newsletter Europe des Patries. Less than a decade ago, the AN were doing straight-armed salutes and praising Mussolini, today they share government with Berlusconi's Forza Italia, and a political group with members of the xenophobic Dansk Folkeparti (Danish People's Party), who emerged at a European level in the 1999 European elections and won 12 percent of votes and twenty-two seats.

In Sweden, there is good news and bad. While the Social Democrats achieved resounding success in the 2001 elections, the Liberals managed to triple their vote – the electorate perhaps attracted by the party's restrictive immigration policies.

Racism and xenophobia have, in recent years, come much more to the fore. At worst, they manifest themselves in the denial of human rights and freedoms to both migrants – the ten to twelve million Third Country nationals – and to visible minorities, the four million black Europeans who are nationals or residents of a particular country. This takes the form of physical violence, support for the nationalistic policies and actions of the extreme right, or subtler discrimination in everyday life. As these minority groups often have little access to the political process and an often underdeveloped capacity to respond adequately to the problems of racism and xenophobia, tension and division among 'white' Europeans and ethnic minorities is on the increase.

Racism is not only socially divisive but, on a political level, discrimination on the grounds of race is potentially harmful to European integration. Firstly, racial discrimination will certainly interfere with free movement of persons and services by preventing victims from obtaining jobs, housing and services, therefore obstructing the single market. Secondly, if the level of protection afforded differs between states, this will discourage minorities from moving to those offering less protection. Racism and xenophobia are, at one level at least, European problems, which warrant a response from the European institutions.

So what has been done? In the mid-1980s, the European Parliament responded to the success of the extreme right by establishing a Committee of Inquiry into the Growth of Racism and Fascism in Europe, the main catalyst being the success in the 1984 European Elections of the extreme right under Jean-Marie Le Pen in France with 11 percent and eleven MEPs. The resulting report, known as the Evrigenis Report after its *rapporteur*, was labelled in 1986 as 'alarmist'. In fact, with the passage of time it has turned out to be, if anything, overcomplacent.

The Report produced a string of Recommendations, including a proposal for a European Race Relations Directive; a reversal in the burden of proof, with organisations having to prove that they were not racist rather than individuals having to prove racism; the establishment of a framework of legislation to ensure that all EU Third Country nationals had the same rights and same duties as everyone else.

However, other than within the European Parliament itself, there was precious little evidence that these proposals were taken seriously. At the time, the European Commission claimed – despite the June 1986 Solemn Declaration on Racism and Xenophobia and the EU Treaty commitments on Fundamental Rights and the Rights of Migrant Worker – that they had no competence in the field.

In 1989, a second and further Committee of Inquiry into Racism and Xenophobia was set up, with Glyn Ford as its *rapporteur*, in response to the success of the extreme right in the 1989 European Elections (seventeen million votes and twenty-two seats), resulting nine months later in a Report.[2] This further Report concentrated less on reiterating the conclusions of the first (which by then were becoming self-evident truths to students of European psephology), and more on identifying action to be taken. However, the Report concluded that the rapid growth in popularity of the extreme right meant urgent legislation was required if ethnic and migrant groups and communities throughout Europe were to be protected. Of its seventy-seven Recommendations, the first three to be adopted included an Annual Debate in the European Parliament on racism and xenophobia, the establishment of the European Parliament's Civil Liberties

Committee, and finally, the setting up of the European Migrants Forum, a proposal that had also featured in the Evrigenis Report.

The Migrants Forum was modelled on the European Youth Forum and was intended as a representative body that would act as a sounding board between Europe's 'Sixteenth State' and the Parliament, Council and Commission. Unfortunately, its members were appointed as individuals and not as representatives of their organisations, which would have made them accountable to their 'constituencies'. Therefore, it chose not to position itself in the niche it was intended to occupy, but instead surrendered its special status by acting as yet another pressure group and not the privileged body it was intended to be. Eventually, as internal divisions subsided, the European Migrants Forum began to reorient itself towards the Community institutions which were the initial intended target of its endeavour; however, it ultimately proved flawed and failed to live up to its early promise, effectively folding in 2000.

In 1992 Article 6 (ex-Article F) of the Treaty on European Union (TEU), committed the Member States to respect fundamental rights, as guaranteed by the European Convention on Human Rights (ECHR).

The European Parliament has placed successive Social Affairs Commissioners Vasso Papandreou (PASOK, Greece, 1987–1993), Padraig Flynn (Fianna Fail, Ireland, 1993–1999) and Anna Diamantopoulou (PASOK, Greece, 1999–present) under considerable pressure to bring forward antiracist legislation. Initially they resisted the challenge, retreating into the arms of lawyers as the Commission claimed, as mentioned earlier, that it did not have a legal basis for action. However, with political will and backbone, even ambiguity can provide opportunity. After all, Jacques Delors, then Commission President, used the Solemn Declaration in 1987 to justify a subvention to the populist antiracist youth group SOS Racism in France when questioned by the then Front National MEP Olivier d'Ormesson. Delors confirmed that initiatives and projects against racism were 'in line with the traditions and principles of human rights' and the granting of a subsidy to an anti-racism association like SOS Racism was also 'in line with the undertakings by the Community institutions' in the 1986 Solemn Declaration.

In 1994, the Parliament pressured Jacques Santer, then President of the Commission, to put responsibility for coordination of action against racism and xenophobia with the European Council within the remit of the Employment and Social Affairs Directorate-General. Here, the Parliament was responsible for pushing the issue up the agenda, as now responsibility for combating racism and xenophobia had a specific place and a group of people formally responsible for addressing it.

Also in 1994, the Consultative Committee on Racism and Xenophobia (RAXEN) was proposed and established by the Council.[3] This initiative was unusual for the Council: since the first direct elections of the European Parliament in 1979, the European Council had limited its interventions to Resolutions condemning racism, anti-Semitism and xenophobia after each new high-water mark tide of racial attacks, racial murders or anti-Semitic incidents. RAXEN constituted high-level recognition of the significance and gravity of the problem, and had been set up as a result of a Franco-German initiative by Kohl and Mitterrand, both facing rising racism in suburbs of major cities, launched at the Corfu Summit in July 1994. However, the initial terms of reference threatened to restrict its function, as it was set up simply to make Recommendations, geared as far as possible to national and local circumstances, on cooperation between governments and the various social bodies in favour of encouraging tolerance, understanding and harmony with foreigners. While its initial Report to the Essen Summit in December 1994 remained within these restraining terms, the Final Report went much further in demanding action at a European level. This Report was presented to the European Council at Cannes in July 1995. It echoed all the European Parliament's demands of the previous decade. It recognised that racism and xenophobia threaten European integration, and acknowledged that national action can only become embedded and effective if it is underpinned by European-level action. It demanded firstly, that during the 1996 Intergovernmental Conference (IGC), a Treaty amendment should be agreed to make it unambiguous that the European Community (an important distinction from the EU) has competence to deal with the fight against racism and xenophobia.

Second, that the European Commission introduce a European Race Relations Directive to make discrimination on the grounds of race or religion illegal for European Community residents.

Third, that a Directive should outlaw Holocaust denial and the distribution of fascist and anti-Semitic material in written or electronic form. This would ban race-hate computer games like 'Concentration Camp Manager'.

Fourth, that a European Monitoring Centre be established to monitor incidents of racism and xenophobia.

Fifth, to ask that the European police and customs liaison organisation, EUROPOL, take responsibility for exchanging information regarding neo-Nazi and neo-fascist organisations, including those linked with football violence between Member States.

Sixth and finally, that its own continuation be recommended until the requested Treaty changes are ratified, whereupon the responsibility would shift to the appropriate Community institution with the enlargement of its terms of reference to include free movement.

Three of the proposals have been implemented to date, the most important probably being the establishment of a European Union Monitoring Centre in 1997. In fact, the final outcome was that the Consultative Committee's mandate was renewed 'to study, in close co-operation with the Council of Europe, the feasibility of a European Monitoring Centre on Racism and Xenophobia'.[4] This was done and a full proposal presented to the European Council in Florence. The study was approved and the Consultative Committee instructed to continue its work. At the Dublin European Council, it was reiterated that the Council wanted to press ahead and to see the launch of such a centre at the Amsterdam European Council. The term 'close co-operation' came under intense scrutiny as the Council of Europe attempted to hijack what was essentially a European Union initiative. To have anything more than close cooperation would draw the teeth of such a centre by a double dilution of its work: first by expanding its area of concerns to include the whole of the Council of Europe; secondly by making it a 'joint venture' with the Council of Europe, placing inevitable limits on matching financial contributions.

A breakthrough came in 1995 with the European Commission's first ever Communication on the subject, which was coupled with a Council proposal to designate 1997 as the European Year against Racism. The Year supported a number of projects, ranging from grass-roots programmes and regional initiatives to high-profile national and international events attended by stars from the world of sport and show business. This represented a watershed after more than a decade's work.

The Communication sets out key areas for further action to be built into existing policy instruments. The key areas are grouped under seven headings:

- promoting integration and opening pathways to inclusion;
- promoting equal opportunities and reducing discrimination;
- raising public awareness and combating prejudice;
- preventing racist behaviour and violence;
- monitoring and punishing racist crime;
- international cooperation;
- the question of European-level legislation.

The Communication also stated the Commission's intention to press for a specific competence discrimination clause in appropriate Community legislation. In 1997, the introduction of Article 13 (ex-Article 6a) into the Amsterdam Treaty increased the EU's capacity to ensure its founding principles are respected. This finally became operative with the formal ratification of the Amsterdam Treaty in spring 1999.

> Without prejudice to the other provision of this Treaty and within the limits of the powers conferred by it upon the Community, the Council, acting unanimously on a proposal from the Commission and after consulting the European Parliament, may take the appropriate action to combat discrimination based on sex, racial or ethnic origin, religion or belief, age or sexual orientation.

This allows for the Council to act against discrimination and was the first time that a constitutional document stated that the fight against racist and xenophobic discrimination is the responsibility of the EU. Sexual discrimination was already covered. Since the ratification of the Amsterdam Treaty, the European Commission has bought forward three anti-discrimination measures: the Anti-Racist Directive, which was overwhelmingly approved in May 2000; an Anti-Racist Action Programme; and a more general proposal against discrimination in employment across the whole spectrum of discriminated groups.[5]

The Action Plan was part of the Commission's plan to encourage future European-level initiatives to combat racism, similar to the Amsterdam Treaty. It proposed to 'adopt legislative initiatives on the basis of Article 13 of the Amsterdam Treaty, (integrate) action against racism into Community policies and programmes, and develop and exchange 'new models to combat racism'.

The EU used its powers to protect fundamental rights in 2001 when the European Parliament, by a huge majority, condemned the formation of an Austrian government coalition, which included Jörg Haider's Freiheitliche Partei Osterreichs (FPÖ) (Freedom Party). Haider clearly demonstrated, through both words and actions, that he deserved to be excluded from normal democratic discourse, and when the party won a huge number of seats in the general elections of 1999, MEPs voted for the first time in the EU's history to impose diplomatic sanctions against Austria *if* its new government actually violated the 1997 Amsterdam Treaty – Article 7 – which could suspend an EU country for 'serious and persistent' breaches of democracy, human rights and the rule of law. Haider stepped down from formal leadership of his party in response to the controversy and concentrated instead on his role as First Minister of the state of Carinthia, but has now resumed his role, while the government coalition has collapsed. The EU established a Group of Wise Men who were to assess whether or not the sanctions imposed by the EU should be lifted. It concluded that there was no clear evidence that the aforementioned Article was being violated.

The European Union, embracing the principles of dignity, freedom, equality, solidarity, citizens' rights and justice, signed a Charter of Fundamental Rights of the European Union, in 2000. The European Union Charter of Fundamental Rights sets out in a single text, for the first time in the European Union's history, the whole range of civil, political, economic and social rights of European citizens and all persons resident in the EU.

Yet, despite the fact that much has been done at EU level to combat the rising tide of racism and xenophobia within the Community, the problem that made this kind of legislation necessary has not gone away.

The European Union is in and of itself a multicultural community. Alongside the rainbow cultures of the fifteen states are the smaller communities from across Asia and Africa spread throughout the Union. Immigration has had a positive cultural and economic impact. Already, more than 20 million out of the 370 million population of the EU work in a state of which they are not in fact citizens. The large majority of these are Third Country nationals. Therefore, it is essential to ensure they have fundamental civil and political rights. Simple measures must be supported to extend the rights of this 'nation' which makes up Europe's seventh largest 'state', falling behind only Germany, the U.K., Italy, France, Spain and the Netherlands.

It should be made simple to acquire nationality after five years' unblemished residence in a country, and the children of immigrants born in a country of the Union should be granted automatic citizenship. Where necessary, the acquisition of dual nationality should be permitted. It is ludicrous that hundreds of thousands of people born and brought up in the EU, with no real ties with their parents' or grandparents' home country, and in some cases no knowledge of their language, are considered to be foreign nationals.

There is a danger, with the single market, of creating a group of second-class citizens: European residents who are not citizens of Member States, and Member-State nationals who, because of their skin colour, are increasingly likely to be discriminated against and exploited. One only has to come through passport control at Brussels or Barcelona, Manchester or Milan to see the two-tier treatment in operation.

Such policies of commission and omission coupled with rising racism and anti-Semitism have mutually reinforced each other. Tougher policies against immigrants 'prove' to the racists and their fellow travellers that they were right, 'There is a problem.' Rising racism allows 'public opinion' to legitimate the actions of reactionary governments. Consequently, violent youth feels racial violence is acceptable. There is an increasing rise in racist attacks on the Union's ethnic minority citizens and asylum seekers.

There is still much to be done, then, and legislation must be forthcoming and effective. However, it would be naïve to believe that Treaty amendments alone can eliminate the racist menace and bring harmony to communities divided by the issue of race and nation. Legislation, education and employment are all necessary but not sufficient conditions: legislation to lay down clearly and police the limits of intolerance; education to ensure that future generations do not repeat the mistakes of the previous ones; employment to undercut the extreme right-wing slogans which, in Le Pen's version, intoned 'Three million immigrants, three million unemployed, three million immigrants too many'. This frighteningly echoed the Austrian Nazi slogan of the 1930s: '400,000 Jews, 400,000 unemployed, 400,000 Jews too many'; all too tragically, we know what happened to the Jews.

A society in which one group is deliberately disadvantaged by another is not full democracy, and a Member State in which this practice is increasing both in frequency and openness cannot claim to be so. Legislation is clearly only the first step in what will be a long march to tolerance and welcome.

Notes

1. More recently, in March 2002, Pim Fortuyn, a right-wing populist of the Leefbaar Nederland Party in Holland won seventeen of forty-five seats on Rotterdam City Council.
2. Ford (1992).
3. I served on it from 1994 to 1998 when it finished its work
4. During this period, the European Union Monitoring Centre, based in Vienna, by chance held its official opening ceremony with President Prodi and European Parliament President Nicole Fontaine. Uninvited, the Austrian Government gatecrashed the party and they found themselves mobbed by the media and ignored by the guests.
5. Initially Commissioner Padraig Flynn planned to introduce the Directives and Action Programme, but this was blocked with the fall of the Santer Commission when the interim Commission decided not to introduce any new business while awaiting its replacement. In the end it was under Commissioner Anna Diamantopoulou that the Directives were agreed in June 2000 and the Action Programme commenced in 2001.

Reference

Ford, G. 1992. *Fascist Europe*. London: Pluto Press.

Riding the Tiger: the Difficult Relationship between NGOs and the Media

Marc Peirs

This text is purposely and necessarily biased. It is biased in two ways: it presents the point of view of a journalist, and of a Belgian. Moreover, it wants – or at least tries – to be a text with a stance, an opinion, that can make the reader nod with amusement or with anger – whatever. This said, it will be clear that this text does not pretend to be scientifically correct. Rather it is rooted in the praxis of the author, who is a Belgian journalist.

Life on Mars

The 'Bible' for NGO workers, *The Earthscan Reader on NGO Management* (Edwards and Fowler), contains no less than thirty chapters on all conceivable aspects of running an NGO. Chapter titles deal with a variety of subjects such as: 'NGO performance: what breeds success?', or: 'The role of gender in NGO's'. But about media contacts or press handling one does not find a word, certainly not a whole chapter dedicated to this subject. In the index to the book we looked for the word 'media', but that proved a fruitless effort. Striking? Not for a Belgian. In the overview of Flemish and bilingual Dutch–French Belgian NGOs, the so-called *NGO Atlas* (2001), the staff of each organisation is listed according to the department they belong to and the tasks they have to perform: neither a department like 'press relations', nor a job like 'press officer' is to be found in the guide. 'Is there life on Mars?' asks rock singer David Bowie in one of his earlier songs. My answer is: 'Yes. Mars is inhabited by NGO-people.'

Let us be tolerant and look beyond the intellectual borders of both books I have mentioned. In fact, let's think worldwide. When I use the search engine 'Google' to ask for all references combining the words media, training or management and NGO, Google replies, 'no results found'. No results found.

Admittedly, there is one commercial link, which looks promising at first sight. But, upon closer examination it proves to be a link to the website of 'IIG Associates – Security Services and Riot Management'. And that hardly sounds like an NGO.

In spite of all these obvious signs of a complete lack of interest in the media, only a madman would claim that the press is not important for NGOs and the causes they advocate. In NGO offices all over the world, loud cheers are heard whenever the organisation is mentioned in media-reports. Rightly so. Media attention is vitally important for a modern organisation. It is through the media, and only through them, that an NGO's message can reach the general audience as well as the circles of political and economic decision makers. These two target audiences are equally important. The general audience is needed for its ideological, moral and most of all financial support, whereas the attention of the decision makers needs to be grasped as an essential first step to establish all kinds of desired changes (structural, legal, political etc.). At one time, these audiences could be easily reached through intermediaries like churches, encompassing social organisations and/or political parties. In the past two decades, all of these partners have seen their power to influence opinions and behaviour of the public decrease dramatically. Today, only the media can function as a loudspeaker for reaching a broader audience. But the NGOs do not own the loudspeakers. Moreover, most of them barely know how to operate such an installation. Why is that the case?

Entertain Us

Far too often, people working in NGOs believe that the moral righteousness of their cause is sufficient guarantee to receive media attention: the junta in Myanmar, for example, is so obviously disgusting that of course the media will join us in the fight for establishing an international boycott. Spaniards in tight ballet-like clothes, who pester animals to death by using sabres, are clearly acting cruelly: a campaign against bullfighting will surely get backing from an all non-Spanish media. I doubt it. Or perhaps the clitoridectomy of women in Islamic parts of black Africa, something so clearly backward that a text venting anger and denouncing the practice will undoubtedly be published with pleasure on the opinion pages of the newspaper. It is not.

Such a story is often not good enough for today's media. It is considered to be too marginal, too far away, too poorly documented, too abstract, or – worst of all in the eyes of reporters – too well known. And yet, even the most cynical journalist would want the famines in the Third World to end, animals not to be tortured and the Amazon forest not to be destroyed. NGO people ask grumpily: 'Why isn't the media giving the right amount of attention to all our great causes?'

A first set of reasons can be found in the media themselves. To name only two of the most important reasons: the change in mind-set of many media houses, which switched from a political to a commercial logic, and the self-image of the modern reporter who wants to be a professional rather than a do-gooder.

It is widely known, for instance, that the Belgian media in the last two decades has gradually cut itself loose from its political-ideological roots. This process has yielded a more professional, objective and free press. The newspapers in particular exemplify this. In the same movement the Flemish public broadcasting company, VRT, freed itself from political interference to a large extent. The same is true, albeit to a lesser extent, of its French-speaking counterpart RTBF. From the outset, the (younger) privatised television and radio stations were born in a commercial rather than a political cradle. From the point of view of a journalist it is, of course, a great relief to be able to work without being bothered by politicians, who would more than likely object to this or that particular report.

On the other hand, the newly discovered freedom from political interference is immediately constrained by a new obligation for media houses. They want and need to create profit. The medium is no longer an ideological but a commercial tool. This leads, consciously or not, to a different way of covering the news. Foremost is the style of presentation, but also the content and the angle chosen. Increasingly, the rule applied is that the public gets what the public wants. And this is not necessarily identical with what the individual reporter would like to cover. It appears that foreign news, especially, is not very attractive to the reader, viewer or listener. On an ordinary Wednesday of an ordinary week (20 March 2002), the nine Flemish newspapers had a total of 281 pages. Of these, not more than eight are dedicated to foreign news. Moreover, seven of these eight pages are to be found in just three of the nine papers examined; to be precise, in the three top papers *De Morgen*, *De Standaard* and *De Financieel-Economische Tijd*. These findings corroborate totally all kinds of surveys on the audience's taste and are even more powerfully sustained by the huge amount of copies sold by a popular paper like *Het Laatste Nieuws* (with a circulation of around 340,000 copies, by far the biggest-selling Flemish daily). This newspaper focuses entirely on local and national news, with an emphasis on entertainment and sport.

Therefore, the individual reporter is not exactly begging for copy delivered from a NGO. While his older colleague – riding on the waves of the May '68 rebellion – may have been more of a do-gooder, this role today is not at all sought after by the young contemporary journalist. The survey *Tussen Woord en Daad* (Of words and deeds), which was conducted among journalists by the Belgian King Boudewijn Foundation think-tank, showed once more that the vast majority of reporters define their task as one of informing the public. The idea that journalists should lend a voice to the non-vocal groups in society or become a tool to help create a better world is widely rejected amongst reporters. Journalists like to see themselves as information-professionals, not as teachers – let alone as preachers.

Two Princes

In a media culture that emphasises profits, and where a journalist considers himself primarily as a professional creator of content; the criteria for newsworthy facts follow a cold-blooded logic, rather than a moral or idealistic view. In this sense, media and NGOs adhere to two different styles of thinking. They look at the world through different spectacles, while observing the same facts – like in the well-known story in which two princes stand on different shores of the same river; neither is able to cross the deep water and join the other.

This is not the place to develop the criteria for defining what would or should be news. They include obvious elements, such as conflict, being the first/biggest/last … to be/do something, the number of people affected, fact as opposed to idea, trustworthiness of the source, and so on. Most of all, and often overlooked by people working in NGOs, 'the news' implies the mentioning of something that was not known before. Exactly this point explains why some NGO stories do not receive attention in the media. There is a civil war with a lot of bloodshed and kidnapping in Colombia? Yes, we know and we have known that for years. The story may be sad, awful and full of deep analysis, but it is not news. At least, it is not news until the moment when an internationally famous Colombian or an ordinary Belgian is kidnapped, when a few dozen people are killed all at the same time, or the U.S. Marines invades territories held by rebels. Then we have news. Then something happens.

A second problem is the difference between education and information. Information provides neutral facts and data and gives opinions from all sides involved. What the reader, viewer or listener does with this information is entirely up to his or her own discretion. Education, on the other hand, tries to make people aware of situations as a first step towards a desired change in patterns of behaviour. Naturally, education borders on information. A report about the poverty of Nicaraguan small coffee growers can be written according to all the journalistic patterns and also used in a leaflet promoting fair trade products, e.g. Nicaraguan coffee. But in most cases it is immediately clear to the journalist that what he receives from the NGO, although disguised as a press kit or a newsletter, is actually a text written for educational purposes. These texts are always rich in bias (only one point of view is presented, usually that of the *campesino* (Spanish for peasant) Ramón and poor in specific data. Quotes from the poorly known Ramón are followed by general statements starting with vague formulas like 'lots of', 'most of', etc.). This material may well serve as a method for gaining the audience's sympathy for Ramón and his likes, but no reporter will quote it as a reliable source of information. To put it bluntly; informing the public about the factual developments, the root causes and effects of a crisis, is, information. Thus, a journalist's task is, to create a public awareness that something should be done about it. This belongs to the field of education – a field inhabited by NGOs, not by the media.

Having said all this, it should be added that NGOs also seem to possess the rare talent for unintentionally killing good opportunities to be mentioned in the media. Their amateur-like approach as think-tank often gives the impression that people working for NGOs hide themselves from reporters. Whenever a Belgian journalist calls an NGO later than 5 p.m., he might at best be greeted by an answering machine. Everybody has left for the day and the NGO is too short-sighted to pay for a mobile phone and permanent Internet access at home for the spokesperson. Furthermore, NGO people still need to be educated in the basics of dealing with journalists. For example, a press meeting cannot be held at 6 p.m. At that time newspapers are approaching their deadlines, whereas television reporters have already passed it. Similarly, it is not wise to organise the press meeting on a day already packed with important news. And it is most recommendable to provide footage for radio and television and pictures for papers and magazines.

Come Together

Respecting these practical basics, and letting go of the misapprehension that the moral imperative of the message per se provides an entrance ticket to the theatre of the media, there are a lot of new but, unfortunately, poorly used ways for NGOs to obtain access to the media. NGOs should never forget that they are able to offer something the media needs like a mammal needs fresh air; an interesting content. NGOs should also remember that to receive coverage from the media, they must compete with political parties, heads of industry, farmer and trade unions, mass murderers, soccer teams and the European Union, to name but a few. There is only one mantra to allow NGOs to stand out from all these competitors who each want to be caressed by the media – they have to 'ride the tiger without being eaten'. It is crucial that they adapt their media strategy to what the media wants without giving up their proper role and identity. Let us explore five practical recipes to receive attention in the media:

The path of the humble man. NGOs often take their own cause or line of thinking as a starting point to attract the media. Even if for some years there is no news at all coming from, for example, the Philippines, any NGO specialised in battling poverty in the Philippines should not view this as a reason to temporarily stop bombarding the media with pleas for attention. It is far smarter to glue the NGO cause to an external, newsworthy fact, e.g., elections in the Philippines, or a Philippine writer winning the Nobel Prize for literature. Otherwise, NGOs are just bothering the media with press releases nobody reads or cares about.

The path of the faraway man. NGOs, especially those active in the Third World movement, have an enormous treasure they hardly use: their men and women in the field, who are right on the spot where it happens. Belgian practice shows, alas, that NGOs hardly ever have the reflex to inform the media of the existence of these potential eye witnesses in the case of conflict, disaster, *coup d'état* or an election. Of course, it might happen that Our Man in Havana could be awakened by a reporter calling at an ungodly hour.

The path of the fast man. Thanks to their (supposed) antennas in local communities, faraway countries and specialised organisations, NGOs should be able to react swiftly whenever newsworthy events occur in their field of interest. Collecting information, selecting a spokesperson and writing and sending a press release can be done in a matter of just a few hours. This is something which is proved and practised daily by commercial enterprises. NGOs can be as fast as these heads of industry.

The path of the empathic man. Due to the increasing tendency to define media as a commercial tool, papers, magazines, radio stations and, to a lesser extent, television stations, try to hit a well-defined target audience. The Dutch monthly *Woef!* targets the dog-lover, *The Economist* aims at the well-informed liberal intellectual, and the French television channel Arte tries to seduce the highbrow culture-junkie. In turn, NGOs should adapt, edit and rewrite their unique messages attuned to their target media. Within the AIDS-prevention NGOs, it is common practice to guide the reporter to exactly the information and the angle he needs. The journalist is able to ask and receive data on the use of condoms or on AIDS victims, but he can also ask for an interview with a person who is infected with HIV – a typical specimen; a male, around 40 years of age and gay. Imagine an NGO campaigning in favour of the poverty-stricken Nicaraguan coffee growers. For the top newspapers, an overview of prices and production during the last ten years is necessary, along with background information on the structure of landowning in the coffee-growing region. For television, some footage from the location is necessary. For a human-interest magazine, an interview with poor Ramón is necessary – fly him over.

The path of the reliable man. Most of all, NGOs should begin to invest in making themselves known to the media as reliable sources of high-quality information. A modern NGO should act as a data bank for precise information and as a think-tank where the media can always find an eloquent interviewee on the themes the organisation specialises in. This implies, in the view of the Belgians, that the NGO chooses a few themes in which to specialise. This process can be called branding. In the same way that commercial enterprises like Pampers, Bic or Lego have taken the branding process one step further by replacing the name of a product by the name of their brand, so can NGOs brand themselves by proving to be the undeniable specialist in the matters they stand for. In the long run, the name of the NGO itself stands for 'newsworthy quality'. Greenpeace can be pointed at as a forerunner in this trend.

Break on Through

It sounds simple – learning to deal with the media, establishing a good relationship with the press in general and specialised journalists in particular. But for NGOs it is anything but easy. It requires time, people and money – in one word, it calls for professionalism. Some NGOs know that very well and have attended to the problem:

> Unfortunately, a NGO's working efficiently with mass media is rather an exception than the rule. Many new NGO's are preoccupied with looking for resources to

implement projects, plans, programs, but do not give proper attention to public relations work, strive for creating positive image of their organization and do not consolidate in order to shape strategies on governing public opinion. Does every public organization have an expert on public relations? A sociological survey can give an exact answer, but it seems that the answer will be mostly negative. We know that such experts could make the journalists' job easier. You will agree that a well prepared press release, a selection of pictures, and a clear comment addressing the target audience makes the chances of the material to be published more likely. And this means that such experts for NGO's should be trained.

Is this an excerpt from a text of a long-standing, respectable Grand Old Lady within the rich and experienced Western NGOs? No. It is a quote from Victor Tsoy, chairman of the public association 'Rabat Malik' ... from Uzbekistan. NGOs emerge everywhere. But the sad examples at the beginning of this text prove that the road ahead is long and winding.

My Home Town

Today's world is as lively as it is confusing. This is even more so in big cities. For the Flemish and the Dutch, this is hardly new. Next to Singapore, Flanders and The Netherlands are the most densely urbanised regions of the world. Also in other regions of the world, cities are growing like mushrooms. Today almost half of the world's population lives in an urban context.

It is not surprising that social scientists such as sociologists and anthropologists join city planners and architects in their focus on the city in a variety of fields such as demographic, political and cultural life. The city is the melting pot in which all kinds of opportunities and threats converge. For NGOs it is a challenge to adapt to this societal reality. A long list of social scientists directs their attention to the many-sided phenomena that come with urbanisation. I mention a few of them that are important for NGOs to make an effort to rethink their contacts with the press. First of all, the spreading of American culture (or the globalisation of culture, one might say) happens mainly through the cities. Secondly, cities attract many immigrants, both from the surrounding countryside and from abroad. Hence, they are the primary arena of struggle between those who advocate and those who reject the multicultural society. The importance of this discussion for NGOs is obvious. Advocates of the New Right are now using the notion of culture as a substitute for race, while sticking to the old racist ideological ways of thinking and speaking. Thirdly, cities seem to induce in their inhabitants a desire to stress individuality (me, myself and I), thus helping to (re)create a new identity. In its most visual form the emphasis on individuality turns to fear of the other. Some people try to curb their fear by barricading their property with fences and alarm systems, or by hiring private security guards. In this manner, the city becomes literally a battlefield for the competition between identities.

Indeed, at the core of these societal developments is the discussion of identity in a globalised and urbanised world and how it can be situated. It has long been accepted that a single person performs various roles and hence adopts different identities: a father or mother, a saleswoman or technician, a David Bowie or Britney Spears fan, a member of a trade union or of a soccer team, a citizen of London or of Amsterdam. Moreover, these identities can change in the course of a lifetime. The point social scientists nowadays make is twofold. First, an undeniable fact is that urbanisation confronts every one of us with a huge variety of identities living in one's city. Secondly, the definition of one's identity is no longer a matter of family, political loyalty or economic position: instead it is rooted in culture – hence in information and communication.

This brings us back to the media and their important role in the battlefield of identity definition. In a world where all traditional tools for defining identity and rallying people are under attack, the media can become the most important, if not the only, go-between for the contact between the different identities. NGOs should learn to talk to their audiences in the language of their identity, and that presupposes their mastering of that language. If culture and identity become the major themes in the urbanised world of today, then the media are the obvious partners for the NGOs.

References

Benthall, J. 1993. *Disasters, Relief and the Media*. London: I.B. Tauris.

De Ekstermolengroep. 2000. *Don Quichote Voorbij*, 11.11. Brussels, NCOS/11.

Edwards, G. and Fowler, C. 2001. *The Earthscan Reader on NGO Management*. London: Penguin.

S.N. 2001. *NGO Atlas 2001*. Brussels: Coprogram.

Knops, G. 2002. *Tussen Woord en Daad*. Brussels: Koning Boudewijn Stichting.

Tsoy, V. 2002. 'Shall We Become Social Partners?' www.cango.net.kg

URBAN CROWDS MANIPULATED: ASSESSING THE AUSTRIAN CASE AS AN EXAMPLE IN WIDER EUROPEAN TENDENCIES

André Gingrich

Introduction

Joerg Haider took over the leadership of the Austrian Freedom Party (FP) in 1986. At that time, the FP held just above 5 percent of the country's electorate. Its leaders before Haider pursued a 'liberal' orientation, mostly in the interest of small business and the middle classes, while the FP was a minor partner, then, in a coalition government with the Social Democrats (SP) (1983–86).

After Haider took over the FP in 1986, the Social Democrats refused to continue that coalition, because of Haider's more radical and rightist orientation. From 1986 until 1999, the country then was ruled by a coalition of Social Democrats and Christian Democrats (People's Party, VP), while Haider's FP remained in parliamentary opposition. During that time, the FP's influence rose from those 5 percent in 1986 to the 27 percent in 1999, which alarmed Europe.

By 1999, Haider's FP thus had managed to become the most successful rightist party in elections, in any European Union country. Inside Austria, they became the second strongest party in the country, behind the SP and just ahead of the VP. Quite obviously, this success was based on a huge growth of influence and support among the urban population, including workers and employees – many of whom formerly had supported the SP. The result of the 1999 elections helped to install, early in 2000, the new VP–FP coalition government, which, for a few months in 2000, was confronted by massive international protests and boycotts.

As a reaction to these protests, Joerg Haider nominally stepped down from his party's formal leadership, while retaining a strong influence behind the scenes in his position of governor in Carinthia, one of Austria's nine provinces (or federal states). While his own party thus became the first rightist and populist party in the national government of an EU country, it turned out that this was only the tip of an iceberg. After that 2000 breakthrough in Austria, a number of comparable parties came to government during subsequent years in other EU countries as well, such as in Italy, Denmark, and the Netherlands – not to speak of Portugal, Norway, or of Le Pen's success in the French presidential elections, of the significance of the Vlaams Blok in Belgium, or of Blocher in Switzerland, and so forth.

By late 2002, however, that first rightist breakthrough to governmental power had already entered its first major crises: in the Netherlands as well as in Austria, the rightist parties in government engaged in such intense internal struggles that in both countries it became necessary to call for new elections, which seemed to result in certain setbacks for these rightists. For the FP, opinion polls from autumn 2002 even went as far as predicting that voters' support would shrink down to about half (13 percent) of what it had been in 1999. At the very least, the 2002 elections made it obvious that within two and a half years in government, Haider's FP had lost much of its former support among urban crowds.

In this article, I will discuss some of the major factors that led to the success (1986–99) and the failure, perhaps an initial failure only (2000–2002), of Haider's FP among the urban population in Austria. Simultaneously, I will consider how this development relates to some dimensions of racism in urban Austria. First, however, I will discuss a number of features which Austria, in this context, shares with several other countries in the EU. These features will then be assessed in the second section, through their specific relevance for Austria, by exploring the internal contradictions that led to the VP–FP-coalition's downfall in 2002. Finally, some conclusions will be drawn from this case study.

Economic Chauvinism and Cultural Pessimism

In a world of increasing globalisation, and in a context of European integration and enlargement, it would be extremely one-sided to treat a case like Austria only by its particular and unique features. For this reason, I begin with some of the wider and comparable dimensions.

Party politics is only one indicator, of course, of racism, which is the central topic of this publication. Focusing on one type of party only, within the wider, interactive spectrum of Western European party politics, narrows down even further the heuristic value of that indicator. Bearing in mind the very limited scope of such an approach, we may nevertheless begin by assessing the rise of new rightist parties in Western Europe, such as Haider's FP, as one such limited indicator for the rise of racism in metropolitan areas. In this perspective, let us first take a look at the evidence. Which are the countries of Western Europe (EU and EEA, the European Economic Area) where new rightist parties have already gained some considerable influence in their respective national parliaments, and where has this not, or not yet, been so?

The answer to this question reveals that by the early twenty-first century, the new right has not yet managed to establish itself in the national parliaments of three among Europe's five largest countries. That is, in the parliaments of Britain, Germany and Spain, representatives of such parties are not, or not yet, installed. In addition, and in spite of Le Pen's symbolic success at the 2002 presidential elections, the influence of the rivalling two Fronts Nationaux remains limited (below 10 percent) in the French Assemblée Nationale. Italy, therefore, is the exception to this situation among Europe's 'big five'. Otherwise, the rise of new rightist parties has not yet made it quite into the main demographic and economic centres of Western Europe, in the early years of this century.

Where, then, have these parties been particularly successful, if not in the centres of Western Europe? Most of their initial success is rooted in Western Europe's periphery. It may well be, and it is indeed likely, that similar parties will strive to establish themselves also in Western Europe's centres. Alternatively, it is also possible and perhaps even more likely that the established centre and left-of-centre parties in Western Europe continue adopting more rightist policies themselves, in order to prevent their new rivals' ascent to power.

Examining Western Europe's small-country periphery now a bit closer brings out Portugal as another kind of exception – similar, in a reverse sense, to the exception of Italy among Western Europe's 'big five'. Among those small Western European countries, where by the first years after 2000 rightist parties do have significant positions in national parliaments or governments, Portugal does represent a case of 'below mean average income' in Western Europe. Or, to put it more bluntly, Portugal is small and relatively poor. In most other small, 'below average income' countries (e.g. Ireland, Greece) no such parties are influential. By contrast, the other small countries in question represent 'above mean average income' examples in Western Europe and, in fact, in the world: Denmark, Norway, Netherlands, Belgium, Switzerland and Austria represent Western Europe's 'small, affluent' countries par excellence. (Remarkably, Sweden is not, or not yet, part of this list.)

Insofar as the rise of racism in metropolitan areas of Western Europe is embodied and enacted by new rightist parties, this development therefore has one of its core bases in 'small, affluent countries'.

In view of this first evidence, let me repeat that the rise of racism in Western Europe takes on many different forms.

Racial riots, such as in Oldham and other areas of northern England, are one form. In Germany, burning homes of refugees and asylum seekers, damaging Jewish cemeteries and institutions and the lynching of African migrant workers are similar forms. Likewise, mob attacks in Spanish Andalusia are another parallel to the Oldham riots and burning asylum houses in Germany. One may indeed ask the awesome and tantalising question, how the presence of such openly racist mob violence, in Britain, Spain and Germany – that is, in three among Western Europe's 'big five' – relates to the absence of rightist parties in these countries' parliaments? Furthermore, that awesome question may be complemented by a second question – namely, how far the almost complete absence of such openly racist mob violence in most of Western Europe's 'small, affluent' countries relates to the presence of new rightist parties in these parliaments and governments? Perhaps a reliable answer lies along these lines:

the new rightist parties pull most potential for open racist mob violence away from the streets, by transforming it into covert, institutionalised racism.

Only one among the many different forms which the rise of racism takes on in Western Europe, therefore, is embodied in new rightist parties. From the turn of the century, this 'distinct party form' of Western European racism has been particularly successful in 'small, affluent' countries. This was achieved by encouraging, and by channelling away, open mob racism into more covert, institutionalised racism. Such 'distinct party forms' of racism, in turn, have managed to impose their own agenda upon existing mainstream parties. In turn, these 'mainstream party forms' of racism either have joined forces with the 'distinct party form' (as in many small, affluent countries), or they so far have managed to prevent the rise of distinct party forms by being themselves 'racist enough' for such a clientele (as in several other Western European countries).

On a conceptual level, and leaving still other forms of racism aside, we thus have put the rise of new rightist parties in context, by distinguishing between 'mob racism', 'mainstream party racism', and the new right's 'distinct party racism' for Western Europe, and by indicating some of the potential and actual interrelation between these three. Furthermore, we have identified Austria as a 'tip of the iceberg' case example for the rise of 'distinct party racism' in Western Europe, which had 'small affluent' countries as its core base. Are there, then, any common factors that can be identified as promoting the rise of such specific, 'distinct party' racism among most 'small, affluent' countries of Western Europe?

By way of a working hypothesis, I propose to consider such factors that are rooted inside the very properties of these countries, namely their common qualities of being affluent and small.

I have already indicated that 'affluence' here is understood not in GNP terms, but rather in terms of mean average income: Affluence thus refers to the regular income situation of the broad population. In this sense, we are dealing here with countries that all rank among the world's top ten or, according to statistical criteria, among the top twenty at least. In addition, these also are countries with a particularly high concentration of the population in urban areas. This high degree of urban affluence includes factors which, for a British or a U.S. employee or worker, sound like utopia, or like paradise lost: free public schooling of a high standard; high coverage of medical services through compulsory semi-public health insurance; obligatory unemployment insurance, distributed in case of need on a decent level for several months; an annual minimum of four weeks of paid vacation, and so forth. Based on their rather high income taxation, these are 'public welfare societies' with overall income and living conditions for the average child, adult or elderly person that are far higher than elsewhere. Now in the eyes of many in these countries, the benefits from their 'public welfare societies' are put at risk by the current phase of globalisation, and by globalisation's additional European variants, namely immigration, and the integration and enlargement of the EU.

One basic approach by 'distinct party racism' in Western Europe, in mobilising support, is to manipulate many of these concerns and fears of urban working people about the future of public welfare, and of the public welfare state. For most working people, these concerns and fears have to do with their material and social well-being, with belonging to a sheltered, functioning public life, with which they often identify. Many may even have a sense that this public welfare society is, to an extent, also 'their own' achievement, to the point that they 'own' it.

Now, a sense of belonging, and even of property, is still far away from a racist attitude. Distinct party racism, however, tends to exaggerate the results and the dangers of immigration, of integration (which implies that the rich countries in the EU pay for the poorer EU members), and of enlargement by (usually) poorer new EU members. Through this exaggerating manipulation, concerns about well-being, belonging and owning are transformed into fears of downward mobility. These fears are then turned into an aggressive attitude about defending that which is feared to be in danger. I call the ensuing mass attitudes of 'aggressively defending one's own' (attitudes which already reflect the impact of distinct party racism) by the term 'economic chauvinism'.

Basically, economic chauvinism postulates that immigration, EU enlargement and EU integration bring in illegitimate claims by 'inferior others' to sell out what is 'ours'. Distinct party racism induces, encourages, and strengthens economic chauvinism, and argues in various forms that those illegitimate claims by others come from inferior, parasitic, criminal, greedy, lazy, etc. 'others'.

Economic chauvinism may arise in different places and at different times – but in Europe's 'small, affluent' countries, it is particularly active and widespread, given the actual unevenness of living conditions between these 'small islands of wealth and affluence' and their closer and wider neighbourhood. Apart from their respective local agenda, all rightist parties in Western Europe's small, affluent countries have these programmatic features in common: they are all against immigration, and in one way or another, they are against EU enlargement and against too much EU integration.

A second commonality goes hand in hand with economic chauvinism. I call it 'cultural pessimism'. Basically, this concerns questions of nationhood and national identity, as well as related questions such as language, religion and education. Former governments of these small and affluent countries did little to prepare their populations for the unavoidable processes of interacting in these fields with people of other languages, religions and of other forms of education. With new waves of immigration, and with the ongoing processes of the EU's integration and enlargement, popular concerns about these small, affluent countries' cultural futures have been growing. In one of its most popular forms, these concerns are articulated by the worried question: What will become of our small country (region) in this changing world? Being concerned about one's cultural future is not racist, and is not nationalist – in fact, such concerns may become quite creative. What distinct party racism has done, however, is to manipulate these concerns, and to transform them into the fearful conviction that 'we will lose our language, our religion, and our educational values' for good, unless they are protected by radical means. Such radical means, it is postulated, are necessary to safeguard national culture from its destruction by inferior and more powerful outsiders. That conviction about an almost inevitable loss of one's cultural future lies at the core of cultural pessimism. In this regard, as in the realm of economic chauvinism, distinct party racism points its finger in two directions: to the top, i.e., to the EU centres in Brussels, and to the periphery, i.e., to immigrants and to incoming new and simultaneously less affluent, EU member countries.

In this regard, Western Europe's new rightist parties follow a strategy that is parallel to the right and to the far right in the United States: polemics against Washington (or New York) combine with hate language against Hispanic and other immigrants there. In similar ways, the rightist parties of Western Europe argue against 'Brussels' (dominated by the 'big five'), and against those 'from outside the EU'. Western Europe's distinct party racism thus constructs a hierarchical, tripartite cosmology: the bottom and top levels are aggressive and dangerous 'others', the middle level is the collective endangered 'us'. The bottom level consists of economically and culturally 'inferior' immigrants and new EU members; the top level is 'Brussels' and its allies (the big five and aspects of globalisation led by the U.S.A.), who are seen as being perhaps more powerful economically, but not as superior in cultural terms. With economic chauvinism and cultural pessimism, distinct party racism mobilises against key opponent and enemy groups that it identifies along these tripartite, hierarchical terms. Haider's FP was most successful in this struggle.

Austria as a Case Example of Rightist Success and Failure

I have already indicated In the introduction that in Austria, the rise of the FP occurred within a relatively long time span of more than thirteen years, from 1986 to 1999. In this process, Haider used primarily cultural pessimism for initially gaining mass support for the FP, while economic chauvinism was brought into focus only at a later point.

The initial chapters of Haider's success story thus dealt with cultural pessimism, facing the priorities of the late 1980s and early 1990s. The Waldheim affair, Austria's entry procedure into the EU, and the collapse of communism in Austria's immediate neighbourhood provided these priorities. In the Waldheim affair of 1986, a domestic electorate had put into effect, for the first time, a centre and right-of-centre voter's majority, which, in spite of strong international reactions, brought the ex-Secretary General of the UN into the office of Austria's state presidency. Not only did that new majority signal options for more practical and less symbolic political tasks; but in addition, this also combined with a variant of Austrian nationalism that emphasised some emotional continuity with its Nazi past. Haider saw these possibilities, and seized power in his party in the same year. When, soon after, the mainstream SP and VP coalition parties entered into negotiations about Austria's EU entry, they left largely unguarded any kind of Austrian patriotism. A sense of Austrian nationhood had been a relatively recent phenomenon, born out of feeble First Republic loyalty (1918–38), out of weak anti-Nazi resistance (1938–45), and thus largely being a result of the founding process of the Second Republic (1945–55). That founding process primarily was credited to the two mainstream parties, VP and SP. Austrian patriotism therefore was usually associated with these two parties, until the late 1980s. By contrast, the FP had originally been founded by 'ex-Nazi supporters turned democratic'. Until the late 1980s, the FP had maintained a diffuse pan-Germanic orientation, which is irreconcilable with Austrian patriotism.

When SP and VP negotiated Austria's EU entry, however, the FP suddenly discovered Austrian patriotism. Within a few years, Haider cleaned his party's outward appearance of any explicit signs of political pan-Germanism, and transformed its surface into that of loyal Austrian patriots and nationalists. Although the plebiscite about Austria's definite entry into the EU resulted in a 'pro' vote by two-thirds (1991), the remaining third constituted a solid base for Haider's anti-EU policy in the years to come. Meanwhile, the communist world had imploded. Illegal immigration to Austria from these countries rose dramatically, and neutral Austria's traditional, post-Second World War role as a 'bridge' between East and West became obsolete. In this context, Haider's FP began to mobilise for Austria's entry into NATO, for gaining more 'security and protection' – a point on which he was failed by the majority of Austria's population, who continue to prefer neutrality over NATO membership. After this setback, the FP transformed the 'security and protection' topic from an international into an even more explicit domestic agenda for more police and for less immigration. Roughly by the mid-1990s, it became obvious that Haider attracted voters not only from the Christian Democrats, and from those who otherwise would not vote at all, but also from the SP. Since 1970, all national governments had been led by the Social Democrats as the strongest party. After a quarter of a century of Socialist Federal Chancellors, there was a growing sense of a need for urgent political change, in an international setting that had been transformed so radically. Widespread public opinion associated the SP's leadership with saturation of power, estrangement from the 'common people' and their needs, with no visions for the future, and with mismanagement and personal abuses.

It was only during this period that Haider's FP began to give top priority to an economic agenda. Haider's various apologetic statements about Nazism raised a lot of domestic and international protest. Yet while these statements sought to enhance and continue the 'new' nationalism from the Waldheim period, the FP's main agenda began to focus on something else: mismanagement and public spending by the SP-VP government, job security for Austrians, and illegal immigration. In a way, cultural pessimism became integrated and subordinated to this economic agenda: in several cultural campaigns, for instance, Haider's FP attacked public funding by the SP administration for what the FP labelled as 'perverse', 'blasphemous' or 'anti-patriotic' art.

Gradually, the economic priorities of the FP became clear: more public funding for police and army; almost no more funding for NGOs and for cultural concerns; a 'flat tax', copied from the U.S. Republican agenda; and a cash sum for mothers, in the form of a 'children's cheque', in order to encourage them to stay at home instead of seeking jobs in the labour market. Most important, of course, was a stop for any immigration from outside the EU, and tough measures against illegal resident immigrants, plus, at the core, a drastic privatisation programme for large sectors of what was still owned by the state.

The FP's economic agenda thus combined a rigid 'law and order' protection of the domestic labour market with a relatively radical neoliberal programme of privatisation. That neoliberal programme did not, however, include any privatisation of unemployment and health insurance, nor of primary and secondary education. The FP's programme thus carefully avoided any plan to privatise the central pillars of the welfare state, but went as far as possible in all other fields. With this agenda of economic chauvinism and of cultural pessimism, the FP gained their 1999 landslide victory of 27 percent. Since then, no rightist populist party in Western Europe has achieved better results in national elections. Although by 1999 the unemployment rate in Austria was among the lowest three in the EU, Haider's FP successfully managed to reach out to the urban poor, that is to say, to the employed working people. His party therefore was able to convince major segments of the urban (and rural) population that his programme would meet their economic and cultural concerns about the future. After being in national government for less than three years (early 2000 to late 2002), however, the FP became stuck in internal contradiction to such an extent that their coalition government collapsed.

This 'failure' and the 2002 collapse of the VP–FP coalition may only be a provisional one. As in the Dutch case, the Austrian rightist party is certainly capable of learning from some of its avoidable mistakes. The 2002 collapse nevertheless reveals a number of contradictions and tensions that can be identified as being inherent in such parties. These inherent tensions are bound to stay, no matter how well a more coherent party organisation, and a more efficient charismatic media performance might manage to cover up such internal contradictions. In countries like Austria or the other 'small, affluent' EU member states, any party that wants to seize governmental power has to gain some influence among the urban working strata. By 1999, Haider had gained particular influence among a larger proletarian segment of young males, and among elderly workers disappointed in the SP. To an extent, this amounted to a protest vote against a stagnating post Second World War domestic order, led by Social Democrats, amidst a rapidly changing world.

Once within government, Haider's FP had to seek ways to implement their programme, with its most painful consequences as early as possible, in order to then safeguard some enduring support among urban voters from 1999 for the next elections. In this key task of theirs, the FP failed completely. It became evident very soon that the 'pro-proletarian' element inside the FP (represented by Haider and by a few government members) had less and less to say in economic and financial matters. Rather, it was the big and small business wing of the FP that set the terms for government policies, together with the leading business circles inside the VP. This joint constellation produced one wave of privatisation after another, one wave of cutting down subsidies after the next, one series of new fees followed by another. Within only two years, every urban household in the country had less income at their disposal than before, while unemployment began to rise. Although the FP–VP government had virtually stopped any new immigration, this did not improve the domestic employment situation at all. Although the FP–VP government had promised to boost the economy and to cut national budget deficits, the results for a vast majority of urban households, and for their budgets, were clearly negative. By and large, many among the urban working crowds who had been seduced into a protest vote, and into opting for cultural pessimism and economic chauvinism, became increasingly disappointed with the FP.

In order to try and prevent any further estrangement from popular support, Haider attempted to return to his party's leadership, and to mobilise cultural pessimism and economic chauvinism again – by threatening to veto the Czech and Slovak Republics' entry into the EU, and by calling for an income tax reform. On both points, he met considerable resistance not only from the VP government partner, but even more importantly, among the neoliberal wing of his own party. When the most prominent members from that wing resigned for these reasons from government, the whole coalition collapsed. Among those who still supported the FP disappointment grew even further, in view of how this collapse came about.

Drawing some Conclusions from the Austrian Case?

Neither the Dutch nor the Austrian case provides any simple lesson. It would be quite inappropriate, for instance, to conclude that once in government, rightist parties soon manoeuvre themselves into such difficulties that these coalitions would implode anyhow, on their own. While, at the time of writing, it is not even certain that the 2002 elections will actually succeed in ousting these parties from the Dutch and Austrian governments, the additional Italian example demonstrates that distinct party racism also is capable of overcoming such a setback: in Italy, after all, a first right and right-of-centre government coalition under Berlusconi was voted out of government in the 1990s, only to come back to power in 2001.

Urban crowds, it seems, do not learn quickly from such experiences, and tend to allow several rounds of successive manipulation. Any conclusions from the Austrian case, it seems to me, have to focus on medium-term effects, therefore, rather than on any short-term 'how-to-do' considerations. I propose to identify such medium-term conclusions in the comparative realm of cultural pessimism, and of economic chauvinism, and to combine them with the particular conditions of each case. In the Austrian example, such particular conditions include the country's proximity to five out of ten new incoming EU countries, the strong element of small business in its economy, its relatively recent emergence as a nation and, very importantly, the country's reluctance to seriously deal with its Nazi past. All of these factors combine with the more comparative aspects of cultural pessimism and economic chauvinism, on which

I nevertheless have concentrated here for the sake of the argument. (For some of the elements mentioned here as being particularly Austrian, see Gingrich 2000 and 2004).

For a wider context and debate, as in this volume, I propose to consider three medium-term conclusions from the Austrian case.

1. Economically, 'distinct party racism' always seeks to mobilise interests from various segments of society. Gaining employees' and workers' support for their purposes is crucial for these parties, but these interests inevitably will be frustrated when neoliberal government policies are implemented. This inevitable frustration, however, does not automatically lead away from rightist influence. These are not the unemployed masses from earlier decades, who might be satisfied with 'new jobs' alone. It seems to me that developing new visions for maintaining and adapting welfare societies is indispensable for profoundly challenging economic chauvinism at its roots. These roots include a manipulation of 'belonging' and of 'owning'. A serious challenge to these roots thus cannot ignore these notions, but has to address them up front. This, to my mind, cannot avoid a new, economically based notion of 'sharing'.

2. Politically, 'distinct party racism' obviously cannot be countered by overtaking it from the right. When still in government, Austrian Social Democrats themselves attempted throughout a decade to pursue 'mainstream party racism', in view of immigration, to quite a considerable extent. Far from keeping distinct party racism at bay, this was counterproductive, by publicly legitimising and upgrading racist attitudes in general. The Dutch or Scandinavian cases point exactly in the same direction.

3. Culturally, 'distinct party racism' represents a programme of a twofold, rigid seclusion against the current phase of globalisation: seclusion against current and further aspects of globalisation (Hannerz 1996) in Western Europe, such as in EU integration, EU enlargement, and against most aspects of legal and illegal immigration. This is portrayed as the 'only way out', otherwise national culture would be destroyed and lost. This manipulation and enhancement of cultural pessimism can only be seriously challenged if it is directly addressed. In one way or another, the alternative to cultural pessimism lies in envisioning a future in which the legacy, and the creativity, of these small European countries and their cultures have a stable home within increasing, globalised arenas of cultural diversity (Appadurai 2000).

Acknowledgments

For their help in discussing various aspects of this chapter, I am grateful to Sylvia Haas (Vienna), Ulf Hannerz (Stockholm), Rik Pinxten (Ghent), and Marshall Sahlins (Chicago). Earlier versions of this paper were presented in December 2001 in Ghent, and in March and May 2002 at the anthropology departments of New York University and of the University of Chicago.

Bibliography

Appadurai, A. 2000. 'Grassroots Globalization and the Research Imagination'. *Public Culture* 13, 1: 1–19.

Gingrich, A. 2000. 'A Man for All Seasons: An Anthropological Perspective on Public Representation and Cultural Politics of the Austrian Freedom Party'. *The Haider Phenomenon in Austria*, R. Wodak, and A. Pelinka, eds. New Brunswick and London: Transaction Publishers: 67–91.

———— 2004. 'Race Falling, Racism Rising? Methods of Analysis, Pieces of Austrian Folklore, and the Wealth of Small Nations'. *Racism in Europe. Special Issue of Ethnos*, P. Hervik, and M. Gullestad, eds.

Hannerz, U. 1996. *Transnational Connections: Cultures, People, Places*. London: Routledge.

Some Reflections on Culture and Violence

Erwin Jans

'Whenever I hear the word culture, I reach for my gun.' These infamous words were uttered not so long ago in the very heart of Europe by Nazi propaganda chief Joseph Goebbels. A few years ago the same words came back to me, but ordered in a different way, as an answer to Goebbels' statement. They were spoken by a Moroccan stand-up comedian, Ahmed Snoussi, alias Bziz. He said: 'Whenever I hear a gun, I reach out for the word culture.' Tempting as it is to see in this reversal and reappropriation of Goebbels' phrase the possibility of the mobilisation of culture and its achievements as a resistance to the physical and moral aggression in society, it is too naive and too simple a perspective on the relationship between culture and violence. To mobilise culture against violence is to forget about the violence of culture itself. It is the notion of culture itself that has to be examined. In many contemporary discourses knowledge of and respect for one's own culture and the culture of the other are articulated as efficient non-violent strategies against racism and xenophobia. However, we should not forget that a long intellectual history intertwines the notions of culture and national character, on the one hand, and race, on the other hand. It is only after the Second World War that the use of the word race became highly problematic, but not its underlying concept, as Paul Gilroy makes clear:

> After 1945, the effects of the Nazi genocide made respectable academic opinion shy and cautious about openly invoking the idea of racial difference in purely biological terms. In those conditions, the concept of culture supplied an alternative descriptive vocabulary and a more acceptable political idiom with which to address and simplify the geographical, historical, and phenotypical variations that distinguished racialized inequality. (Gilroy 2000: 281)

In other words: the terrible injustice, the violence and the brutality justified by the ideology of 'race' found shelter under the roof of 'culture'. It should make us aware of the complexities and ambiguities involved in the fluency with which the word 'culture' is used in all kinds of contemporary political, cultural, social and sociological discourses.

Being professionally involved in modern theatre, I want to start my contribution by returning to one of the decisive moments in the construction of the Western theatre, which is also one of the decisive moments in the construction of Western culture: the emergence of Greek civilisation. The 'wonder' of Greek civilisation and its artistic, intellectual and political achievements have been celebrated as the single most important source of Western culture. The word 'wonder' tries hard to ignore the troubling question about the sources of Greek civilisation itself. This question of origins is the question of culture and of identity par excellence. In a very personal essay on the tragedian Aeschylus, the Albanian writer Ismail Kadare raises an intriguing and disturbing question concerning the origins of Greek culture. Why, Kadare asks (1995), was the ancient Greek civilisation so obsessed by the Trojan War? Why, from Homer to the tragedies of Aeschylus, Sophocles and Euripides, were so many of the stories that were told in one way or another stories about that war that took place so many centuries earlier? The answer Kadare gives is purely hypothetical but impressive and provocative in its assumptions about culture and cultural identity: 'In the same way as someone recalls a long forgotten crime committed in his youth, the Greek people, at the moment of its full maturity, woke up to the regret over a crime committed in its youth. Eight hundred years earlier it had suffocated the Trojan people in its sleep' (1995: 56). Greek literature and Greek tragedy are, according to Kadare, ways of dealing with this crime, ways of dealing with the collective guilt of the Greek people for having destroyed another culture. From that moment onwards Greek literature and Greek tragedy are haunted by the ghosts from the burning ruins of Troy. What impressed me in this hypothesis of Kadare is his vision on culture, on what culture is and what it excludes, and on how what is excluded comes back and defines and defies by its very exclusion that culture. What Kadare tells us about culture or civilisation is that it is always based on a crime that is forgotten, denied or repressed. It is the same as what the philosopher Walter Benjamin meant when he wrote that no document of civilization is not at the same time a document of barbarism. In other words: culture and violence are deeply involved. To understand better what is at stake when the word 'culture' is used, we should become aware of its traumatic and explosive contents. I use words like 'trauma' and 'explosion' on purpose in order to refer to the physical and psychic destructions involved in those contemporary conflicts that have national, ethnic, religious or cultural identity as their main issue.

We use the word 'culture' when we talk about the highest achievements of mankind: the arts, philosophy, science, and our political institutions. For the nineteenth century English writer and thinker Matthew Arnold, culture was the reservoir of the best that was known and thought in a society. He believed that culture could soften, although not neutralise, the destructive effects of a modern, aggressive and materialistic urban life. By reading Homer, Dante and Shakespeare, by listening to the Flemish polyphony, Mozart, Händel and Beethoven, by looking at paintings or sculptures by Van Eyck, Michelangelo and Da Vinci, we keep permanently in touch with the best that mankind created. By doing so we get a deeper understanding of ourselves, of our tradition and of our society. We also use the word 'culture' to talk about the highest personal ideal: the ideal of being a 'cultured' or a 'cultivated' person. However, being an ideal, culture is also always, as Werner Hamacher points out convincingly, 'culture's shame for perhaps not being sufficiently culture': 'No culture is Culture, culture itself, no culture can measure up to its claim to be culture. It is, therefore, not a possession, this culture, but a projection and a reproach, an attempt to reach a goal – itself, that other – that is by definition unattainable: ever another culture, and each time guilty of not being the other culture and of not being whole'. (Hamacher 1997: 284). Culture is always a split concept, a permanent conflict between its realisation and its goal, its ideal and its insufficiency. Culture, in other words, introduces from the onset conflict in cultures and conflict between cultures. The consequences of this interpretation of culture are far-reaching. Culture is used as a polemical term for the distinction between culture and non-culture, culture and nature, culture and barbarism, and so on, and thus as a weapon in the struggle against other cultures, as an instrument of denunciation and barbarisation of other cultures: 'Culture is always also a declaration of war'. (Hamacher ibid.: 286)

The above-mentioned miracle of the fifth century in Athens was historically partly due to the national pride of Greece after having defeated the Persians in the sixth century B.C. It is one of the great achievements of Greek civilisation to have given a voice to the defeated. This achievement took place in Aeschylus' tragedy *The Persians* (1985). Aeschylus, who distinguished himself as a warrior during the Persian Wars and lost a brother in battle, gave voice to the pain, the misery, the lament of those who were defeated. The tragedy is a proof of the humanism and the deep empathy the Greeks were capable of. With these words, the messenger in the tragedy announces the defeat of the Persian army:

> O cities of wide Asia! O loved Persian earth,
> Haven of ample wealth! One blow has overthrown
> Your happy pride; the flower of all your youth is fallen.
> To bring the first news of defeat's an evil fate;
> Yet I must now unfold the whole disastrous truth:
> Persians, our country's fleet and army are no more. (Aeschylus: 130)

But in his English translation Philip Vellacot misses an important point, which is brought to the surface in the French translation by Paul Mazin. Here, the last two lines run as follows: 'Et pourtant, il me faut déployer devant vous toute notre misère, Perses: l'armée barbare tout entière a péri!' (Aeschylus 1982: 117)

The Persian messenger uses the word the Greeks used to talk about the others: the barbarians. The Dutch translation by Herman Altena uses 'the non-Greeks' as translation. (Aeschylus 1994, 61). It is in the end not a Persian who is speaking – for how could he refer to himself as a barbarian? – but a Greek. In any case, it shows the antagonism (the 'symbolic' violence) between Greeks and Persians even at a moment where the highest point of empathy (of being 'cultivated') was reached.

This silencing of a difference at the heart of Greek culture was repeated once more in the nineteenth century. In his highly discussed and thought-provoking book, *Black Athena: The Afro-asiatic Roots of Classical Civilization*, Martin Bernal (1985) analyses the major shift that took place in the study of Greek civilisation in the first half of the nineteenth century. He makes a distinction between what he calls the Ancient Model and the Aryan Model. According to the Ancient Model, the ancestors of the Greeks had lived around the Aegean in idyllic simplicity until the Phoenicians and rulers from Egypt arrived and acquired territories, built cities and founded dynasties. They introduced many of the arts of civilisation, notably, irrigation, various types of armaments, writing and religion. (Bernal 2001: 27). Already in the fifth century this idea of cultural dependence was not much appreciated by the Athenians, as the pan-Hellenic, anti-barbarian passions clearly prove. The other model, the Aryan Model, sees Greek civilisation as the result of the conquest of the Aegean basin from the north by the Hellenes, speakers of an Indo-European language. The Aryan Model took over from the Ancient Model in the beginning of the nineteenth century because, according to Bernal, it fitted into the new cultural identity Europe was constructing in that period.

Bernal distinguishes four different forces affecting the social and ideological environments of scholars in the late eighteenth and early nineteenth centuries: (1) the establishment of the paradigms of progress; (2) the triumph of romanticism; (3) the revival of Christianity; and (4) racism (ibid.: 28). Bernal adds: 'Although it was only one of four factors behind the fall of the Ancient Model, racism became the major ideological force by which the Aryan model achieved and maintained its dominance from 1850 to 1950' (ibid.: 31). That period is the period of imperialism and colonialism that saw the emergence of racist theories and ultimately fell into the abyss of fascism and Nazism, leading to the extermination camps of the Second World War.

In his study, Martin Bernal looks for a compromise model. Accepting the argument of the Aryan Model that Greek is fundamentally an Indo-European language and that at a certain stage the Aegean basin must have been substantially influenced by the north (as a result of conquest or migration), he does not want to exclude the possibility of substantial cultural influence from the south and the east as well: 'It is plausible to suppose that, rather than being the result of a pre-Hellenic substrate, the non-Indo-European elements in the Greek language and culture were largely later Semitic and Egyptian superimpositions on an Indo-European base. Possibly these were the result of conquest and elite settlement around the Aegean, and certainly they came from trade and diplomatic contacts between Egypt and the Levant, on the one hand, and the Aegean, on the other' (ibid.: 27). This is not the place to go into the details of Bernal's thesis and the arguments of his critics. What his analysis makes clear, however, is that a pure origin of culture does not exist and that purity (and for the same reason racism) is not a fact but always a political or ideological rewriting of fact. The French philosopher Jean-Luc Nancy formulates it as follows: 'Every culture is in itself "multicultural", not only because there has always been a previous acculturation, and because there is no pure and simple origin, but at a deeper level, because the gesture of culture is itself a mixed gesture: it is to affront, confront, transform, divert, develop, recompose, combine, rechannel' (Nancy 2000: 152).

If the essential gesture of culture is conflict and confrontation, it implies that what we call culture, and especially the dialogue between cultures (interculturality or multiculturality), always hides the possibility of aggression, power relations and feelings of superiority. Returning to my field of profession, I want to focus on a theatre performance from the 1980s that on the one hand was praised as a model of intercultural understanding, but that on the other hand also has been interpreted as a culturally imperialistic and Eurocentric work of art: 'The Mahabharata' by Peter Brook. For more than three decades, the celebrated theatre director Peter Brook has been manifesting his interest in working with theatrical traditions and actors from other cultures. In many projects he showed his ability to communicate with actors from very different cultural backgrounds (European, American, African, Asian, etc.). Towards this intercultural communication, he takes a humanist and utopian position. Brook makes a rough distinction between three forms of culture: the culture of the 'state', the culture of the 'individual' and the culture of 'links': 'Both cultures – that of the state and that of the individual – have their own strengths and achievements, but they also have strict limitations due to the fact that both are only partial. At the same time, both survive, because both are expressions of incredibly powerful vested interests. Every large collectivity has a need to sell itself, every large group has to promote itself through its culture and in the same way, individual artists have a deeply rooted interest in compelling other people to observe and respect the creations of their own inner world'. (Brook 1996: 65). The state as well as the individual is, according to Peter Brook, characterised by clearly defined interests and by a will to defend those interests. Recognising the merits and the force of the cultures of the state and of the individual, Brook chooses explicitly for what he calls the 'third' culture, the culture of 'links': 'It has the force that can counterbalance the fragmentation of our world. It has to do with the discovery of relationships where such relationships have become submerged and lost – between man and society, between one race and another, between the microcosm and the macrocosm, between humanity and machinery, between the visible and the invisible, between categories, languages, genres. What are these relationships? Only cultural acts can explore and reveal these vital truths'. (Brook ibid.: 66) It seems that in the culture of the state and the culture of the individual certain truths and relationships are submerged or ignored, and can only be revealed by a culture of links, i.e. a culture of relationships. An important dimension of the culture of links is the dialogue with other cultures. Brook expresses his great expectations from such an intercultural dialogue, as did the anthropologist Victor Turner when he said:

> Cultures are most fully expressed in and made conscious of themselves in their ritual and theatrical performances. A performance is declarative of our shared humanity, yet it utters the uniqueness of particular cultures. We will know one another better by entering one another's performances and learning their grammars and vocabularies. (cited in Schechner: and Appel 1993: 1)

This (universalistic and humanistic) understanding was what Peter Brook was after in his staging of the great Indian epic 'The Mahabharata'. The performance became the central reference in the ongoing debate on the possibilities and methods of an intercultural theatre. The most passionate and fierce criticism was articulated by an Indian critic and theatre director Rustom Bharucha. His analysis was a 'cold shower' for well-meaning Western interculturalists. Bharucha makes clear from the outset in what tradition he places Brook's performance of 'The Mahabharata': 'It was the British who first made us aware in India of economic appropriation on a global scale. They took our raw materials from us, transported them to factories in Manchester and Lancashire, where they were transformed into commodities, which were then forcibly sold to us in India. Brook deals in a different kind of appropriation: he does not merely take our commodities and textiles and transform them into costumes and props. He has taken one of our most significant texts and decontextualised it from its history in order to "sell" it to audiences in the West' (Bharucha 1993: 68). For Bharucha the work of Peter Brook continues the British imperialistic and colonial enterprise in India. In saying so, he stresses the often hidden or ignored unequal socioeconomic structures underlying the so-called intercultural exchange. Bharucha articulates very explicitly that intercultural projects still execute an (often unconscious) colonial agenda: 'as much as one would like to accept the seeming openness of Euro-American interculturalists to other cultures, the larger economic and political domination of the West has clearly constrained, if not negated the possibilities of a genuine exchange. In the best of all possible worlds, interculturalism could be viewed as a "two-way street", based on a mutual reciprocity of needs. But in actuality, where it is the West that extends its domination to cultural matters, this "two-way street" could be more accurately described as a "dead-end"'(Bharucha ibid.: 2). Bharucha is strongest when he points to the economic and political power relations that underlie intercultural exchange. This detailed analysis and criticism of the performance remains an important document that should make us aware of the many traps of intercultural communication and of culture/multiculturalism as such.

Bharucha himself does not completely avoid the trap of seeing culture as a closed entity. One could ask the question: at what point is one familiar enough with another culture to deal with its cultural and artistic achievements? How much knowledge of context and history is needed? Could Brook ever reach the level of understanding Bharucha wants him to reach? Does Bharucha have that level of understanding himself? Through merely belonging to the Indian culture? Or through study? Is one ever familiar enough with one's own culture? Is culture something one has or can have? To avoid these crucial but difficult questions, culture is often defined in reductive terms. The more, however, a culture perceives and defines itself in terms of purity, unity, sameness, health, authenticity, race, ethnicity, national or cultural identity, the more a culture denies its fundamental and original trauma, its violence against and its exclusion of the other. Belonging to a culture, then, means literally partaking in a crime, prolonging a criminal scene. It means that there is no such thing as a healthy, a pure or a sound culture. Because of the crime that is committed there is something fundamentally *unheimlich* ('uncanny') in culture. Culture can therefore never be a place where we are at home, a 'domus', where we feel members of the same family, of the same herd, of the same blood, of the same race. Extreme right, racist and fascist discourses try to 'redomesticate' the multicultural public space, try to recreate a pure domestic space only for family members, a space that never existed and whose existence as an ideal is only possible because of the repression of initial violence and exclusion. There is no culture of the domus any more. There is only the culture of the polis, of the metropolis. The polis is the culture of what Jean-Luc Nancy calls 'the mêlée' (the mixed). In an essay about and for Sarajevo, one of the recent tragic names of this 'redomestication', Nancy writes: 'A city does not have to be identified by anything other than a name, which indicates a place, the place of a mêlée, a crossing and a stop, a knot and an exchange, a gathering, a disjunction, a circulation, a radiating [un étoilement]. The name of a city, like that of a country, like that of a people and a person, must always be the name of no one; it must be the name of anyone who might be presented in person or in its own right [en proper]. The "proper" name must always serve to dissolve the ego: the latter opens up a meaning, a pure source of meaning; the former indicates a mêlée, raises up a melody: Sarajevo'. (Nancy 2000: 145–46). The melody of Sarajevo was, however, suffocated in a brutal screaming for ethnic cleansing.

Western culture (and maybe culture itself) is by definition urban culture. We cannot talk about modernity without talking about the modern city and the way it fundamentally changed our perception of ourselves in relation to the other, to the others, to other cultures. It is in the streets of the modern city that culture meets its traumatic history. Walking through the city of Brussels, as I do every day, I am confronted with the Belgian colonial past and its marginalisation of Africans in Belgian society; with the immigration from North Africa and the social disruption of a whole community; with the consequences of the fall of communism in Eastern Europe; with the European and Belgian laws concerning political and economic refugees. The public space in the modern multicultural city has become the scene of our traumatic and violent history.

Let me return for a moment to Kadare. He seems to argue that there is a moment of maturity in cultural development. That moment of maturity is the moment of recognition of the initial crime that founded culture. Is it possible that at the beginning of this third millennium there are certain signs of the maturity Kadare was talking about? The maturity to face the crimes underlying culture? The maturity to face colonialism, imperialism and its terrible consequences? To face fascism, Nazism, Auschwitz? To face racism, xenophobia and intolerance in all its visible and invisible appearances? To face the challenges and the demands of the multicultural society?

The rescue of culture lies in its affirmation of cultural self-suspicion, says Werner Hamacher (Hamacher 1997: 285). Culture is always in crisis, because it is crisis itself. At the height of the political and cultural achievements in the age of Pericles and the Acropolis, Greek tragedy confronted the Greek citizen with 'das Unbehagen in der Kultur', the uncanny in (his) culture. The work of art can be, using the vocabulary of the anthropologist Victor Turner, a liminal or liminoid space, a transitional space where existing and fixed cultural identities are questioned, decentred, dislocated and opened up to a process of doubt, reflexivity and change. But at the same time the field of art is not a Garden of Eden protected against ideology, power and interests. The world of art and culture, artistic institutions, museums, art galleries, theatres, publishing houses reproduce the mechanisms of exclusion of the society they belong to. This has enormous consequences for non-Western artists or for artists living in Europe and coming from the ex-colonies or the migration countries. There has always been an interest in the other cultures. This interest has had and still has a multitude of names: orientalism, exoticism, primitivism, ethnic art, world music, etc. but these names stand for processes of commercialisation, fetishisation, commodification, processes of appropriation of the other into the same.

It is important that a culture becomes aware of the symbolic violence at work in its very heart. It means that a culture has to rethink and reconstruct itself. A culture of the mêlée is a culture based on a new set of questions, as is made clear by Paul Gilroy:

> Can we improve upon the idea that culture exists exclusively in localized national and ethnic units – separate but equal in aesthetic value and human worth? What significance do we accord to the histories of imperialism and white supremacy that are so extensively entangled with the development of modern aesthetics, its storehouses, collections, and museums and the anthropological assumptions that governed their consolidation? How, if we can reject the over-simple diagnoses of this situation offered by ethnic absolutism, might we begin to frame a trans- or cross-cultural criticism? What role does expressive cultural creativity play in mediating or even transcending racialized or ethnically coded differences? What recognition do we give to the forms of non-national and cross-cultural practice that are already spontaneously under way in popular-cultural and disreputable forms, many of which have supplied important resources to the transnational social movement against racism? (Gilroy 2000: 247–48)

Let me concentrate for a moment on the Flemish theatre – my professional field of work – and list some concrete questions that can be asked, not to accuse or to condemn but to open up a discussion on this symbolic violence that is also a violence of representation. How many actors and directors of Moroccan, Turkish or African origin are working in the Flemish theatres? How often are performances in the Arabic language or in other languages programmed? Are the new urban subcultures artistic expressions represented on the official stages? What kind of strategies are developed to communicate with new audiences? Are there many youngsters of non-European origin in the theatre schools? If not, what are the reasons for their absence? Do journalists and critics write in a well-informed way about non-European theatre or dance performances? Do our theatres stage non-European plays? Do festival organisers visit the festivals in Beirut, Damascus and Tunis or do they only go to Berlin, Avignon and Edinburgh? What is the role and function of government policies in all this? These are questions that involve the notions of power and representation, of cultural identity and artistic assimilation.

Creativity is not a human faculty that is developed outside of the socioeconomic and political ideological context. It is always also related to mechanisms of cultural dominance, recognition and exclusion, to the laws that regulate the positions of the centre and the margins in the artistic field.

When we talk about a multicultural society, we have to take it seriously on all levels, politically as well as culturally. Only then do we have the chance to deal with the traumas of history and to reach out for what the sociologist Paul Gilroy calls 'a different view of culture, one which accentuates its plastic, syncretic qualities and which does not see culture flowing into neat ethnic parcels but as a radically unfinished social process of self-definition and transformation' (Gilroy 2000). Or, in the words of Nancy: 'The mélange, therefore, is not. It happens; it takes place. There is mêlée, crisscrossing, weaving, exchange, sharing, and it is never a single thing, nor is it ever the same' (Nancy 2000: 150–51).

References

Aeschylus. 1985. *Prometheus Bound, The Suppliants, Seven Against Thebes, The Persians*. Translated with an introduction by Philip Vellacot. London: Penguin Books.

———— 1994. *De Perzen*. Translated with an introduction by H. Altena. Baarn: Ambo.

———— 1982. *Tragédies*. Presented and translated by P. Mazin. Paris: Gallimard.

Bernal, M. 1985. *Black Athena: the Afro-asiatic Roots of Classical Civilization*. London: Pergamon.

———— 2001. 'Race, Class, and Gender in the Formation of the Aryan Model of Greek Origins'. *Unpacking Europe. Towards a Critical Reading*. S. Hassan and I. Dadi, eds. Rotterdam: NAi Publishers.

Bharucha, R. 1993. *Theater and the World. Performance and the Politics of Culture*. London and New York: Routledge.

Brook, P. 1996. 'The Culture of Links'. *The Intercultural Performance Reader*. P. Pavis, ed. London and New York: Routledge.

Gilroy, P. 2000. *Between Camps. Nations, Cultures and the Allure of Race*. London: Penguin Books.

Hamacher, W. 1997. 'One 2 Many Multiculturalisms'. *Violence, Identity and Self-Determination*. H. de Vries and S. Wever, eds. Stanford, CA: Stanford University Press.

Kadare, I. 1995. *Eschyle ou le grand perdant*. Paris: Fayard.

Nancy, J.L. 2000. *Being Singular Plural*. Stanford, CA: Stanford University Press.

Schechner, R. and Appel, W., eds. 1993. *By Means of Performance. Intercultural Studies of Theatre and Ritual*. Cambridge: Cambridge University Press.

NATURALISING DIFFERENCE AND MODELS OF COEXISTENCE: CONCLUDING COMMENTS

Laura Nader

The subject matter in this collection may be read as reflecting a microcosm of contemporary global changes: the movement of cheap labour, the presence of both racism and tolerance, the power of the Islamic 'scarf', casteism versus racism, the colonialist language of race in modern garb, social repertoires and governance, the management of diversity and far right politics, institutionalised racism, and the inevitable primacy of difference, especially in places like Europe, India, Singapore and the United States. While the variety of topics is seemingly endless, there is a way of thinking here, one that contains anguished descriptions of racial problems and racial solutions – the dark side of difference – that is incomplete. The following comments are meant to enlarge the scope, perhaps to provide a distancing from the papers to redirect responsibility specific to Europe's problems with difference while also giving historicity and insight into the cultures that form the background of some immigrants.

Although I am not a race expert, I found the papers fascinating. Prior to attending the conference on 'Racism in Metropolitan Areas' I had come across a book review of *Race Experts* by historian Elisabeth Lasch-Quinn (New York Times, 9 December 2001). It was specifically about (as the subtitle indicates) 'How Racial Etiquette, Sensitivity Training, and New Age Therapy Hijacked the Civil Rights Revolution.' It was about the racial-problems industry and the racial-solutions industry, both flourishing after the Civil Rights movement in the United States. The problem of 'bridging equality and difference has become a major preoccupation of our time' the author impatiently notes. Lasch-Quinn focused on New Age therapy, with its insistence on 'the persistence of cultural differences into the workplace.' Her point of view is unmistakably clear: diversity trainers have difficulty acknowledging the proposition that any differences may be superficial compared with an appreciation of what all human beings have in common. In other words, the author explores the ways in which

the reification of race gets perpetuated by means of misguided expertise deeply
invested in social engineering, and deeply invested in difference as a 'problem.'
I am getting ahead of myself, because the papers at hand taught me a good deal
about the contributions and problems that result from more or less fixed frames
of reference that sometimes accompany expert knowledge. They also force one
to ask why and when is difference an issue at all?

Some scholars highlight the state as the key issue in naturalising difference.
Edwin Wilmsen reminds us (Wilmsen and McAllister 1996: 14) that the
pursuit of homogeneity by the nation-state is something that has been observed
all over Europe and the Western world more generally, sometimes involving
debate about when a state is a nation-state. In the nation-state context
immigrants are a 'problem', something not natural, something abnormal. Such
a stance favours the integration of migrants or their repatriation. In other
words, there are *implicit* assumptions about what a state or a nation-state is and
the place of diversity therein. In the words of Jan Blommaert and Jef
Verschueren (1995: 110), 'present-day migration is presented as an aberrant
form of human behaviour and the very presence of foreigners is a problematic
deviation from a natural state of affairs'. As a result, abnormalisation of the
foreigner is normalised. Thus, one purpose of the papers in this volume might
be to question the idea that homogeneity is normal, because if 'homogeneity is
the norm, the natural solution to problems caused by diversity is
rehomogenisation' (ibid.: 112), with all the totalitarian connotations of the
concept. To what extent do the papers in this volume problematise the absence
of diversity or homogeneity or resistance to diversity while at the same time
assuming that the flows of globalisation are inevitable? In other words, to what
degree have scholars dealt with contradictions such as the easily accepted
notion that Europeans are *by nature* tolerant, thereby suggesting that problems
that arise with the flow of labour must be inherent in the migrants themselves?

Troy Duster opens discussion with a pragmatic observation about the
movement of capital investment and labour across national boundaries and the
concomitant creation of an endemic and systematic pool of high youth
unemployment in locales as distant from one another as Australia, the United
States, Europe or Asia. Duster warns that attention has been fixated on racial
quotas instead of on the shrinking labour force, a point that was underscored by
other participants. Eric Seward wrote a sympathetic analysis of the decline of
employment in the British textile industry in Britain's northern towns, where he
also describes disturbances provoked by right-wing males, but the focus is on the
disturbances to the social order while the opposing males do not speak to us about
these issues. Peter Hervik writes of Denmark and the asymmetric relationship
between tolerator and tolerated, between immigrants and Danes, or between
orientalism and occidentalism and the shift from culturalism to racism; cultural
differences are seen as incompatible. But then there are many kinds of Danes.

The input from Dipankar Gupta asserts that India has caste democracy and
stresses that casteism is not racism under a different name. His position becomes
interesting when he tells us that Catholics in India prefer the term racism for acts
of discrimination, which, Guy Poppe tells us, got the Dalit Catholics some

attention at the race conference in Durban which caste might not have. Sumit Sarkar encounters the 'language of race', first with British colonialism and later in Hindu chauvinist ideology. Differences appear as 'problems' under many guises, but Don Robotham questions the inevitable primacy of difference, the absence of the victim's voices, the absence of and recognition of contradiction, and the essentialising of racist whites as well as victims.

One question that none of the papers delve into are the similarities resulting from a globalised corporate culture, one that is predominantly American in style. For all the differences described, many Europeans and migrants to Europe drink Coca-Cola or some such drink, watch TV, follow corporate fashion, use computers, etc. We might ask what makes for similar consumer behaviour and could not some of these common consumer tastes work to exaggerate a need for difference for purposes of identity? In other words, if we examine the driving forces behind exaggeration of difference, we might disaggregate the 'problem' of racisms much as Talal Asad (1990) did for Britain in the wake of the Rushdie affair. The causes of recognising differences are situational: unemployment is but one example. Fixing hate behaviour is another, as in October 2002, when a British person who shouted abuse at a Muslim neighbour was found guilty and ordered to do community service for a new offence of religion-based aggravated behaviour (Times Literary Supplement 7 February 2003: 2). The person in Britain so convicted could easily have been charged under previous laws with just threatening and abusive behaviour, thereby avoiding the issue of difference.

Emanuel Marx warns that ethnic stereotypes facilitate contacts between strangers but laconically concludes: 'the weak attack the even weaker instead of organising against the real culprits, the large economic organisations and the agencies of the State'. The latter, the power of the state and economic interests, are something that Mary Judd takes for granted in her story of Singapore, where the management of diversity is arrived at through legislating harmony in various guises. J.S. Gundara goes beyond race to Islamophobia (without mentioning the deep history of European crusades and Ottoman incursions into Europe) and cultural differences. But Gundara reminds us that London has been multicultural since medieval times, before Islam's arrival.

Solutions to urban racism are implied and embedded in these papers, but educational solutions enter with Johan Leman, who makes a plea for educational adjustments to diversity. Finally, Glyn Ford and André Gingrich speak about the power and location of right-wing parties, which appear, it seems, in smaller, marginal locations of Europe where strong social safety nets may be threatened by expanding needs of new immigrants.

The single speaker, who was most certainly not a race expert, was a CEO. He did not leave a paper, but in his oral delivery he asserted the need for Germany to import 10 million workers over the next ten years, without comment on what this might mean for national social organisations, let alone what it might mean for the 'racial problem". The CEO darted out of the door before questions could be asked. Mid-nineteenth-century social engineering that separated economic life from social and political life by means of the free market institutions made possible his kind of thinking about an economy independent of social good (Gray 1998: 1–21). The CEO was unaware, apparently, of the catastrophes generated by the so-called self-regulating market system, although he most certainly must have been aware of Europe's demographic turning point and its concomitant population decline and rapid aging.

Curiously, although there are two papers from the Indian subcontinent, there are no papers written by social scientists from the societies that send many immigrants to Europe – North Africa, Africa south of the Sahara, Turkey – and little is said about corporate or other power structures that are implicated in processes of contemporary movements of peoples; nor was class stratification a central issue although inequality is a major part of people's lives, 'causing resentment among the deprived and anxiety among the privileged ...' (Berreman 1981: 4)

There is a need to stretch the usual social science *area* paradigms. This entails some hard thinking about paradigms of difference, power and change. Furthermore, because social scientists are products of their own culture, it is useful to deconstruct earlier die-hard race constructors who represent a way of thinking about difference between the so-called developed world and the rest that is hegemonic (that is, interpenetrating and instrumental) and that sometimes is found even in the most sympathetic accounts of racism and policy recommendations.

Twenty-odd years ago, Edward Said spoke about academic paradigms in *Orientalism* (1979). In relation to orientalist scholars he asked: 'how does orientalism transmit and reproduce itself from one epoch to another...an orientation that depends on a positional superiority which puts the Westerner in a position of privilege, an orientation shot through with various kinds of racism or collective ideas that identify 'us' and 'them', all non-European peoples who lived out there in their own then colonized lands.' He wanted to reveal the eye that was seeing peoples of the East.

Many of these non-European people are now not in their own lands. They are in Europe or the United States, or in Australia, for example. Those previously colonised have come to live with the colonisers under conditions of a fallen colonialism and a weakening of the industrial manufacturing sector. The cultural domination of which Said wrote has followed the immigrants. We still speak of the 'other' whose cultural practices are more 'other' than ever in spite of, or because of, modernising proximities. The scope of othering practices still includes accepted and uncritical essentialisms about Islam, women, sexuality, violence and work ethics, even though in Europe the exotic may be now absent. We need an expanded frame, one that is illustrated by a letter to the *New York Times* (Deirdre M. Higgins, 27 October 2002):

> Having taught overseas, I had many students who wore abayas and adhered to strict Muslim traditions. They were some of the most charming, intelligent and self-confident women I have ever met ... In contrast when I returned to America I found a culture where millions of women were having their skin injected with botulism toxin to appear prettier, younger and more marketable and to erase any signs of personality from their faces ...

The author concludes that Saudi women might consider some of our customs to be downright barbaric. The point of such observations is not only to reduce the hubris surrounding focus on difference, but also to reveal the commonalities: both European-American cultures and Arab Islamic cultures are patriarchal, although male dominance in each place is expressed differently (Nader 1989).

Throughout my participation in this conference, the word 'coexistence' kept coming to mind. I don't recall that the word cropped up in our discussions, but I thought of Spain and the high cultural Spanish achievements that Muslims and Jews made in art and literature. I thought of the Damascus market, segregated as it is right up to the beginning of the twenty-first century into Islamic, Christian and Jewish sections and frequented by peoples of all three religious groups. I thought of Carleton Coon's best-selling book (*Caravan*, 1958), in which he spoke about the Middle East in terms of a mosaic, a division of economic labour amongst separately residing groups – nomads, villagers, city peoples – and I thought of the many different religions that make up the Middle East, and the 'People of the Book', as Muslims, Jews and Christians are called. I recalled seeing a sign at the entrance to old Cairo in the 1970's – 'We are peoples of old Cairo – Moslems, Christians and Jews who live together in peace' – co-existence as an ideal.

Peace, of course, is a relative concept. So too is order. One can document past instances of intense rivalries and factionalism in the Middle East, while at the same time acknowledging that Abdel Nasser's 1956 revolution was a bloodless revolution. It is also possible to document the French and British colonial use of minority groups, pitting one against the other to manage and control other minority groups. I thought of the Ottoman Empire's lasting power (over five hundred years) and wondered whether its duration might in some degree be related to the millet system of government that allowed minority self-governance in critical areas of law and religion (actually an Ottoman form of indirect rule). I think one can make a case for a coexistence model, one that is positively valued in these older parts of the world where long-term social survival – and economic viability – depended on learning to respect difference.

Let us pursue this representation for a moment longer by remembering a reverse-flow-immigration from Europe to the Middle East – expatriates, they were sometimes called. We might try to imagine how contemporary Europeans would feel if they were dealing with comparable numbers of powerful immigrants. For the Middle East, there has long been transit traffic due to war, raiding, trade, colonialism or pilgrim traffic. North African seaports were heterogenic due to immigration of hundreds of thousands of Frenchmen, Spaniards and Italians, who came to constitute a majority or a very large minority of urban inhabitants (Issawi 1969: 108–9). Charles Issawi notes that in 1907 'foreign citizens constituted 25% of the population of Alexandria and 28% of Port Said, although they formed only 2% of the total Egyptian population.' After 1914, Aleppo (Syria) took in around 50,000 Armenians and Lebanon even more. Under French control, the law was used to legitimate French settlers in Algeria, Tunisia and Morocco (Leveau 1986). French settlement in North Africa was a result of colonial rule, one based on positional superiority and military power. Rémy Leveau illustrates the attitude of these 'visitors' to Morocco by quoting the words of an administrator:

> Without further delay, it is advisable to seek out those lands which could be reserved for colonization ... The amount of land appropriated should always be measured in such a way as to leave the local population with enough land to fulfil their needs for existence and normal development. (quoted in Milliot 1922: 142)

These were uninvited and unwanted European immigrants who, because of military and other colonial instruments of power poached on Arab lands, taking what they wanted until their Moroccan 'hosts' ousted them, and only a few decades ago created a state more or less in the European sense!

Janet Abu-Lughod, famous for her work on Arab cities such as Cairo, notes (1989: 183) that 'Islam works to overcome class cleavages, cultural cleavages, and to decrease social distance even among people who are objectively very dissimilar.' Urban structures, with the ubiquitous presence of quarters of mixed *class* origin are one example. The quarters are highly segmented in the face of drastically changing conditions and prevailing insecurity. In other words, in one part of the world from which immigrants to Europe come, they are used to accommodating difference. Over long time periods, they accommodated to comings and goings by residential means that involve the creation of quarters (sub-cities they are sometimes called), which are at times heterogeneously composed. In addition, their culture places a high value on hospitality and recognition of the 'People of the Book'. And they have done this for centuries.

In Baghdad in the 1940s, the Jewish quarter had a population of about 100,000 people. Arraham Zilkha (2002: 120–26) tells the story of growing up happily in the oldest of Jewish diasporas until the fighting in Palestine meant that 'life in Iraq would no longer be the same. A rising wave of nationalism created an atmosphere of intolerance toward minorities ... the slow wave of emigration became a mass exodus and the community began to disintegrate.' Many of his large extended family did not want to leave the oldest Jewish diaspora, 'which had lived under the reign Nebuchadnezzar, Cyrus, and Haroon al-Rashid ... witnessed the rise of Islam, the Mongol invasion, and the modernization of Iraq.' Such a changed environment reflected the powers of European dominance, itself a kind of globalisation, one that results in an 'atmosphere of intolerance toward minorities'.

Even in the early twentieth century, in Saudi Arabian cities, Soraya Altorki and Donald Cole (1989) tell us: 'Rich and poor were mixed within any neighborhood, and people in the same neighborhood were of mixed origins...much of such old cities have been abandoned in light of recent modernizing which brought skilled, semiskilled, and unskilled workers from Africa, Asia, Europe, North and South America' (ibid.: 120) to Saudi Arabia, now a state power. Altorki and Cole tell us that in 1970 expatriates in Saudi Arabia represented an estimated 14.3 percent of the population and 27 percent of the work force. Ten years later they had increased to form an estimated 30.9 percent of the population and 53.3 percent of the workforce: 'expatriates can be hired very cheaply compared to what Saudi Arabians demand'. (ibid.). The

Saudis are also now managing rapidly increasing numbers of temporary workers with state interest in mind. Prior to 1975, expatriates of all classes were almost all other Arabs – Jordanians, Yemenis, Syrians, Palestinians, Sudanese, Hadramis and Iraqis. Now numbers come from all parts of the world.

My point here is simply to note that what is happening in the economically developed world must be seen as happening in world terms. The 'problem of racism', or paradigms of difference, are part and parcel of hegemonies. This observation means not looking at racism as unconnected to history, and not looking at Muslims, in this instance, specifically from a western angle only, which of course, does not obviate looking at Europe from a European perspective. Many population changes in the East in the nineteenth and twentieth centuries were convulsive particularly because of the domination by unwanted European and U.S. powers. The consequences are still with us. In contemporary Europe, people are probably not considering the history of European colonialism when reacting to or participating in racial acts. There is need for a world history model of education, one that makes connections between local and global, between nations, states and the politics of difference, between unemployment and global capitalists who think solely of company profits rather than social and political consequences of free-market economic activities that are not constrained by what they call externalities.

This raises the question of how much change and what rates of change amount to tolerable change in Europe or in any society. Today, Europeans are 'supposed to be tolerant' to non-European difference while coping with the European Union's perhaps unprecedented erasure of difference within Europe itself. Most Westerners have no idea of the havoc European settlers caused in the Arab world. Nor do they make connections between migrating to another land as a dominant group (as with the North African, French, Italian and English colonial settlers) or migrating to Europe as subordinate and dependent workers or as professionals. When the French went to North Africa they took the land, even though they legally justified the take. They neither worked for the land, nor did they always buy the land, all the while asserting the right to legally extract natural resources. While this history is undoubtedly in the mind of immigrants, most Europeans have no sense of payback when North Africans, for example, move to European countries. As we learn from critical historians, what is owed to whom is shrouded in provincial education systems and talk of race and racism, or xenophobia, or Islamophobia.

People are even less tolerant when Muslim outrage surfaces, as in the wake of the Rushdie affair (Asad 1990). In that affair the English had no tools for understanding why Muslims were not 'behaving' in the 'host' society, why they were not integrating with British society. Talal Asad (ibid.: 457) framed the crisis in terms of overload. The British are already overloaded with developments that threaten their identity: integration into the European community, demands of Welsh and Scottish nationalists, the civil war in Northern Ireland, and now immigrants from ex-colonies. Rather than phrasing the problem as one of racism, Asad sees the issue as 'yet another symptom of British, post imperial identity in crisis', and not, as most commentators represented the Rushdie affair, as an 'unhappy instance of some migrants with difficulties in adjusting to a new and more civilized world' (ibid.: 457). Do immigrants extend the scope of British life, Asad asked, or are they tolerated by the authentic British? Asad analyses John Patten's interventions in the Rushdie affair, Patten being the home minister responsible for race relations. He asks whether the threat is about freedom of speech or about the 'politicization of a religious tradition that has no place within the cultural hegemony that has defined British identity over the last century.' (ibid.: 462). In his riveting critique Asad concludes: 'I would argue that in insisting that the fundamental issues to be contested by immigrants can all be reduced to the problem of racism, radical critics have made it difficult to theorize difference' (ibid.: 471).

A central concern for Asad is about how the British rule and intend to rule a diverse population some of whom are British citizens, and what he sees as a form of indirect rule, an old colonial policy. Again, race experts shrink from the larger context, from the central hegemonies of racial disturbances that involve workers or Danes who are bothered by the 'scarf', an apparently powerful symbol of difference, or the racist right-wing parties that are emerging in the periphery of Europe. Asad is moving us into the upper echelons of liberal policies, policies that are imbued with an attitude about difference as problematic. Such an attitude used to be called the White Man's Burden.

In an interesting book on the politics of marginality (*The Politics of* Difference, exdited by Wilmsen and McAllister 1996), John Comaroff reminds us (Ibid.: 162) that the notion of 'modernity' has always involved the removal of difference and as a result the inevitable demise of cultural localism is seen as something abnormal at best. Abnormality is got rid of either by removing the abnormal or homogenising them. But diversity is not disappearing in the face of 'modernity' – quite the opposite is happening. If homogeneity is the norm then a reaction or exclusion to foreigners is perfectly normal (Blommaert and Verschueren 2003: 104–22), but as Blommaert and Verschueren also note the European self-perception, is the 'Noble European', who is *by nature* tolerant. The concluding remarks of these two authors is dark indeed: 'the same societal ideology based on the norm of homogeneity which underlies attitudes toward minorities in Western Europe poses risks for the reemergence of some form of fascism'.

My reaction to dark-side analyses of social problems is to look for the assets, in this case the assets that migrants bring to Europe, and to wonder why more race experts do not observe that the lack of recognition of assets is part of the ideology of difference, which exhibits itself in racism. When Europeans remove the difference, they also remove the assets by only focusing on difference and its dark side. Those who study migration processes often list the assets as in the following example:

> Highly-skilled migration is the type of migration currently most popular with the governments of receiving countries. Since the 1980's, the United States, Canada and Australia have set up privileged entry systems to attract entrepreneurs, executives, scientists, professionals and technical specialists. More recently, western European and some East Asian countries have followed suit … Attracting Indian IT professionals has become a global competition, while the health services of countries like Britain, could

not run without doctors and nurses from Africa and Asia. This type of migration can represent a 'brain drain' – that is a transfer of human capital from poor to rich countries ... Low-skilled migration was crucial to post-1945 industrial growth in most rich countries, but is now generally rejected on the grounds that it is economically unnecessary and socially harmful. NIC's continue to import unskilled labor, often for construction or plantation industries...The reality, as Saskia Sassen pointed out years ago (Sassen 1988), is that global cities are based on dualistic economies, where the luxury consumption needs of elites create demand for new armies of low-skilled workers for construction, garment manufacture, food processing and service industries. The demographic and educational situation of local populations means that they cannot fulfil these roles, and low-skilled migrants are vital. Use of irregular migrants and asylum seekers has become a systematic need, which is covertly pursued by holders of economic and political power. (Castells 2002: 1151–52).

The same author notes that forced migration is linked to the failure to build strong economies in certain regions of the world, a structural aspect of globalisation about which our disappearing CEO might have something to say. Thus, the old myths of national homogeneity have been undermined in reality if not in changing ideologies, especially in global cities. And so we have policies of incorporation: assimilation, exclusionary policies and multiculturalism. But what of coexistence, which is different from government policies of multiculturalism? Or what of the history of Europe itself whose people have moved freely over each other's lands making and taking human and material contributions? What about brain drains from the Third World to the First?

My point here is that the two conversations about difference and cultural intermingling should be intertwined in order to move beyond differential thinking. While hostile encounters have, to some extent, defined Europe so too have the fruits of Islamic culture. Bringing the commonalities together in any conversation on race and racism is bound to turn a stream of fresh ideas upon our unexamined notions and habits, adding new vitality and cultural richness. Might not our educational apparatus include knowledge of humans moving about the globe, a sense of real world history that allows people to place the local in the global, a history that looks both horizontally and vertically, allowing for considerations of power and the politics of difference make a difference? And might we not separate policy implications from hegemonies and the theorising of difference? Emphasising difference to facilitate exclusion has long operated as a feature of control and domination, a position unbecoming to any larger vision of world peace and prosperity.

In an incisive analysis of the increasing instability of global capitalism, John Gray, in his book *False Dawn* (1998), reminds us of a mid-nineteenth-century English experiment in social engineering: to free economic life from social and political control by means of a new institution – the free market. The emergence of this new institution broke up the more socially rooted markets that had existed for centuries in England, thereby leaving behind the idea that economic life need be constrained by social needs. This Great Transformation is now a worldwide phenomenon in which there is no place for a diversity of cultures. Its pursuit as a universal good produces the social dislocation that some see under the rubric of racism, with little room for ideas of coexistence, and less responsibility for what universalist economic policies mean for the social fabric worldwide. Elisabeth Lasch-Quinn's polemic – that race experts are moving in the wrong directions since any differences may be superficial compared with what all human beings have in common – may be what spurred the recent worldwide objection to unilateral war. On the other hand, Aldous Huxley might argue that difference is not a problem for democracies although it may be for totalitarian regimes.

References

Abu-Lughod, A. 1989. *Before European Hegemony – The World System A.D. 1250–1350*. New York: Oxford University Press.

Al Sayyad, N. and Castells, M., eds. 2002. *Muslim Europe or Euro-Islam – Politics, Culture, and Citizenship in the Age of Globalization*. New York: Lexington Books.

Altorki, S. and Cole, D.P. 1989. *Arabian Oasis City – The Transformation of Unazzah*. Austin: University of Texas Press.

Asad, T. 1990. 'Multiculturalism and British Identity in the Wake of the Rushdie Affair'. *Politics and Society* 3: 455–79.

Berreman, G.D. 1981. 'Social Inequality: A Cross – Cultural Analysis'. *Social Inequality Comparative and Developmental Approach*. G. Berreman, ed. New York: Academic Press.

Blommaert, J. and Verschueren, J. 1998. *Debating Diversity: Analyzing the Discourse of Tolerance*. London: Routledge.

Castels, S. 2002. 'Migration and Community formation under Civilizations of Globalization.' *International Migration Review* 36 (winter): 1143–68.

Issawi, C. 1969. 'Economic Change and Urbanization in the Middle East'. *Middle Eastern Cities. Ancient, Islamic, and Contemporary Middle Eastern Urbanism: A Symposium*. I.M. Lapidus, ed. Berkeley: University of California Press: 102–21.

Gray, J. 1998. *False Dawn – The Delusions of Global Capitalism*. New York: The New Press.

Lasch-Quinn, E. 2001. *The Race Experts – How Racial Etiquette, Sensitivity Training, and New Age Therapy Hijacked the Civil Rights Revolution*. New York: W.W. Norton & Co.

Lapidus, I.M., ed. 1969. *Middle Eastern Cities – A Symposium on Ancient, Islamic, and Contemporary Middle Eastern Urbanism*. Berkeley: University of California Press.

Leveau, R. 1986. 'Public Property and Control of Property Rights: Their Effects on Social Structure in Marocco.' *Property, Social Structure, and Law in the Modern Middle East*. A.E. Mayer, ed. Albany: State University of New York Press.

Milliot, L. 1922. *Les terres collectives: Etude de legislation marocaine*. Paris: Leroux.

Nader, L. 1989. 'Orientalism and the Control of Women'. *Cultural Dynamics* 2: 323–55.

Said, E.W. 1979. *Orientalism*. New York: Vintage Books.

Wilmsen, E.N. and McAllister, P. 1996. *The Politics of Difference – Ethnic Premises in a World of Power*. Chicago: University of Chicago Press.

Zilkha, A. 2002. 'By the Rivers of Babylon (Psalm 137)'. *Remembering Childhood in the Middle East: Memoirs from a Century of Change*. Collected and edited by Elizabeth Warnock Fernea. Austin: University of Texas Press.

Notes on Contributors

Troy Duster is Professor of Sociology at the University of California, Berkeley. He specialises in the research (and research based action) on poverty and the job perspectives of urban minorities in the U.S.A.

Glyn Ford is a former MP of the United Kingdom, and member of the European Parliament. He specialises in studies and legislation on racism and discrimination within the EU.

André Gingrich is Professor of Social Anthropology at the University of Vienna. He is doing research on North African societies and cultures, and on the rise of extreme right in the European context today.

Jagdish S. Gundara is Professor in Intercultural Studies at the Institute of Education, University of London, U.K. He holds the UNESCO Chair on Intercultural Education and publishes widely on racism and education for citizenship.

Dipankar Gupta is Professor of Political Theory at the J. Nehru University of New Dehli, India. He has published in the field of social theory and Hindu social and political structure.

Peter Hervik is a social anthropologist at the University of Copenhagen, Denmark, and formerly at the University of Oslo, Norway. His research focuses on the rise of rightist movements and racist groups in Denmark.

Erwin Jans is the Drama Director of various international theatre companies. He is presently Director at the RO-theater of Rotterdam, The Netherlands.

Patrick Janssens was Chairman of the Social Democratic Party of Flanders, Belgium and since 2003 Mayor of Antwerp, Belgium.

Mary Judd is a cultural anthropologist who is serving as a senior officer of the World Bank. She has competences in intercultural communication and interaction in different parts of the world.

Johan Leman was Director of the Royal Commission on Racial Equality of Belgium until 2003, and is currently Professor of Anthropology at the Catholic University of Louvain. He specialises in migrant studies in Europe.

Emanuel Marx is Professor of Cultural Anthropology at the Hebrew University, Israel. He works in the field of intercultural interaction and conflict.

Laura Nader is Professor of Cultural Anthropology at the University of California at Berkeley, U.S.A. She initiated the study of legal anthropology and publishes substantially on the interface between anthropology, law and ethical issues.

Marc Peirs is a journalist for Flemish radio and part-time lecturer in communication studies. He specialises in the communication of NGOs, offering interface means for NGOs.

Rik Pinxten is Professor of Cultural Anthropology at the University of Ghent, Belgium. He works mainly in comparative anthropology, with a focus on identity and religion.

Guy Poppe is a senior journalist for Flemish radio and television. He focuses on Third World issues and cultural politics.

Ellen Preckler is Junior Interface Officer of the city of Ghent, facilitating the interaction between policy circles and youth movements in urban contexts.

Donald Robotham is Professor of Anthropology at SUNY, New York, U.S.A. His work concentrates on urban anthropology, the Caribbean and the impact of tradition on the urban dwellers.

Robert A. Rubinstein is Professor of Cultural Anthropology and Director of PARC at Syracuse University, NY, U.S.A. He works in political and medical anthropology, and in the study of intercultural conflict resolution.

Sumit Sarkar is Professor of History at the New Dehli University in New Dehli, India. He works primarily on the recent history of India, and on the impact of Hindu social systems on the present state.

Eric Seward was a senior officer of the Commission on Racial Equality of the United Kingdom, stationed in London. He retired in 2004.

INDEX